Legal Secretary's
Word Finder and Desk Book

Theresa M. Reilly

Legal Secretary's
Word Finder and Desk Book

Parker Publishing Company, Inc.

West Nyack, New York

© 1974, *by*

PARKER PUBLISHING COMPANY, INC.

West Nyack, N.Y.

Library of Congress Cataloging in Publication Data

Reilly, Theresa M
    Legal secretary's word finder and desk book.

    1. Legal secretaries--United States--Handbooks,
manuals, etc. 2. Law--Terms and phrases. I. Title.
KF319.R4   340'.02'4651   73-17136
ISBN 0-13-528588-7

Printed in the United States of America

The Scope and Practical Value of This Book

Speed and accuracy are essential in the law office. Accurate use of legal terms is important; documents are permanent records, and an undetected misspelled word is perpetuated, because an *exact* copy has to be made of any legal document. Whether new or fully experienced, the legal secretary will at times encounter unfamiliar terminology, and under the pressure of speed she will need to have available a simple reference tool. It is not feasible to have on the desk of each stenographer a voluminous law dictionary such as lawyers use. What the secretary needs is an accessible book—a streamlined dictionary—containing the most frequently used legal words and expressions.

The *Legal Secretary's Word Finder and Desk Book* contains approximately 2,500 words constantly used in legal work. The list has been tested in a variety of law offices; for example, in situations representing corporate, tax, patent, litigation, real estate, theatre, publishing, estates, criminal cases, mergers, banking, the fashion world, civil rights, and various other aspects involving legal work.

While working in law offices, time and time again the author has noticed legal stenographers consuming a great deal of time in searching for the correct spelling of a word, or in attempting to decipher shorthand notes when they were not familiar with word meaning or usage. Also, many legal stenographers perform routine duties day after day without understanding the meaning of legal terminology, the significance of legal documents, or possessing even a rudimentary knowledge of the structure of the American legal system and the hierarchy of the Federal and State Courts.

The *Legal Secretary's Word Finder and Desk Book* will (1) assist the legal secretary in transcribing dictated material more efficiently and more intelligently by having at hand a ready reference to legal words and expressions, their definitions and abbreviations; and (2) give the legal secretary a basic understanding of the scope and significance of the legal profession.

The book is divided into five parts. Each part covers a particular aspect of reference material for the legal secretary:

Part I   Word division and meaning of approximately 2,500 commonly used English and Latin legal terms.

Part II   Abbreviations of legal and medical terms as well as abbreviations commonly used in citation reports.

Part III   Words presenting spelling difficulties, such as, plurals of certain words, compound terms, words ending in "able" and "ible."

Part IV   A brief summary of the hierarchy of the Court system of the United States of America.

Part V   Commonly used legal forms; for example, acknowledgments, affidavits, verifications, attestation clauses, minutes, bills for services rendered, and other forms used in an attorney's office.

The need for a book of this type is evidenced by several specific and typical incidents. During the past 15 years, I have found that the highest rate of error frequency in composition work and transcription is the misspelling of words. While a shorthand outline may be written correctly, the spelling may be inaccurate. Misspelled words also constitute a significant number of errors made by beginning employees and even by experienced employees. For the beginning secretary, this book should be a deterrent to poor workmanship, careless errors, and needless corrections. For the experienced secretary, it may be a new approach to saving time and energy. Specifically,

    —it is a powerful and incredibly simple reference tool;

    —it will help the secretary supply the correct word when she cannot decipher shorthand outlines, or when she is using a transcribing machine and cannot understand a low or mumbled voice;

    —it will motivate the secretary to check the correct spelling of a word rather than "guess" at the spelling.

Occupational demands of the legal field require that secretaries be able to produce under pressure of time. A secretary who has this legal dictionary on her desk will be inclined to consult it immediately when in doubt about the spelling of a word. She will not have to disturb the office by asking another secretary how to spell a word, nor will she have to spend time going to the law office library in order to consult the more comprehensive lawyer's dictionary. The use of this legal word finder will lead to a better quality of work, greater job satisfaction on the part of the secretary, and significant increases in productivity.

The *Legal Secretary's Word Finder and Desk Book* will be useful not only in law offices, but also in the legal department of large corporations, in banking, insurance, law schools, libraries, educational institutions, and indeed in any field where the English language is used as a medium for written legal communication.

–Theresa M. Reilly

CONTENTS

Legal Secretary's
Word Finder and *Desk Book*

Part I

PART I, "Legal Words and Expressions," comprises the bulk of the book and pertains directly to vocabulary. A limited legal vocabulary is more serious than lack of knowledge of technically correct shorthand outlines. Reference, when necessary, to the material contained herein, should enable the legal secretary to become more competent in the performance of her transcription work.

Certain legal concepts can be expressed only in Latin terminology, and lawyers use such terminology almost as readily as English words and phrases. Since Latin is rarely taught in schools at the present time, not many stenographers have heard of the Latin words and phrases which are practically indigenous to the legal profession. Consequently, a list of the most frequently used Latin words and expressions is included in this chapter on vocabulary.

This book will be used again and again by the secretary as the need arises to check the spelling, word division, or meaning of English and Latin words commonly used in legal work. Definitions of words should help the secretary enlarge her legal vocabulary so that she will be able to communicate more intelligently with lawyers and clients.

Legal Words and Expressions

A. Words Frequently Used in Legal Documents, Forms, and Letters; Their Syllabic Accents and Division at Ends of Lines

(The markings show possible places at which words may be divided at ends of lines.)

A

aban/don/ment — the act of leaving a wife or husband; the surrender, relinquishment, disavowal, or cession of property or of rights.

abate — to quash, beat down, or destroy, as in the case of a nuisance or an objectionable writ.

abate/ment — reduction; termination; rebate; effect on action when defendant pleads writ to be defective.

abdi/ca/tion — the renunciation or abandonment by a person of an office, trust, or sovereignty to which he is entitled.

abduc/tion — the unlawful taking or retention of any female for purposes of marriage, concubinage, or prostitution; illegal taking away by force or enticement of person.

aber/ra/tion — act of wandering from the usual way or normal course.

abet — to give aid, to assist, especially in the commission of a criminal offense; exertion of a force, physical or moral, joined with that of another in the perpetration of a criminal offense.

abey/ance — the condition of being undetermined; the condition of a freehold when there is no person in existence in whom it is vested; a state of suspension.

abjuré	forswear; renounce formally; repudiate.
abor´/tion	act of procuring the miscarriage or premature delivery of a pregnant woman.
abor´ tive trial	a trial in which no verdict is reached involving no misconduct of a party.
abrá/sion	superficial tearing of skin.
abridǵ/ment of damages	reduction of damages by order of court.
ab´ro/gate	to annul, repeal, or destroy; to annul or repeal an order or rule issued by a subordinate authority; to repeal a former law by legislative act, or by usage.
abro/gá/tion	the nullification of a law or obligation by an authoritative action.
abscond´	to go away suddenly and secretly; go off and hide.
absorp´/tion	assimilation.
ab´stract, n., adj.	summary comprising the principal parts of a larger work.
abstract´, v.	to separate; to take away.
ab´stract of ti´tle	endorsed history of title to real property.
ab´struse	hidden; concealed; difficult to comprehend or perform; hard to be understood.
abut´	to end at; to border on; to reach or touch with an end, as where a lot touches the highway.
accep´/tance	an official recognition of authority or of a claim; the actual or implied receipt and retention of that which is tendered or offered.
accep´/tor	the person who by writing the word "accepted" and his signature on the face of a bill of exchange becomes responsible for its payment.
accep´/tor su´pra pro´/test	the acceptance of a bill of exchange by a person other than the drawee, voluntarily and without consideration.
acces´/sory (/ries)	a person who in some manner is connected with a crime, either before or after its perpetration, but who is not present at the time the crime is committed; anything joined to another thing.
acces´/sory after the fact	one who helps a criminal to evade or elude capture or arrest.

acces'/sory before the fact	one who encourages, counsels, or induces another to commit a criminal act.
accom'/mo/da/ted party	the person for whose benefit another known as the accommodation party signs a bill or note as maker, drawer, acceptor, or endorser, thereby lending the credit of his name to the former.
accom/mo/da'/tion endorse'/ment	endorsement by which responsibility is assumed should default occur.
accom/mo/da'/tion endor /ser	a person who has endorsed a bill or note for the purpose of lending the credit of his name to another party.
accom/mo/da'/tion paper	a bill or note which one has signed as a maker, drawer, acceptor, or endorser for the purpose of lending the credit of his name to another.
accom/mo/da'/tion party	a person who has signed a bill or note as maker, drawer, acceptor, or endorser for the purpose of lending his name to the credit of some other person.
accom'/plice	a person who knowingly, voluntarily, and with common intent with the principal offender unites in the commission of a crime.
accord'	n., a satisfaction agreed upon; v., to bring into agreement.
accord' and sat/is/fac'/tion	an agreement or document settling a suit or claim; agreement to discharge a contract.
account'	a device for grouping and summarizing the changes caused by business transactions.
account' book	ledger in which is kept record of commercial transactions.
account cur'/rent	an open or running or unsettled account between two parties; the antithesis of an account stated.
account stated	sum of money agreed upon as the amount due from one person to another.
accred'it	to give credit to; to accept as true.
accre'/tion	a gradual increase in land due to natural causes, as out of the sea or river.
accroach'	to exercise power without due authority.
accru'/al	that which accrues; something growing or developing to be added or attached to something else, as interest to principal.

accrue'	to come as a natural product or result.
accrued' divi'/dend	a dividend which became due and has either been paid or not paid.
accrued' expense'	charges incurred but not yet paid.
accrued in'ter/est	interest figured at a given time between the regular dates for payment.
accru'er clause	express clause in gifts by deed or will to tenants in common, providing for rights of survivorship.
accu/mu/la'tive judg'/ment	a judgment which is to take effect upon expiration of a prior judgment.
accu/sa'/tion	a charge of wrongdoing.
Achilles' heel (use apostrophe)	a vulnerable point, as in an argument.
Achilles ten /don (no apostrophe)	a joining muscle in the calf of the leg.
acknowl'/edge	admit to be true; recognize the authority or claims of; recognize or certify in legal form.
acknowl'/edg/ment	formal declaration before authorized official, by person who executed instrument, that it is his free act and deed.
acqui/es'/cence	a tacit approval or at least an indication of lack of disapproval. Acceptance, perhaps without approval, as acquiescence in decision.
acqui/si'/tion	the act by which a person gains possession of property.
acquit'	to set free, release or discharge as from an obligation, burden, or accusation. To absolve one from an obligation or a liability; or to legally certify the innocence of one charged with crime.
acquit'/tal	the setting free of a person who had been charged with a crime.
ac'ro/nym	a word composed of the initial letters or syllables in a phrase or title.
act of God	an accident or circumstances arising from natural cause without human intervention.
ac'tio in rem	in the civil and common law; an action *for a thing;* an action for the recovery of a thing possessed by another.
ac'tion	a proceeding in a court of law.

ac'tion /able	that which furnishes legal grounds for an action.
ac'tion in per/so'/nam	an action against the person, founded on a personal liability; an action seeking redress for the violation of a *jus in personam* or right available against a particular individual.
ac'tion to quiet title	one in which plaintiff asserts his own estate and declares generally that defendant claims some estate in the land, without defining it, and avers that the claim is without foundation, and calls on defendant to set forth the nature of his claim, so that it may be determined by decree.
ac'tual no'tice	having been told condition exists.
ac'tual or con/struc'/tive	existing or implied.
ac'tu/ary	one engaged in the work of calculating the cost of carrying a risk, the amount of insurance premiums, the value of future interests, life estates, and annuities.
adduce'	cite as pertinent or conclusive; to bring forth in argument.
adeem'	to revoke.
ademp'/tion	extinction or withdrawal of legacy by testator's act, equivalent to revocation or indicating intention to revoke.
adhe'/sion	molecular attraction exerted between surfaces of bodies in contact.
adja'/cent	lying near, but not necessarily touching.
ad'jec/tive law	that category of law that designates the proper what, when, and how to bring a legal issue into judicial consideration and judgment.
adjoin'/ing	contiguous; in contact with.
adju'/di/cate	to give judgment; to render or award judgment.
adjudi/ca'/tion	judgment, decision, or sentence of a court.
adjure'	appeal to earnestly; to command or bind by oath.
admin'i/cle	confirmatory evidence; corroboration.
admin'/is/tra/tive	of or pertaining to the management of a business or of public affairs; executive responsibilities and functions are indicated.

admin´/is/tra/tive law	the law that controls, or is intended to control, the administrative operations of government.
admin´/is/tra/tor	one who administers; in the most common usage, the personal representative of a decedent's estate.
admin´/is/tra/tor with will annexed	one appointed administrator of deceased's estate after executors named in will refused to act.
admin/is/tra´/tress or admin/istra´/trix	female to whom letters of administration have been granted. (PL., administratresses; administratrixes or administratices)
ad´mi/ralty (/ties)	the law of the sea and the practice pertaining thereto; courts with jurisdiction in admiralty cases.
ad´mi/ralty court	a court having juridiction over maritime offenses.
admis´/si/ble ev´i/dence	evidence of such character, the court is bound to receive it.
admis´/sions	confessions, concessions, or voluntary acknowledgment made by a party of the existence of certain facts.
admit´ to pro´/bate	to judge the validity of a will and give it legal effect.
adop´/tion	approval, as the adoption of a statute; legally taking into one's own family the child of another.
adsorb´	to gather on a surface in a condensed layer, as when charcoal adsorbs gases.
adsorp´/tion	the adhesion of gas or liquids to solid bodies in contact.
adul´/tery	voluntary sexual affair between a married person and one who is not the wife or husband.
adum´/brate	to indicate by a vague or partial disclosure; to foreshadow.
adven/ti´/tious	accidental, not inherent; arising sporadically or in other than usual locations.
adverse´ pos/ses´/sion	an open possession and occupation of real property under an evident claim or color of right; enjoyment of property in defiance of another person's legal title.

advis'/edly	acting with a prepared mind, not on the spur of the moment; with deliberation.
ad'vo/cate	to summon counsel; n., one in the role of a pleader for another in court.
advow'/son	the right of presenting a nominee to a vacant ecclesiastical benefice.
aegis (PRON. ē'jis)	under the patronage or sponsorship of.
affect'	to influence; to act upon; to produce an effect.
affi'/ance	to pledge; to engage to marry.
affi'/ant	a deponent; one who makes an affidavit under oath.
affi/da'/vit	a sworn statement made under oath before an authorized person.
affi/da'/vit of serv'/ice	an affidavit intended to certify the service of a writ, notice, or other document.
affir/ma'/tion	an unsworn statement.
affreight'/ment	the act of hiring a ship to transport goods.
a'gency	relationship between two or more persons by which one party is authorized to do certain acts for or in relation to the rights or property of the other.
a'gency tar'/iff	tariff issued by an authorized agent for transportation lines.
a'gent	a person authorized by another to act for him; one entrusted with the business of a principal.
a'gent pro/voc' a/teur (PL., agents provocateurs)	secret agent generally inciting actions or declarations that will incur punishment; instigator.
aggrieved'	unjustly injured; unjustly caused grief or trouble.
agi'o (PRON. a gi'ō)	percentage paid as premium for exchange of currency; rate of exchange.
agio'/tage (PRON. a gi ō'tag)	speculation on fluctuation of public securities.
agrar'/ian	of or pertaining to fields, or to a division or distribution of land.
agree'/ment	a mutual understanding; also the writing or instrument that is evidence thereof.

aid and abet′	help, assist, or facilitate the commission of a crime, promote the accomplishment thereof, help in advancing or bringing it about, or encourage, counsel, or incite as to its commission.
a′lias	otherwise; also called; as formerly.
al′ibi	the plea of having been elsewhere than at the scene of a crime at the time of its commission.
al′ien	an unnaturalized person of foreign birth.
al′ien/able	transferable to the ownership of another.
al′ien/ate	to convey or transfer property to another.
aliena′/tion of affec′/tions	the actionable wrong committed against a husband by one who wrongfully alienates the affections of his wife, depriving him of his conjugal right to her consortium—her society, affections, and assistance.
al′i/mony	money paid by a husband for the support of a wife legally separated or divorced from him.
al′i/quot part	a number contained within a larger number an exact number of times.
all fours	cases, decisions, etc., materially alike.
alle/ga′/tion	the assertion, declaration, or statement of a party to an action, made in a pleading, stating what he expects to prove; a statement made under oath without proof.
allege′	to make a statement of fact; to state positively.
alli′/ance	a banding together; a confederacy.
al′lo/cate	to allow an appropriate proportion; to allot
allo/cu′/tion	a formal or authoritative exhortation or address.
allonge′	a paper attached to a note or bill of exchange to create additional room for endorsements; a rider.
allu′/sion	a passing, casual, or incidental reference; an insinuation; a suggestion.
alum′na (PL., alum′/nae)	a female who has attended or graduated from a particular institution of learning.
alum′/nus (PL., alum′ni)	a male who has attended or graduated from a particular institution of learning.
amanu/en′/sis	one who takes dictation; a secretary.

am'bi/ent	completely surrounding or encompassing.
am'bit	an enclosing line or limit; a boundary line.
ambiv'a/lence	the existence of contradictory thoughts or emotions.
amend'	to alter formally by modification, deletion, or addition.
amend'/ment	a correction or revision of a writing to correct errors or better to state its intended purpose.
amerce'/ment	money penalty imposed upon an offender by a court.
am'i/ca/ble	friendly.
ami'/cus cur'/iae	a person who interposes and volunteers information upon some matter of law in regard to which the judge is doubtful or mistaken, or upon a matter of which the court may take judicial cognizance; friend of the court.
am'nesty	an act by which a government grants a general pardon for an offense, usually exerted in behalf of certain classes of persons, rarely exercised in favor of single individuals.
am'or/tize	to provide for the payment of a debt by creating a sinking fund or paying in installments.
amo'/tion	a removal; election; deprivation of possession or ownership; especially, the judicial removal from office of a corporation officer.
anam/ne'/sis (PRON. anam/nē'/sis)	a preliminary case history of a medical or psychiatric patient.
an'cil/lary	aiding; attendant upon; subordinate proceeding, usually to administer estate in one state under will probated in another state.
an'cil/lary admin/is/tra'/tor	one who administers an estate in one state under a will probated in another state.
and/or	a concocted ambiguity; conjunctive disjunctive.
an'no/tate	to mark or note by way of explanation; in annotated statute books, decided cases involving the statute are cited following each section of the statute.
anno/ta'/tion	a concise statement of the holding of a case, appended to a section of constitution or code of statutes, showing the application of such or a similar section in an actual case.

annu'i/tant	one who is entitled to a series of equal payments made annually.
annu'/ity	an incoming sum calculated on an annual basis, though it may be payable in other than yearly periodic installments.
annul'	to render void; to invalidate.
annul'/ment	the act of canceling or making void.
anon'y/mous	without a name.
ante-nup'tial agree'ment	a contract made between a man and a woman in contemplation of their marriage to one another.
ante-nup'tial set'tle/ment	contract between a man and a woman before marriage, but in contemplation and generally in consideration of marriage, whereby the property rights and interests of either the prospective husband or wife, or both of them, are determined, or where property is accrued to either or both of them, or to their children.
anti/no'/mian	one who holds moral law is of no use, faith alone being necessary.
appeal'	application to a higher court for review and decision.
appel'/lant	a person who takes an appeal from one court to another.
appel'/late	pertaining to the taking of an appeal, as appellate court, appellate procedure; of a higher jurisdiction.
appel'/late juris/dic'/tion	the power and authority to re-try or review an issue that has already been heard in a court of lesser jurisdictional power.
appel/lee'	the party in a cause against whom appeal is taken; in some courts, a "respondent."
appen'/dix (PL., appen'/dixes; appen'/di/ces)	additional or supplemental material, an abbreviated record on appeal.
ap'po/site	well adapted to the purpose; relevant; appropriate.
apprais'al	opinion of expert as to true value of real or personal property.
apprais'al value	the value recorded through a written estimate.
appre/cia'/tion	gain in value.

appur´/te/nance

a thing belonging to another or principal thing and which passes as an incident to the principal thing; for example, addition of a shed or garage to a building or piece of land; an adjunct.

apro/pos´
  (PRON. a pro pō´)

adj., opportune; pertinent. adv., to the purpose; incidentally.

ar´bi/ter

person or agency vested with power to decide a controversy.

ar´bi/trage

the computation of differences in rates of money exchange and in the market values of securities for the purpose of profiting by sales and purchases in different places.

arbit´/ra/ment

an arbitrator's decision or award.

arbi/tra´/tion

the submission, for determination, of disputed matter to private unofficial persons selected in a manner provided by law or by agreement.

ar´bi/tra/tor

one chosen to settle differences between two parties in controversy.

ar´chives

a place where public records or other historical documents are kept.

arm's length

at a distance.

arraign´

to call a defendant to the bar of the court to answer an indictment.

arraign´/ment

the act of calling before the court a person accused of a crime so that he may be advised of the charge against him.

arrest´

to deprive a person of his liberty by legal authority.

ar´ro/gate

to assert a claim to, or take, something without right; to exercise authority which one does not have.

ar´son

the unlawful and malicious burning of a building or other property.

ar´ti/cles

a group of clauses forming a contract; divisions of a constitution, a statute, charter, or of any other written statement of principles, terms, or conditions.

articles of
  incor/po/ra´/tion

the charter or the organic law of a corporation.

ar´ti/fact

product of human workmanship, especially of simple primitive art.

ar ti/fice	a clever trick or stratagem; craft; trickery.
arti/fi′/cial bound′/ary (/ries)	boundary created by man, not by nature.
arti/fi′/cial per′/son	an entity created by law or by authority of law, given the attributes of a natural person; for example, a corporation.
ascen′/dant	an ancestor in direct ascendancy line, as a parent or a grandparent.
as, if, and when agree′/ment	a contingent agreement.
asper′/sion	slander; defamation; a derogatory criticism.
aspor/ta′/tion	the removal of things from one place to another—a requisite to constitute the offense of larceny.
assault′	an intentional, unlawful threat of corporal injury to another by force, or force unlawfully directed toward the person of another, under such circumstances as create well-founded fear of imminent peril, together with apparent ability to execute the attempt.
assault′ and bat′/tery (/ies)	the unlawful touching of a person with the intent and purpose of actually doing physical injury, with a reasonable ability to carry the intention into execution.
assessed′ valu/á tion	a listing and valuation of property as a basis upon which taxes are to be collected.
assess′/ment	the process of apportioning an amount to be paid, as an assessment of damages or taxes.
as′sets	property of value that is owned; anything possessed that can be used to pay debts, legitimately.
assignee′	the person to whom an asset, right, or security has been made over.
assign′er OR assign′or	a person who transfers a right, whether he be an original owner or an assignee.
assign′/ment	the transfer of title or interest by means of a written document.
assize′	a trial or hearing in the nature of an inquest before a sworn jury, without evidence of witnesses.

assump´/sit	action to recover from breach of contract; a promise or contract, not under seal, on which such action may be brought.
astute´	sagacious; of keen penetration or discernment; shrewd.
attach´/ment	a legal process placing a debtor's property in the court's hands until the case is decided.
attain´/der	the extinction of civil rights and capacities of a person who has been convicted of treason or felony and sentenced to death.
atten´u/ate	to make thin; to weaken or reduce in force or intensity; to lessen in value.
attest´	authenticate officially; affirm to be true; to certify.
attes/ta´/tion	the act of signing a document to affirm the witnessing of an action.
attes/ta´/tion clause	the clause at the conclusion of a document, denoting that the persons signing are witnesses.
attorn´	to agree to become tenant to one to whom reversion has been granted.
attor´/ney (PL., attor´/neys)	an agent; one legally appointed by another to transact business for him.
attor´/ney at law	one qualified to appear in court to prosecute or defend.
attor´/ney´ gen /eral (PL., attorneys general or attorney generals)	chief law officer of a state or nation who represents the government in litigation.
attorney-in-fact (divide only at hyphen)	one who is authorized by another to act in his place and stead, such authority being usually conferred by a written instrument called a power of attorney.
attor´/ney's daybook	a diary or journal in which are briefly recorded the actions taken on any case being handled by the firm and any matters requiring attention at some future date; the time expended is also recorded.
attor´/ney's lien	the right of an attorney at law to hold or retain in his possession the money or property of a client until his proper charges have been adjusted and paid; it requires no equitable proceeding for its establishment.

attri/bu´/tion	that condition under the income tax laws whereby a situation is created and wherefrom certain resulting consequences flow.
attri´/tion	the act of wearing down by mechanical friction; act of weakening by harassment; sorrow.
au´dit	a formal or official examination and verification of accounts, vouchers, and other records, the purpose being to determine their accuracy and to show the condition of a business.
au´di/tor	a person appointed and authorized to examine accounts and accounting records, to verify balance sheets and income statements.
aus/tere´	harsh in manner; severe in discipline of self and others; grave; serious.
aus/ter´/ity	severity of manner or way of life.
authen/ti/ca´/tion	official attestation of a written instrument in order to render it legally admissible in evidence.
aux/il´/iary (/ries)	giving support; assisting; subsidiary; additional; used as a reserve.
avails	in wills, the corpus or proceeds of an estate after payment of debts; proceeds; benefits.
aver´	v., to allege; to plead; to assert. n., property; substance.
aver´/ment	a positive statement of fact.
avoid´	shun; evade; invalidate; cancel.
avoid´/ance	rendering void; nullifying.
award´	to grant, concede, or adjudge to; to give or assign by sentence or judicial determination; for example, the court awards an injunction, a jury awards damages.
avow´	to acknowledge and to justify an act done.
avul´/sion	sudden loss or addition to land from the estate of one to that of another by the action of water.

B

bail	the means of procuring the release from custody of a person charged with a criminal offense or with debt, by assuring his future appearance in court and compelling him to remain within the jurisdiction.

bail bond	a bond given as security for the purpose of obtaining release of a person in custody.
bailee´	party to whom personal property is delivered under contract of bailment.
bailer´ OR bailor´	party who bails or delivers goods to another under contract of bailment.
bai´/liff	a sheriff's deputy or constable; a minor officer of the court.
bail´/ment	a delivery of personal property by one person to another in trust for a specific purpose, with an agreement that the trust shall be faithfully executed and the property returned or duly accounted for when the special purpose is accomplished.
balance-of-payments def´i/cit	the excess of money going out over money coming in.
bald	unadorned; undisguised; plain.
bank accep´/tance	acceptance of a bill of exchange by a bank or other credit-loaning institution.
bank endorse´/ment	endorsement of commercial paper, such as checks and promissory notes, usually made by writing the name on the back of the paper.
bank note	a promissory note issued by a bank, payable to bearer on demand.
bank/rupt	an insolvent person.
bank´/ruptcy (/cies)	placement of an insolvent business under the administration of the court to protect the creditors.
bar	lawyers as a group are frequently referred to as "the bar"; in England the bar is the place where the accused stands in a court.
bar´/ra/try	in maritime law, an act by a shipmaster hurtful to the owners of a vessel or its cargo; repeated deliberate attempts to cause resort to the courts.
bar´/ris/ter	(English law) an advocate; a counselor learned in law who has been admitted to plead at the bar and who is engaged in conducting the trial or argument of causes—to be distinguished from the attorney who draws the pleadings, prepares the testimony, and conducts matters out of court.

base coin	adulterated or alloyed coin.
basis (PL., bases)	the bottom or base of anything, or that on which it stands or rests; a groundwork or fundamental principle.
bas´/tardy pro/ceed´/ings	action against the father of an illegitimate child to compel support.
bat´/tery	any unlawful touching, beating, or other wrongful physical violence or constraint, inflicted on a human being without his consent.
bat/ture´	land formed by accretion.
bear´er	the holder of negotiable paper not payable to a specified person.
being duly sworn	having taken an oath; bound by an oath.
bel´/lows file	a heavy cardboard container with alphabetized or compartment sections, the ends of which are closed in such a manner as to resemble an accordion.
bench (lower case)	the seat where a judge sits in court; tribunal for the administration of justice.
Bench (upper case)	the office or dignity of a judge; the place where justice is administered; the persons who sit as judges.
bench war´/rant	order issued by a judge, for the arrest of a person.
bene/fi´/ci/ary (/ies)	person who is to receive money or property from an insurance policy, will, etc.
bene/fi´/ci/ar/ies, third party	persons who are not parties to a contract, agreement, or written instrument, but who are to receive the promised consideration or sum portion of it.
bequeath´	to hand down to posterity; to give or leave personal property by means of a will.
bequest´	a legacy; a gift of personal property by a will.
berm or berme	strip of land along a dike; a narrow path.
bête noiré (PRON. bā t-nwar´)	anything that is an object of hate, dread, or special aversion, whether a person, task, or object; black beast.
bian´/nual	occurring twice a year.
bicam´/eral	consisting of, or based upon, two legislative bodies.

bien´/nial	occurring every two years; continuing or lasting for two years.
bien´/nium (PL., bienniums ALSO biennia)	a period of two years.
big´/amy	act of marrying while the spouse of a former marriage is still alive and the former marriage is still in force.
bilat´/eral	affecting reciprocally two sides or parties.
bilat´/eral con´/tract	contract formed by an offer requiring a reciprocal promise.
bill	a document in the form of a law; a denomination of paper money; the amount owing on an account; a listing of things offered to patrons or customers.
bill´/heads	sheets of paper with the firm's name printed and with appropriate space for listing charges.
bil´/lion	in U.S. and France, a thousand million; in Great Britain and Germany, a million million.
bill of attain´/der	a legislative act which inflicts punishment without a judicial trial.
bill of excep´/tions	formal statement in writing of exceptions taken to opinion, decision, or direction of judge, delivered during the trial of case.
bill of exchange´	an unconditional order in writing by one person to another, signed by the person writing it, requiring the person to pay on demand, or at a fixed time, a certain sum in money to order or to bearer.
bill of lad´/ing	an itemized list of a shipment, signed by the carrier for the shipper's protection.
bill of par/tic´u/lars	itemized statement of facts and claims on which an action or claim is based.
Bill of Rights	term used to designate the first ten amendments to the Constitution—the amendments that protect the personal rights of individuals.
bill of sale	a written instrument evidencing the transfer of title to personal property described therein from a seller to a purchaser.

bill of sight	form of customhouse entry, allowing consignee to see goods before paying duty.
bind′er	a memorandum or agreement notation that is to take effect until the execution of a formal agreement.
bind over	to hold on bail for trial.
blank endorse′/ment	bare signature of payee endorsed on a negotiable instrument.
blue laws	strict statutes or ordinances, particularly those which affected observance of the Sabbath.
blue-sky laws	laws protecting the investing public against exploitation; term apparently originated in the expression concerning the credulous as "dumb enough to buy the blue sky, if it is offered to him."
board	a group of people, appointed or elected, with authority to share the management or direction of a business or a trust.
bog′us	spurious; sham; U.S. counterfeit.
bo′na fide (PRON. bō′në fī de)	good faith; in all sincerity; without fraud.
bond	the obligation secured by a mortgage or deed of trust; a corporate obligation; one who acts as surety or bail.
book value	the value of capital stock as indicated by the excess of assets over liabilities.
bot′/tomry	Marine Law: a contract, of the nature of a mortgage, by which the owner of a ship borrows money to make a voyage, pledging the ship as security.
bowd′/ler/ize	omitting or modifying text which is considered to be indelicate.
box file	a box that opens conveniently in order to file papers between alphabetized guides that are fastened to the inside of the box.
boy′/cott	a conspiracy to prevent the carrying on of business by threats, intimidation, coercion, or withdrawal of patronage.
breach	violation of right, duty, or law.

breach of con'/tract	failure, without legal excuse, to perform any promise which forms the whole or part of a contract.
brib'/ery	the receiving or the offering of any gift, favor, or money in order to influence a person in his behavior in the line of duty or a trust.
bridge'/man	an attendant acting between judge, clerk, and attorneys in Criminal Court.
brief	a written or printed document, prepared by an attorney to serve as the basis for an argument upon a cause in an appellate court, and usually filed for the information of the court; it contains the points of law which the lawyer desires to establish, together with the arguments and authorities upon which he rests his contention.
brief'/ing	the preparation of papers and information needed for presenting or defending cases in court.
budg'et	a plan laid out showing how much money will be required to meet the needs of various departments of the government; a plan for spending.
bu'reau	a department of a municipal or state government; in the Federal government, usually a department within a department, a subdivision of a department.
bur'/glary	unlawful entry into the dwelling house of another with the intention of committing a theft.
by-laws	rules by which a corporation conducts its business; also rules and regulations adopted for their government by clubs, societies, and other organizations.

C

cache (PRON. cash)	n., a place, usually in an unfrequented area, where supplies are stored; the word implies concealment. v., to hide or store in a cache.
cachet'	seal used especially as a mark of official approval; an indication of approval carrying prestige.

ca′dre (PRON. ka′der OR kad′rē) (PL., cadres)	nucleus; framework; core of officers and men necessary to the training of a new military unit.
cal′/en/dar	schedule; tabulation of time.
cal′/en/der	press; a machine in which cloth or paper is smoothed or glazed.
cal′/umny	libel; defamation; slander.
cam′ /era	judge's chamber; a vault; photographic apparatus.
canard′	an absurd story; false report; a hoax.
can′on	law or rule; doctrine; criterion.
can′/vas	n., cloth.
can′/vass	v., to solicit; counting vote returns.
ca′pias	form of writ directing arrest.
cap′i/tal	money used for the production of wealth; the entire assets of a corporation.
cap′i/tal as/sets	nontrading assets such as land, building, machinery, etc., necessary for operating a business.
cap′i/tal stock	shares of stock issued by a corporation, and outstanding; the total of all corporate liabilities and obligations.
cap′i/tol	building occupied by a State legislature; the building in Washington used by the Congress of the United States.
cap′/tion	the heading or title of a legal document.
car′/nal	pertaining to the body, its passions and its appetites; sensual; animal.
car′ /rier	person or company engaged in transporting merchandise or passengers for hire.
car′/tage	the cost or act of hauling freight.
carte′ blanche′ (PRON. kärt′ blänsh)	a blank card; freedom to act in a situation as one thinks best.
case law	law as evidenced by adjudged cases in distinction to statutes or other sources of law.
cash flow	the aggregate of net income plus the amounts allowed for depreciation of plant and equipment and amortization of patents and licenses for the use of patents.

cas'/u/alty	an unfortunate accident, especially one involving bodily injury or death.
cat'/a/pult	an ancient military engine for throwing darts, stones, etc.
cate/gor'/ical	having no qualification or reservation; precise; absolute; explicit; direct.
caus'al	arising from a cause; constituting or implying a cause.
ca'veat (PRON. kā' ve at)	a notice to beware; a formal notice to refrain from some action pending a decision by the court.
cav'eat emp'tor (PRON. kā' ve at emp' tor)	let the buyer beware; a maxim of the common law expressing the rule that the buyer purchases at his own risk.
cav'eat ven'ditor (PRON. kā 've at ven'/di/tor)	let the seller beware.
cen'/ser	a vessel.
cen'/sor	n., a person who examines books, plays, etc., for objectionable material; v., to suppress; to delete objectionable material.
cen'/sure	blame; severe criticism; condemnation.
cen'/tric	located in or at center.
cer/tio/ra'ri	an appellate proceeding for re-examining the action of an inferior tribunal or as an auxiliary process to enable the appellate court to obtain further information in a pending cause.
chain of title	successive conveyances of land.
chal/lenge	n., an objection; an exception. v., to object; to take exception to.
chal'/lenge for cause	a challenge to a juror for which some cause or reason is alleged.
cham'/bers	the place, other than the courtroom, where a judge transacts the business of the court.
cham'/perty	a bargain made by one not a party to a suit to bear expenses of litigation in consideration for a share of the matter sued for.
chan'/cel/lor	a judge in a court of chancery or equity in various states of the United States.
chan'/cery	equitable jurisdiction: the system of jurisprudence administered by courts of equity.

change of ven'ue	the removal of a suit begun in one county or district to another ounty or district for trial; removal of a suit from one court to another court in the same district.
Chap'/ter X pro/ceed'/ing	a proceeding in bankruptcy under which all assets are completely liquidated for the payment of claims in proportion to their priority and amount.
char'/la/tan (PRON. shahr'luh t'n)	a quack; a cheat; an imposter.
char'/ter	n., a grant of rights in the conduct of a business.
char'/ter par'/ty	written contract for the hire of a ship or plane for a given voyage.
chaste	virtuous; undefiled; free from obscenity.
chat'/tel	a movable article of property; not connected with the ground so as to become a part of the real estate.
chimer'i/cal	unreal; fantastic; imaginary.
chose (PRON. shō z)	a thing; a chattel; a personal right.
chose in action (PRON. shō z)	a personal right not reduced into possession, but recoverable by a suit at law.
cir/cum/am'/bi/ent	surrounding.
cir/cum/duc'/tion	annulment; cancellation; avoidance.
cir/cum/stan'/tial ev'i/dence	evidence that tends to prove a fact by proving related facts and therefore affording reasonable interference of the occurrence of the fact in issue.
cita'/tion (PRON. sī tā'shen)	call or summons to appear in court; a reference to an authority or precedent.
civ'il	pertaining to the citizen or to the community.
civ'il ac'tion	an action brought to enforce a civil right; an ordinary action as distinguished from a'criminal action.
civ'il law	private law as distinguished from criminal law.
claim	a demand for money or property; the assertion of a demand or the challenge of something.
claim'/ant	one who makes a claim; a voluntary applicant for justice.

Class A stock	a grade of stock between common and preferred.
clean bill of lad'/ing	a bill of lading which contains nothing in the margin qualifying the words in the bill itself.
clean receipt'	receipt signed without any notation of an exception.
clear ti'tle	good title, free from litigation and palpable defects.
cli'/ents	the customers of a law office.
close cor/po/ra'/tion	a corporation whose stock is in the possession of only a few persons; a "family corporation."
closed-end	adj., having a fixed capitalization of shares traded on the open market instead of being redeemable on demand daily.
closely held	stock that is unlikely to come on the market for general sale while held.
clo'/ture (PRON. klō'cher)	method of ending debate and securing immediate vote upon a measure before a legislative body.
cloud on ti'tle	an obstacle to clear title to property.
coa'gent (PRON. ko ā'jent)	an agent acting jointly with another agent.
co a/li'/tion	an alliance; a fusion.
code	a systematic body of law.
codex (PL., codices)	code or collection of laws.
code plead'/ings	system of simplified procedure prescribed by statutes.
cod'i/cil (PRON. kod'i sil)	an addition to or qualification of one's last will and testament.
cod'/ing	the process of underscoring or marking the subject, title, etc., under which a letter or paper is to be filed.
cog'/nate	blood relative traced through the mother or other female.
cog'/ni/zance	acknowledgment; recognition; judicial hearing of a cause.
cohab i/ta'/tion	state of dwelling together, as a man and wife.
cohe'/sion	act or state of uniting or sticking together.

col´/late	v., to verify the number and order of sheets; to examine; to arrange.
col/lat´/eral	cash or other security used to guarantee the fulfillment of an obligation.
col/lat´/eral an´ces/tor	used to designate aunts, uncles, and other relatives of older generations.
col/lat´/eral descent´	descent to collateral relatives, as from brother to brother, cousin to cousin, etc.; descent from a common ancestor, but not in a direct line.
col/lat´/eral facts	facts which are not directly connected with the principal issue in dispute.
col/lat´/eral note	a borrower's note, given to a lender, stating terms of deposit of security on the loan.
col/lat´/eral trust bond	a bond secured by a pledge of security other than real property.
col/la´/tion	the comparison of a copy with the original document.
col´/lege	an organized association of persons having certain powers and rights, and performing certain duties or engaged in a particular pursuit.
col/lo/ca´/tion	a classification of creditors for the purpose of paying them in proper order.
col/lu´/sion	secret understanding to use fraudulent means to make gains.
col´/or/able	specious; pretended; deceptive.
com/mand´/ite	a special partnership; limited liability company.
com mer´/cial	embracing business activity.
com´mer´/cial pa´per	short-term negotiable instruments arising out of business transactions.
com/mis´/sion	an authority; a writ; a group of people appointed or elected, with authority to perform certain acts of a public nature.
com/mis´/sioner of deeds	an officer empowered to take acknowledgements and to perform acts of the same nature as those performed by a notary public.
com/mit´/ment	an order to send one to prison or to an asylum; a pledge or declaration.
com´/mon car´/rier	one who holds himself out to the public as carrying goods or persons for hire and for all persons indifferently.

com'/mon e'ra	the Christian era (C.E.)
com'/mon law	unwritten law, receiving its binding force from custom, usage, and judicial decisions.
com'/mon-law mar'/riage	a marriage entered into without ceremony, evidencing a mutual agreement to assume the relationship of husband and wife.
com'/mon-law plead'/ing	pleading regulations developed in the English courts of common law.
com'/mon stock	stock ordinarily issued by a corporation, without extraordinary rights or privileges.
com/mu'/nity	a society or body of people living in the same area, under the same laws and regulations, who have common rights, privileges, or interests.
com/mu'/nity prop'/erty	property owned in common by a husband and wife as a kind of marital partnership.
com/mu'/ta/tive con'/tract	contract in which each of tl parties gives or receives an equivalent.
com/par'a/tive law books	law books of foreign countries.
com/par'a/tive neg'/li/gence	doctrine by which the negligence of the parties is compared, in the degrees of "slight," "ordinary," and "gross" negligence, and a recovery permitted, notwithstanding the contributory negligence of the plaintiff.
com/pen'/dium (PL., compendia)	synopsis, abridgment, or digest.
com/pen'/sa/tory dam'/ages	payment for sustained loss that is in direct proportion to the amount of value lost.
com'/pe/tent	legally qualified; fitting; suitable.
com/pla'/cent	self-satisfied; pleased.
com/plain'/ant	one who applies to courts for legal redress.
com/plaint'	allegations made by one who institutes suit at law.
com/plai'/sant	gracious; affable; agreeable; disposed to please.
com'/ple/ment	that which completes or is required to supply a deficiency.
com'/pli/ment	an expression of praise, commendation, or admiration.
com/po/si'/tion	an agreement, made upon adequate consideration, between an insolvent debtor and his

creditors, whereby the latter agree to accept a dividend less than the whole amount of the claims, to be distributed *pro rata* in discharge and satisfaction of the whole.

com/pound'/ing a fel'/ony

forbearing to prosecute a felony for a consideration.

com'/pro/mise

an agreement to terminate, by means of mutual concessions, a controversy over a claim which is disputed in good faith or unliquidated.

comp/trol'/ler (OR con/trol/ler)

a corporate or public officer in charge of the financial affairs of the corporation or public body.

con/cealed' dam'/age

damage that is not evident until goods are unpacked.

con/cealed loss

a loss that is not evident on delivery.

con/ceal'/ment

withholding of something which one knows and which one is bound to reveal.

con'/cept

a general notion; the immediate object of thought in simple apprehension.

con/cep'/tual

pertaining to the forming of concepts.

con/clu'/sion of fact

an inference drawn from the subordinate or evidentiary facts.

con/clu'/sion of law

the court's statement of what the law on a controverted point is, as distinguished from an order or judgment.

con/clu'/sive ev'i/dence

facts in evidence which are so convincing as to support verdict or findings, but are not absolutely beyond contradiction.

con/com'i/tant

accompanying; attending.

con/cor'/dat

an agreement; a covenant; an agreement between church and state as to ecclesiastical privileges.

con/cur'/rent

happening at the same time; acting in conjunction.

con/demn'

to expropriate property for public use; to adjudge a person guilty.

con/di'/tional sale

a sale wherein the seller retains title to the goods, although possession is delivered to the buyer, until some stipulated condition is performed.

con/di´/tion pre/ce´/dent	that which must happen or be performed before some right dependent thereon accrues.
con/di´/tion sub´/se/quent	a condition in a contract which follows liability upon the contract and operates to defeat such liability upon the subsequent failure of the other party to comply with its terms.
con/do/na´/tion	the forgiveness by a husband of his wife, or by a wife of her husband, of a breach of marital duty, with an implied condition that the offense will not be repeated.
con/fes´/sion	a voluntary statement made by a person wherein he acknowledges himself to be guilty of an offense.
con´/fi/dant (mas.) con´/fi/dante (fem.)	person entrusted with one's secrets or confidences.
con´/flict of laws	inconsistency between the municipal laws of different states or countries, arising in the case of persons who have acquired rights, made contracts, or incurred obligations within the territory of two or more jurisdictions.
con/fu´/sion	the mingling of goods of different owners into a common mass.
con/joint´	pertaining to or carried on by two or more persons jointly.
con/san/guin´/ity	a blood relationship; kinship.
con/sec´u/tively	following one after another without interruption.
con/sen´/sual	existing by mere mutual consent without further act or writing.
con/sen´/sus (PL., suses)	general agreement or concord.
con/sid/era´/tion	the cause, motive, price, or impelling influence which induces a contracting party to enter into a contract.
con/signee´	a person to whom goods are transmitted either for sale or for safekeeping.
con/sign´/ment	commitment of goods, usually to an agent or distributor, for sale.
con/sign´ or	one who ships goods to an agent or distributor.
con/soli/da´/ted	combined; united; brought together into a single mass.

con/soli/da′/tion — a bringing together of separate things to make one thing.

con′/sta/ble — a peace officer.

con/sti/tu′/tion — a system of fundamental laws or principles for the government of a nation, state, society, corporation, or other aggregation of individuals.

con/struc′/tive — implied; made out by legal interpretation.

con/struc′/tive no′tice — not actual notice; the substitute in law for actual notice, being based upon a presumption of notice which is so strong that the law does not permit it to be controverted.

con/sum′/mate, adj. OR con′/sum/mate, v. — to finish by completing what was intended; to carry out; to fulfill.

con/tempt′ of court — any act which is calculated to embarrass, hinder, or obstruct the court in administration of justice, or which is calculated to lessen its authority or dignity; refusal to comply with the orders of the court.

con/ter′/mi/nous (ALSO coterminous) — adjoining; a common boundary.

con/tes′/tant — in law, the party who, in proceedings in a probate court, contests the validity of a will.

con/tig′u/ous — in actual contact; adjoining.

con/tin′/gent — conditioned upon occurrence of some future event.

con/tin′/ual — recurring at intervals.

con/tin′u/ance — an adjournment of a cause from one day to another, in the same or in a later term, or to a later hour of the same day.

con/tin′u/ous — going on without stopping.

con′/tract, n. — an agreement upon sufficient consideration to do, or refrain from doing, a particular lawful thing.

con/tract′, v. — to enter into a binding obligation or agreement.

con/tra/ven′/tion — violation of a law.

con′/tre/temps (Sing. and Plural) PRON. kan-tre-ta^n (Sing.) kan-tre-ta^{n}z (Pl.) — an embarrassing or awkward occurrence; a mishap.

con/trib'u/tory neg/li/gence	failure to act prudently and reasonably, or to do that which a reasonable person would not do under the same or similar circumstances.
con/trol'/ler (ALSO comptroller)	chief accounting officer of a business enterprise or institution; a public official who audits government accounts and certifies expenditures.
con'/tro/vert	to oppose by reasoning; to debate.
con/tu/ma'/cious	stubborn; disobedient; perverse in resisting authority.
con/tu'/sion	a bruise; an injury without a breaking of the skin.
con/ver'/sion	any distinct act of dominion wrongfully exerted over another's personal property in denial or against his rights therein.
con/vert'/ible issues	bonds, debentures, or preferred stock giving owner the right to convert to common stock.
con/vey'/ance	transfer of legal title to land; a written instrument under seal transferring the title to land or some interest therein from one person to another.
con/vey'/ance *in pais*	transaction taking place on the land to be transferred.
cop'y/right	the exclusive legal right to publish, reproduce or sell a literary, musical, or such other work.
co/rel'a/tive (ALSO correlative)	reciprocally related; so related that each implies or complements the other.
core/spon'/dent (no hyphen)	third party in a divorce.
co-re/spon'/dent (ALSO correspondent)	fellow respondent.
cor'o/ner's in'quest	an examination made by the coroner and a jury into the causes and circumstances of any death that may have been the result of a crime.
cor'/po/rate con/glom'/er/ate (ALSO free-form; multi-market)	marriage of two or more unrelated companies into a new multi-industry company.
cor/po/ra'tion	a business organization created by law which permits its owners to limit their liability to their investment.
cor/po'/real prop'/erty	property that is material or that has body or substance; thus land is corporeal property; rent is incorporeal.

corps (PL., same, but a distinction is made in speech by adding a "z" sound to the plural)	an organized military body consisting of officers and men, or of officers alone.
cor´/pus (PL., cor/pora)	the main body or corporeal substance of a thing; the principal of an estate or fund as distinct from interest or income.
cor´/pus delic´ti	the body of a crime.
cor´/pus juris	the body of the law; the name of an exhaustive encyclopedia of the law of the country.
cor/re/spon´/dent	one who writes.
cor/rob´o/ra/tive	that which supports with authority and evidence.
cor/rup´/tion of blood	a doctrine whereunder one was disqualified to inherit by conviction of a felony.
co/ter´/mi/nous ALSO con/ter´/mi/nous	having a common boundary.
coun´/cil	legislative department of a city or other municipal corporation.
coun´/sel	lawyer engaged in the management or trial of a case in court.
coun´/selor at law	an attorney who has been duly admitted to the bar and presently qualified to practice law; an advising lawyer.
coun´/ter/claim	claim presented by a defendant in opposition to or deduction from the claim of the plaintiff.
coun´/ter/sign	to add an authenticating signature.
coun´/ter/wills (one word)	another term for reciprocal wills in which the testators name each other as beneficiaries under similar testamentary plans.
coun´/ter/vail/ing proof	proof of a forceful nature against opposing side.
court of equity	court having a chancery or equity jurisdiction, and not being limited by the common law.
cov´e/nant	an agreement reduced to writing and executed by a sealing and a delivery; the paragraphs of a formal lease.
co´vert	concealed; secret; hidden.
cov´er/ture	legal status of a woman during marriage.

covin (kuv´in)	a conspiracy between two or more persons to injure another.
cov´i/nous	collusive; deceitful; fraudulent.
coz´en	to cheat; deceive; beguile.
cred´/ible	believable.
cred´/it/able	deserving of praise.
cred´/its	amounts listed on the right side of an account, as opposed to the debit side.
crim´i/nal	that which has to do with a wrongful act against the law; one who has been legally convicted of a crime.
crim´i/nal intent	the intent to commit a crime; malice, as evidenced by a criminal act; an intent to deprive or defraud the true owner of his property.
crim´i/nal neg´/li/gence	negligence which is proscribed by law and for which punishment is provided as constituting a crime.
crim´i/nate	to charge with a crime; to represent anything as criminal; to censure strongly.
cross-appeal (use hyphen)	an appeal filed by the appellee or defendant in error as an incident of review proceedings instituted by the opposing party.
cross-claim	claim brought by a defendant against a plaintiff in the same action concerning matters in question in the original petition.
cross-complaint	a pleading by the defendant in an action wherein he seeks affirmative relief, relating to or depending upon the transaction on which the action is based or affecting property to which it relates, against the plaintiff or any other party to the action.
cross-examination	the attempt on the part of the opposing counsel to break down the testimony of a witness as given on direct examination.
cross ref´/er/ence	the reference made to another part of the file; a cross reference is used when it is advisable to file a paper under more than one heading.
cul´/pa/ble	blamable; involving breach of a legal duty or the commission of a fault; fault rather than guilt.
cu´mu/la/tive ev´i/dence	additional evidence of the same kind and to the same point.

cu´/mu/la/tive vot´/ing	allowing each stockholder of a corporation as many votes as there are directors to be elected.
cur´/rency (/cies)	circulating monetary medium of a country.
cur´/tesy	the estate a man is entitled to under certain conditions upon the death of his wife; it is a freehold estate for the term of his natural life.
cus´/tody (/dies)	the bare control or care of a thing as distinguished from the possession of it.

D

dam´/age par´/cel	condemned piece of real property.
dam´/ages	a sum recoverable as amends for a wrong; an adequate compensation for the loss suffered or the injury sustained.
da´ta (SING., da´tum)	pertinent facts or premises.
da´tion	a giving or transfer in the fulfillment of a duty; an appointment, as to an office.
da´tive	removable as opposed to perpetual; that which can be given at will.
da´tive tutor	one appointed by a judge to serve as tutor of a minor when the position has not been filled by nature, will, or the effect of law.
dearth	scarcity; lack; want.
de ben´/ture	a written acknowledgment of a debt; an instrument under seal for the payment of money lent.
de ben´/ture bond	a bond not secured by a lien on property of the issuing corporation, being backed by the corporation's general assets and good faith.
de´but	appearance before the public or in society for the first time.
deb´u/tante (fem.) deb´u/tant (masc.)	one appearing before the public or in society for the first time.
dece´/dent	a person who has died and who has left property.
decen´/nial	of or for ten years; occurring every ten years.
deci´/sion	the report of a conclusion reached, especially the conclusion of a court in the adjudication of a case or the conclusion reached in an arbitration.

deci'sional law	law established by court decision, distinguished from statutes enacted by the legislature.
dec/la/ra'/tion	a statement made by witnesses instead of taking the oath; the first pleading of the plaintiff stating cause and complaint and asking relief.
decla'/ra/tory judg/ment	one which simply declares the rights of the parties or expresses the opinion of the court on a question of law, without ordering anything to be done.
decoy (v.)	to entice or lure.
(n.)	a person or a thing which allures.
decree'	an edict; a decision telling what is or must be done.
decree nisi	a provisional decree, which will be made absolute on motion unless cause be shown against it.
defi'/ciency decree'	in a mortgage foreclosure suit, a decree for the balance of the indebtedness after applying the proceeds of a sale of the mortgaged property to such indebtedness.
dec'/re/ment	gradual diminution; the process or fact of decreasing.
decre'/tal order	an order in equity preliminary to the final decree or judgment in the case.
ded'i/mus	writ to commission a private person to do some act in place of a judge, as to examine a witness.
deed	a legal document transferring property from one person to another.
deed in fee	a deed conveying the title to land in fee simple with the usual covenants.
deed of trust	a conveyance of property to one party to be held in trust for another or others.
defal'/cate	to misappropriate funds held in trust.
defal/ca'/tion	includes both embezzlement and misappropriation and is a broader term than either.
defa/ma'/tion	inquiry to a person's reputation—called "libel" when in written form; when by spoken word it is called "slander."
defa/ma'/tion of char'/ac/ter	an attack upon the good name of a person; harming the reputation of a person.
default	failure to perform an act or obligation.

defea´/sance	the clause of a mortgage intended to define the terms and conditions upon which the mortgage shall be satisfied, cease to be security for a debt, and become void.
defea´/si/ble	subject to be defeated, annulled, or revoked upon the happening of a future event or the performance of a condition.
defea´/sible title	one that is liable to be annulled or made void, but not one that is already void or an absolute nullity.
defec´/tive title	the title held by a person who obtains instrument or signature thereto by fraud, force, or fear or other unlawful means, or when he negotiates it in breach of faith.
defend´/ant	a person who is required to answer a charge or suit made by the plaintiff.
def´i/cit	excess of liabilities over assets.
def´i/cit finan/cing	raising of money to meet expenditures which revenues do not cover.
defin´i/tive	having the function of deciding or settling; determining; conclusive; final.
delict	a wrong or injury; an offense against the law.
delim´it	to fix or mark the limits of a territory or country.
delin´/quent	in a state of failing to do what is required by law or duty.
delir´/ium tre´/mens (ABBR. D.T.'s)	a mental disease brought on by the use of intoxicants.
delu´/sion	something that is falsely believed or propagated.
dema´/gogu/ery	the spirit, method, or conduct of an unprincipled politician who leads the populace by appealing to prejudices and passions.
demand depos´it	a bank deposit that can be withdrawn without notice.
demand note	a note that is due at once; one on which suit may be brought without any formal demand.
demesne´ (PRON. demān also demēn)	domain; held in one's own right; lands of the lord himself which were not held by him of a superior.

demise'	the conveyance of an estate, chiefly by lease; to transmit by succession or inheritance.
demur'/rage	charge against a shipper for holding a common carrier's conveyance for loading, such as a truck, railroad car, or ship, beyond the time specified in the agreement.
dene/ga'/tion	denial; contradiction.
den'i/grate	to defame; to blacken.
depo'/nent	a person who gives evidence; one who gives an affidavit or testifies in writing under oath.
depose'	made sworn written statement.
depos'i/tary	the party receiving a document in trust.
depo/si'/tion	a person's testimony given under oath upon interrogatories, not in open court.
depos'i/tory	the place where a document is deposited and kept so that it will be secure.
dep'/re/ca/tory	apologetic; expressing earnest disapproval of; urging reasons against.
depre/cia'/tion	the lessening in worth of any property caused by weather, time, and use, including obsolescence and inadequacy.
depute'	to appoint as one's substitute or agent.
dep'/uty	a person appointed or authorized to act for another.
deraign'	to dispute or contest a claim of another; to trace; to disprove.
deriv'a/tive	not original or primitive; secondary.
derog'a/tion	partial repeal of a law; nullification in whole or in part, as a statute nullifying common-law rights.
descen'/dants	persons born of a certain family or group; offspring; children.
desig'/nee	one who is designated.
detain'er	the wrongful withholding of what belongs to another; writ authorizing the keeper of a prison to continue to keep a person in custody.
detent'	a mechanical locking device.

detente (PRON. dā taⁿt)	a relaxation of strained relations or tensions, as between nations.

detente
(PRON. dā ta^{n}t)

a relaxation of strained relations or tensions, as between nations.

detinet
(det-i'net)

action of debt, for the specific recovery of goods under a contract to deliver them.

det'i/nue

a common-law remedy for the recovery in specie of chattels wrongfully withheld from the plaintiff.

devest'

to deprive.

devise'

a testamentary disposition of land or realty; a gift of real property by the last will and testament of the donor.

devis'ee

one to whom land or other real property is given by will.

devis'or

one who makes a gift of land or other real property by bequest.

devo/lu'/tion

passage onward from stage to stage; transferring from one person to another.

devol'u/tive appeal

an appeal that does not interfere with the carrying out of a judgment appealed from.

diag/no'/sis

etymologically and in its general interpretation, the word signifies a discrimination, a passing of judgment as to physical conditions.

dia/lec'/tics

of or pertaining to the nature of logical arguments; the art of reasoning about matters of opinion.

dichot'/omy

division into two subordinate parts; classification by division, or by successive division, into two groups or sections.

dic'/tum
(PL., dicta
ALSO dictums)

the opinion of a judge that does not embody the resolution or determination of the court.

dilu'/tion

weakening or changing downward the value of previously issued stock as by the issuance of additional stock when not warranted by earnings' growth.

dis/burse'/ments

amounts of money expended or paid out.

dis/charge'

a court order to cancel, dismiss, or to set aside the obligation of a contract.

dis/claim'er

a renunciation or refusal to accept; a denial of interest in the subject matter of a suit.

dis'/count broker	one who discounts promissory notes and bills of exchange, and advances money on securities.
dis/cov'/ert	not under the protection of a husband; not subject to the disabilities of a coverture, applying equally to either a maid or widow.
dis/cov'/ery and inspec'/tion pro/ceed'/ings	pre-trial disclosure proceedings to examine relevant documents or things in the possession of an adverse party.
dis/creet'	wise or judicious in avoiding mistakes or faults; prudent.
dis/crep'/ancy	difference appearing upon comparison; inconsistency.
dis/crete'	disconnected from others; made up of distinct parts; separate.
dis/fran'/chise	to take away a person's citizenship, or his right of suffrage; to deprive of chartered rights and immunities.
dis/her'/ison	depriving of inheritance.
dis/mis'/sal	an order or judgment finally disposing of an action, suit, motion, etc., by sending it out of court, although without a trial of the issues involved.
dis/mis'/sal with prej'u/dice	an adjudication on the merits, and final disposition, barring the right to bring or maintain an action on the same claim or cause.
dis/mis'/sal without prej'u/dice	a voluntary dismissal of an action or proceeding without an adjudication of the cause that would prevent the bringing of a new action upon the same cause.
dis/pa'/rate	distinct in quality or character; essentially different; having no common genus.
dis/pos'i/tive	pertaining to control or disposal; or natural disposition or tendency.
dis/pos'i/tive clause	the clause of conveyance in a deed which provides for the disposition of property.
dis/pos'i/tive facts	producing or bringing about the origination, transfer, or extinction of rights.
dis/sei'/sen OR dis/sei'/zen (PRON. dis-sē-zen)	wrongful dispossession or exclusion of a person entitled to possession.

dis´/so/nance	an inharmonious or harsh sound; discord.
dis/train´	to seize goods or chattels of another.
dis/traint´	a distress; the act of taking and detaining by distress as security for a debt.
dis/tress´	acute suffering; great pain, anxiety, or sorrow.
dis/trib´u/tee	person who is entitled, under the statute of distributions, to the personal estate of one who has died intestate.
dis´/trict attor´/ney	a public officer, elected or appointed, whose chief duty is to prosecute suits on behalf of the state.
divest´(ALSO devest)	to strip or deprive of anything; to take away or alienate property, etc.
dives´/ti/ture	the dispossessing, especially of property, authority, or title.
divorce´	legal dissolution of the marriage ties.
dock´et	a brief entry or the book containing such entries; a list of lawsuits to be tried by court.
doc´/trine	a particular principle taught or advocated.
doc´/trine of dis/cov´/ered peril	same as doctrine of last clear chance; see "last clear chance."
doc´u/ment	an official paper, written or printed, that gives information or proof of some fact.
docu/men´/tary ev´i/dence	evidence supplied by writings and documents of all kinds, as distinguished from "oral" evidence.
domain´	complete and absolute ownership of land.
dom´i/cile	the place where a person has his true, fixed permanent home and principal establishment, and to which place he has, whenever he is absent, the intention of returning, and from which he has no intention of moving.
domi/cil´/iary	existing at, or created at, or connected with the domicile of a suitor or of a decedent.
do´nee (PRON. dō´nē)	receiver of a power.
do´nor	the party conferring a power.
dor´/mant	inactive as in sleep; inoperative.
dos´/sier (PRON. doss-ē-ā)	a bundle of documents all relating to the same matter or subject.

do'tal	pertaining to the separate property which a wife brings to the marriage.
dow'er	the portion of a deceased husband's real property allowed by the law to his widow for her life.
draft	same as bill of exchange; a written order by which one person directs another to pay a sum to a third person, charging it to the maker of the draft.
drawee'	person or institution to whom a bill of exchange is addressed, and who is directed to pay the amount of money mentioned.
drawer'	the maker of a draft or bill of exchange.
dray'/age	the charge made for hauling freight.
due bill	a paper given to a customer who returns ordered goods, granting him credit for such goods against a future purchase.
due care	care which a reasonably prudent man would exercise under similar circumstances.
due pro'/cess of law	a phrase impossible of precise definition; one which asserts a fundamental principle of justice rather than a specific rule of law; law according to settled course of administration through courts of justice.
dun'nage	baggage or personal effects; material used to protect or brace freight to prevent damage in transit from wetting, leakage, or otherwise; loose articles of a cargo.
du'ress	unlawful constraint exercised upon a person whereby he is forced to do some act that he otherwise would not have done.

E

ear'/nest money	a downpayment of part of the purchase price made to bind the bargain.
ease'/ment	a right of the owner of one parcel of land, by reason of such ownership, to use the land of another for a special purpose not inconsistent with a general property in the owner.
easy money	money paid down as evidence of good faith and to bind when an agreement is made.

eccen'/tric	deviating from the recognized or usual practice; erratic; peculiar.
edē'ma	abnormal accumulation of serous fluid.
e'dict	a law or rule of conduct made by a competent authority, usually relating to affairs of state.
educe'	draw forth, as something latent; bring out; elicit.
effect (v.)	to accomplish; to bring to pass; to execute.
(n.)	an impression; a result; a belonging.
ef'flux	the flow of time; outward flow, as of water.
egre'/gious	apart from the herd—i.e., distinguished; remarkably or extraordinarily flagrant.
eject'/ment	action for the recovery of real property and also for damages and costs for unlawful detention of its possession.
elee/mos'y/nary	relating to distribution of charity.
elee/mos'y/nary cor/po/ra'/tion	a private corporation created for charitable and benevolent purposes.
elic'it	to draw or bring out or forth; to derive by reason or argument.
ellip'sis	the omission from a sentence of a word or words which would complete or clarify the construction; asterisks or periods indicating an omission.
eloign (OR eloin)	to remove (oneself) to a distance.
eman'/ci/pate	to release; to set free from any controlling power or influence.
embar'go (PL., embargoes)	restraint on commerce; restriction.
embez'/zle/ment	appropriation of rightful property of another.
em'ble/ments	the products or profits of land which have been sown or planted.
emend'	to correct, usually by textual alterations.
em'i/nent	standing out; notable.
em'i/nent domain	the power to take private property for public use.
emol'u/ment	compensation for services; salary; fees.
empan'el (ALSO impanel)	to select a jury; enroll; enter names on a list.

ena'/bling stat'/ute	a statute which enables one to do what he theretofore could not do.
enact'/ing clause	an orderly, and in some jurisdictions a mandatory, part of a statute, proclaiming the authority by which the statute was enacted.
encash'	to pay drafts, etc., in money.
encode'	change from one form of communication to another.
encroach'/ment (ALSO incroachment)	a movement upon the property, authority, or rights of another; a gradual movement upon and occupancy of the land of another.
encum'/brance (ALSO incumbrance)	the debts owed on property such as taxes and unpaid bills.
endem'ic	peculiar to a particular people or locality, as a disease.
endorse' (ALSO indorse)	to subscribe one's name on the back of an instrument as evidence of receipt or to assign one's interest to another; to approve of; to support.
endor'/see	one to whom a negotiable instrument is endorsed.
endorse'/ment (ALSO indorsement)	a writing on face or back of a legal document.
enfran'/chise/ment	giving franchise or freedom to.
enjoin'	to order or direct (a person, etc.) to do something; to forbid or command by injunction order issued by a court.
enlarge'	to free or set at large, as cattle within an enclosure; to increase in size; to expand; to set at liberty one who is in custody or imprisoned.
en route'	on the journey; along the way.
ensem'/ble	all the parts of a thing taken together, so that each part is considered only in relation to the whole.
entail'(v.) (n.)	to settle or limit succession to real property; a fee limited to the issue instead of descending to all heirs.
entire'ty	a whole of anything, as distinguished from a part of it; an undivided whole, the joint estate of husband and wife.

en´tity | something that has a real existence; a thing; a being, actual or artificial.

entre/pre/neur´ (FEM., entrepreneuse) | contractor; one assuming risk of managing a business.

enure´(ALSO inure) | to operate or take effect; to become of advantage.

eq´ui/ta/ble | just and right; characterized by fairness; pertaining to or valid in equity, as distinguished from the common law.

eq´uity | the mitigating principles, by the application of which substantial justice may be attained in particular cases wherein the prescribed or customary forms of ordinary law seem to be inadequate. [In U.S., equity and chancery are practically equivalent.]

eq´uity plead´/ing | pleading controls developed in the English courts of chancery.

errā´/tum (PL. errā ta) | error in publication.

esca/la´/tion clause | provision in an agreement or contract for a periodic proportional upward or downward adjustment.

escheat´ (n.) | a reversion of an estate to the state when there are no legal heirs or qualified claimants;

(v.) | to be forfeited to the state through lack of heirs.

es´crow | a written document held in custody by a third person until the happening of a prescribed event, or performance of a condition.

eso/ter´ic | confined to a select circle; confidential; adapted exclusively for the enlightened few.

estate´ | an interest in property; the property in which one has a right or interest; the *corpus* of property.

estate by entire´ty (/ties) | an estate predicated on the legal unity of husband and wife, being taken, upon a conveyance or devise to them, to hold as a single person with the right of survivorship as an incident, so that when one dies, the entire estate belongs to the other by virtue of the title originally vested.

estate for years | an estate which must expire at a certain period, fixed in advance.

estate from period to period	an estate continuing for successive periods of a year, or successive periods of a fraction of a year, unless it is terminated.
estate in fee simple	absolute inheritance, clear of any limitation, condition, or restriction to particular heirs.
estate in sev′/er/alty	an estate held by a person in his own right only, without any other person being joined or connected.
estate in suf′/fer/ance	the interest of a tenant who has come rightfully into possession of lands by permission of the owner, and continues to occupy the same after the period for which he is entitled to hold by such permission.
estop′	to stop, bar, or impede; to preclude; to prevent.
estop′/pel	a man's own act or acceptance which keeps him from alleging or pleading the truth or anything to the contrary of what he has accepted.
evict′	to expel from land, a building, etc., by legal process.
evic′/tion	dispossession by process of law: the act of depriving a person of the possession of lands which he has held, in pursuance of the judgment of a court.
ev′i/dence	that which is legally presented as a means of ascertaining the truth, such as through witnesses or objects.
exact in′ter/est	interest computed on the basis of 365 days to the year.
exami/na′/tion before trial (ABBR., ebt)	pre-trial examination under oath of a party to the action or of a witness.
exchange bill of lad′/ing	bill of lading issued in exchange for another bill of lading.
ex-coupon	security sold with current interest payment coupon detached.
ex′cul/pate	to clear from a charge of guilt or fault; to free from blame; to vindicate.
excul′/pa/tory clause	a clause in a trust instrument relieving the trustee from liability for any act performed by him under the trust instrument in good faith.

ex-dividend	without dividend–seller, as owner of record, to receive the dividend paid during a period of closed books in the course of which the transfer of shares was effected; buyer of a stock sold "ex-dividend" is not entitled to current dividend.
exec'u/tant	one who executes or performs.
ex'ecu/ted con'/tract	a contract performed in fulfillment of the object of the contract and the accomplishment of everything required to be done under it.
execu'/tion	a judicial writ directing the enforcement of a judgment.
exec'u/tive	a person or body charged with or skilled in administrative work.
exec'u/tor	a person named by a decedent in his will to carry out the provisions of his will.
exec'u/tors and admin/is/tra/tors	those who are licensed by the probate court to handle the estate of a decedent.
exec'u/tory	that which is yet to be executed or performed.
exem'/plar copy	serving as a pattern, type, or specimen.
exem'/plary dam'/ages	damages given beyond actual loss in order to punish and make an example of the offender; punitive damages.
exem/pli/fi/ca'/tion	an attested copy of a document, under official seal.
exem'/plify	to make an attested copy under seal.
exhib'it	any paper or thing offered in evidence and marked for identification.
ex-interest	without interest.
ex offi'/cio	from or by virtue of the office.
exon'/er/ate	to relieve; to exculpate.
ex'o/ra/ble	susceptible of being persuaded or moved by entreaty.
exo/ter'ic	belonging to the outside world or to the uninitiated (opposite of esoteric).
exot'ic	of foreign origin or character; not native; unusual.
ex par'te	in the interest of one party only; on one side only.

expa'/ti/ate	to enlarge in discourse or writing.
ex'pert	a person selected by court or parties, because of his skill or knowledge, to examine and ascertain and make report of opinion arrived at.
exper/tise' (n.)	expert opinion, commentary, skill, or knowledge.
exper/tize' (v.)	to give professional opinion; to examine and give considered judgment.
expi'ry	coming to an end; the termination of a time fixed by agreement, contract, or law.
explic'it	clearly expressed; leaving nothing implied.
expose' (PL., exposes')	a revelation of something discreditable.
express'	to put into words; to show, manifest, or reveal; direct and not left to implication.
express con'/tract	a contract, the terms of which are stated by the parties; a contract which expresses the intentions of the parties in words.
expro'/pri/ate	to take or condemn, especially for public use by the right of eminent domain, thus divesting the title of the private owner.
expunge'	strike out; obliterate; delete.
ex-rights	stock traded with rights retained or exercised by seller—said of a sale of stock not including such privileges as that of subscribing for additional shares at a stated price.
exscind'	to cut out or off.
extin'/guish	to put out a fire, light, etc.; to discharge (a debt), as by payment.
extra/di'/tion	the surrender of one state or government to another of a person charged with a crime.
extra-dotal prop'/erty	the part of a woman's property under her separate administration and control.
extra/ju/di'/cial	out of or beyond the proper authority of a court or judge.
extra/legal	outside of legal matters.
ex'tra/po/late	to estimate a quantity which depends on one or more variables by extending the variables beyond their established ranges.

extrē'/mis	when a person is sick beyond the hope of recovery, and near death, he is considered to be *in extremis.*
extrin'/sic	not inherent; unessential; from outside sources.
ex-warrants	stock traded with warrants retained or exercised by the seller

F

fac/sim'/ile	an exact copy.
fact	an actual occurrence or logic; questions of fact are for the jury; questions of law are for the court.
fac/ti'/tious	artificial; not spontaneous or natural; developed by fact.
fac'/tor	agent who transacts business or manages affairs for another.
fac'/tor/age	the action or business of a factor; factor's commissions.
fac'/ture	an invoice or bill of goods.
fac'/ulty (/ties)	an ability, natural or acquired, for a particular kind of action; one of the departments of learning, as medicine, law, or theology in a university.
fail-safe	insuring safety in the event of an accident.
famil'/ial	of or pertaining to a family.
fan/ta'/sia	a composition in fanciful or irregular rather than strict form or style.
fea'/sance	doing or performance, as of a condition or duty.
fea'/si/ble	suitable; capable of being done, effected, or accomplished.
Fed'/eral gov'/ern/ment	alliance of states into a union so that central power is erected into a true state or nation.
fee	an inherited right in land; a written account of a charge for services.
fee sim'/ple (PL., fees simple)	absolute ownership of property without limitations of heirs to whom it must descend.

fee tail (PL., fees tail)	property limited to a particular class of heirs.
felo´/ni/ous	malicious; villainous; perfidious; in a legal sense, done with intent to commit a crime.
fel´/ony	an offense punishable by death, or by imprisonment in a state prison or penitentiary; a crime more serious than a misdemeanor.
fen (ALSO fenway)	a marsh or swamp.
feoff´/ment (PRON. fēf´ment)	gift of any corporeal hereditament to another.
feu´/dal sys´/tem	the social, economic, and political system of the Middle Ages under which vassals held land on giving service to the lord owning it in return for protection and the use of the land.
fiat (fi´at)	an order emanating from an authoritative source and in the positive terms of "let it be done."
fiat money	money not convertible into coin or specie of equivalent value.
fic/ti´/tious	false; not genuine; created by the imagination.
fidel´/ity	strict observances of promises, duties, etc.; loyalty.
fidu´/ciary	a person to whom property is entrusted to hold, control, or manage for another; trustee of an estate or director of a corporation.
FIFO	an acronym derived from First-In, First-Out, this being a bookkeeping method of calculating inventory values.
fili/a´/tion	the judicial determination of the paternity of a child, especially of a bastard; the act of being a child of a certain parent.
finan´/cial state´/ment	balance sheet; a statement in writing stating fully assets and liabilities.
find´er	a person who discovers personal property lost by him or another; for the purpose of the crime of larceny by finder, one who discovers lost property with knowledge that it is lost property.
first-hand	from the first or original source.
fis´/cal	pertaining to financial matters in general.
fiscal period	the period of time for which an analysis of the operations of the business is made.

fiscal year	a fiscal year can run from any date in one year to a like date in the year following, usually for tax purposes; whereas, a calendar year begins on January 1st and ends on December 31st.
fixed assets (ALSO capital assets)	nontrading assets such as land, building, machinery, etc., necessary for operating a business.
fixed charges	expenses which must be met, such as taxes, mortgage interest, insurance, depreciation.
fix'/ture	something securely fixed in position; article attached to real estate.
flam'/ma/ble	easily set on fire; combustible.
flot'/sam	part of the wreckage of a ship and its cargo found floating on the water.
flotsam and jetsam	drifting material or persons; flotsam is wreckage of a ship floating on the sea; jetsam is goods cast overboard to lighten a vessel in distress and which sink or remain in the water.
fol'/lower	filing term; an upright of wood or metal that slides along a rod behind the contents of a drawer and serves to hold the cards or folders firmly and in a vertical position.
for/bear'	to refrain from; desist from; cease.
forced sale	sale of property to satisfy claims of creditors.
for'/ci/ble entry	an entry by breaking doors to make an arrest or a search of premises.
fore'/bear	an ancestor; forefather.
fore/clo'/sure	termination of all rights of the mortgagor or his grantee in property covered by the mortgage.
for'/eign cor/po/ra'/tion	corporation organized under the laws of another state.
foreign judgment	judgment obtained in an out-of-state court.
for/en'/sic	pertaining to or belonging to the courts; in the field of public discussion or debate.
for/en'/sic med'i/cine	the science of medicine as connected with the law.
forg'/ery	a criminal offense at common law and under statutes defining the term variously; essentially, the false making or material alteration, with intent to defraud, or, under some statutes, intent to injure.

fo′rum	a court; a tribunal; a jurisdiction; a place where justice is administered; the place of jurisdiction.
fran′/chise	a privilege or right granted by a government or governmental agency.
frank′/ing priv′i/lege	a granting of right to send mail postage-free.
fraud	deception practiced to induce another to part with property or surrender some legal right, and which accomplishes this end.
free alongside	with delivery at the side of ship, free of charges when buyer's liability begins.
free and clear	without encumbrance.
freeboard	the part of a ship's side between the water line and the deck or gunwale.
freeboard deck	deck below which all bulkheads are made watertight.
free-form company	corporate conglomerate; marriage of two or more unrelated companies into a new multi-industry company.
freehold	an estate in fee simple, in fee tail, or for life.
free on board	a term of sale, meaning that the seller agrees to deliver the merchandise aboard the carrier without extra charge to buyer.
free port	port open to all ships and goods without the demand that customs duties be paid.
friendly suit	any suit instituted by agreement between the parties to obtain the opinion of the court upon some doubtful question in which they are interested.
front′/age	the measure in feet or other linear unit of measurement of the boundary between a street or highway and an abutting property.
front foot	1 foot of the width of a plot of land facing on a street, road, or waterfront.
frozen assets	resources that cannot be quickly liquidated.
fruits	civil law—rents and income from real property, interest on money loaned, etc.
ful′/some	offensive to good taste, especially as being excessive; gross; disgusting.

funded debt	an indebtedness in the form of long-term obligations.
fun'/gi/ble	interchangeable; consumable by use, and returnable in kind.

G

gar'/nish	institution of legal proceedings by which a creditor receives his money by attachment of money which would otherwise normally proceed to the debtor; to warn; to notify.
gar'/ni/shee (n.)	the person upon whom a garnishment is served, usually a person indebted to, or in possession of property of the defendant in the main action.
(v.)	to attach the money of an employee through his employer to satisfy a debt.
gar'/nish/ment	a legal process to reach the money or effects of a debtor in the possession or control of another.
gauche (PRON. gōsh)	lacking in social grace; awkward; tactless.
gen'/eral assign'/ment	as an act of bankruptcy—any conveyance at common law or by statute by which one intends to make an absolute and unconditional appropriation of all his property to pay his creditors; share and share alike.
gen'/eral av'er/age	in marine insurance, a proportionate contribution levied on ship and goods to cover necessary sacrifice of a part.
gen'/eral part'/ner	a partner in an ordinary partnership, as distinguished from the special or limited partner in a limited partnership.
gen'/eral release	a surrender of one's claim to the obligated party.
ger/mane'	closely related; pertinent.
ger'/ry/man/der (PRON. gĕr'i man der)	to divide areas into political units to give advantages to one group.
give and bequeath	these words, in a will, import a benefit in point of right, to take effect upon the decease of the testator and proof of the will.
gla'/zer	one who applies glossy coating on china.

gla′/zier	one who fits windows, etc., with glass.
glos′/sary	an alphabetical list of terms taken from a book, appearing in the back of the volume, with explanations intended to be of assistance to the reader.
goodwill	favorable attitude of public toward a business enterprise, being an intangible asset in estimating the value of the company involved.
Gordian knot	pertaining to Gordius, ancient king of Phrygia, who tied a knot (the Gordian knot) which was to be undone only by one who should rule Asia, and which was summarily cut by Alexander the Great; a difficulty that can only be overcome by bold measures.
grand jury	a body composed of a number, which varies from state to state, sometimes six, sometimes 12, and occasionally more than 12, to which is committed the duty of inquiring into crimes committed in the county from which the members are drawn, the determination of the probability of guilt, and the finding of indictments against supposed offenders.
grant (n.)	a conveyance or transfer of real property, especially of public lands.
(v.)	to convey, especially real property.
gran/tee′	a person to whom a grant is made; the party in a deed to whom the conveyance is made.
grant′or	a person who makes a grant; the party to a deed who makes the conveyance.
gra′/tis	without reward or consideration.
gra/tu′i/tous	without valuable or legal compensation.
gra/va′/men	gist; essence; substance; sting; grievance or injury specially complained of; the weight or substance of charge, complaint, or cause.
gre/gar′i/ous	living in flocks or herds, as animals; pertaining to a flock or crowd.
Gross National Product (GNP)	the market value of all the goods and services our economy produces in a given period.
guar/an/tee′ (n.) (PL.,/tees)	a formal assurance given by way of security; assurance of truth, genuineness, etc.; he to whom guaranty is made.

(v.)	to promise; to answer for; denoting action of assuming responsibilities of a guarantor.
guar´/an/tor	one who promises to answer for the debt, default, or miscarriage of another.
guar´/anty (n.) (PL., /ties)	a document promising to perform as stated or agreed upon.
(v.)	to assume responsibility of a guarantor.
guard´/ian	a person to whom the law has intrusted the custody and control of the person, or estate, or both, of an infant, lunatic, or incompetent person.
guardian ad litem (lī´tem)	a guardian appointed by a court of justice to prosecute or defend for an infant in any suit to which he may be a party.
guides	filing term; heavy cardboard sheets of the same size as the folders or cards.

H

habeas corpus (PRON. hā´bĭ es kor´pus)	a writ requiring the body of a person to be brought before a judge or court, esp. for investigation of a restraint of the person's liberty.
hab´/en/dum	clause usually following granting part of deed and beginning with words "to have and to hold."
hab´ it/able	tenantable; reasonably fit for occupation by a tenant of the class which occupies it.
hand money	same as earnest money; money paid down as evidence of good faith and to bind when an agreement is made.
har´/bor dues	fixed charges for a ship's use of a harbor.
hard money	specie; a coin of precious metals, of a certain weight and fineness, with the government stamp thereon, denoting its value as a medium of exchange or currency.
have and hold	phrase used in habendum clause of deed.
headnotes	statements in summary and concise form which appear in law reports at the head of the reported cases, to indicate the propositions decided by a case and the order in which various propositions declared in a case appear in the opinion.

hearsay evidence	evidence given by a witness who speaks not from his own information but from information learned from another person.
heat of pas´/sion	in criminal law, a state of violent and uncontrollable rage engendered by a blow or certain other provocation given, which will reduce a homicide from the grade of murder to that of manslaughter.
hedge	to buy or sell in order to balance a threatened loss in other transactions.
heir legal	an heir who succeeded to the estate of his ancestor by descent under the law of succession, as distinguished from an heir who took possession under a will or a contract.
heirs	those who succeed to either real or personal property of a decedent who dies intestate.
hell and high-water rule	a term for the liberal rule in the construction of the omnibus clause of an automobile liability insurance policy.
hered´i/ta/ments	a comprehensive term, including anything capable of being inherited, be it corporeal, incorporeal, real, personal, or mixed.
her´it/age	what is or may be handed on to a person from his ancestors; inheritance.
hetero/ge´/neous	unlike; differing in kind or nature; consisting of elements or parts that are dissimilar or unrelated.
hia´/tus (PRON. hī ā´tus)	an interruption of continuity; a break, with a part missing.
Hobson's choice	a choice without an alternative (after Thomas Hobson, about 1544-1631, of Cambridge, England, who rented horses, and obliged each customer to take in his turn the horse nearest the stable door or none at all).
hoist by one's own petard	blown up by one's own bomb.
holder in due course	a bona fide holder for value without notice; the holder of a bill, note, or check who is legally entitled to receive payment.
holding company	company controlling subsidiary companies through possession of their stock issues.

holding over	retention of premises by a lessee after expiration of his lease.
hol´o/graph	a writing which is wholly in the handwriting of the ostensible author.
hol´o/graphic will	a will that is entirely written and signed by the testator in his own handwriting.
homestead	the real estate occupied as a home and subject to the right of having it at least partially exempt from levy and forced sale.
hom´i/cide	the killing of one human being by another, whether or not the killing is lawful or justifiable.
homo/ge´/neous	having the same composition, structure or character throughout; uniform; similar or identical in form or nature.
hono/rar´/ium (PL., honoraria)	a fee paid for professional services rendered gratuitously or under such conditions that there is no legal obligation for payment.
hornbook	a rudimentary treatise; elementary text.
hung jury	a jury so irreconcilably divided in opinion that they cannot agree upon a verdict.
husband and wife	the parties to a marriage contract.
hypoth´e/cate	to pledge without delivery of title or possession; to mortgage.
hypoth´e/ca/ted accounts	accounts receivable pledged as security for a loan.
hypoth´e/ca/tion	process of borrowing on securities.
hypoth´e/sis (PL., hypoth´e/ses)	a supposition, a proposition, or principle which is assumed or taken for granted, in order to draw a conclusion or inference for proof of the point in question; something not proved, but assumed for the purpose of argument, or to account for a fact or an occurrence.
hypo/thet´i/cal question	a combination of assumed or proved facts and circumstances upon which the opinion of an expert is asked, by way of evidence at a trial.

I

ibid. (ABBREV. for ibidem)	in the same place.

id	the instinctive impulses of the individual.
id. (idem)	it; that.
iden'/ti/cal	the same exactly.
ideo (PRON. ī'de ō)	therefore; on that account.
ide/ol'/ogy	the aims of a socio-political program; visionary theorizing; systematic body of concepts as relating to life and culture.
id'i/ocy	extreme degree of mental deficiency; senseless folly.
idi/o/syn'/crasy	any tendency, characteristic, mode of expression, or the like, peculiar to an individual.
ille'/gal	unlawful; contrary to law; illicit.
illic'it	not permitted or authorized; unlicensed; unlawful.
illu'/sion	deception; false conception or impression.
illu'/sory	permeated with illusion; deceiving.
im'ma/nent	indwelling; remaining within; inherent.
im'mi/nent	impending; threatening; about to materialize, especially something of a dangerous nature.
immor'al	not conforming to the moral law.
immu'/nity	freedom or protection from obligation, service, or duty otherwise legally imposed.
impair'	to make or become worse; diminish in value, excellence, etc.
impan'el	to select a jury; enroll; enter names on a list.
im'passe	predicament affording no obvious escape.
impeach'/ment	charging with misbehavior in office; challenging or discrediting the credibility of a witness.
imped'i/ment	an obstruction—for example, an obstruction on a highway; a disqualification—for example, insanity barring marriage.
imper'a/tive	not to be avoided or evaded; commanding.
imper'/ti/nence	rudeness; insolence; matter in a complaint, bill, answer, or other pleading not properly before the court for decision at any stage of the suit, particularly, scandalous allegations.

implead´	to sue in a court of justice; to accuse, to impeach; to join in action as party defendant.
im´ple/ment	to give practical effect to and ensure actual fulfillment; to carry out.
implic´it	implied, rather than expressly stated; being without doubt or reserve; unquestioning.
implied´	gathered by implication or induction; understood.
implied con´/tract	a contract inferred from the conduct of the parties, although not expressed in words.
implied cov´e/nant	a covenant in law; a covenant which may reasonably be inferred from the whole agreement and the circumstances attending its execution.
implied trust	a trust which comes into existence through the application of intention to create a trust as a matter of law.
implied war´/ranty	a statement, description, or undertaking by the insured under a policy which binds the insured as though expressed in the contract.
im´post	something imposed or levied, such as tax or duty.
im´po/tency	inability to engage in, or lack of capacity for, normal sexual intercourse; a term applying to both male and female.
imprac´/ti/ca/ble	that which cannot be put into practice with the available means.
impress´/ment	act of seizing for public use; forcing into service, particularly public service or military service.
impri/ma´/tur	an official license to print or publish a book, etc.
improve´/ment	a valuable addition made to property to enhance its value.
inac/ces´/si/ble	in a place which cannot be reached.
inad/ver´/tence	absence of intention; heedlessness.
ina´lien/able	incapable of being alienated, surrendered, or transferred.
ina/ni´/tion	lack of vitality or vigor; lethargy.
inau/gu/ra´/tion	the installation into office of a person elected or appointed to a high office of state.

incen´/di/ary	pertaining to the malicious burning of property; one guilty of arson; a person who stirs up trouble.
in´cest	the crime of sexual intercourse between persons related by blood or marriage within the degrees in which marriage is prohibited.
inchoate (PRON. in kō´it)	recently begun; incomplete; contracts are inchoate until they are executed.
inchoate interest	an interest which may ripen into a vested estate.
inci/den´/tally	by the way; naturally appertaining.
incip´i/ent	just beginning to exist.
inclo´/sure	a fence, wall, hedge, rail, or other tangible obstruction protecting premises against encroachment.
incom/bus´/ti/ble	incapable of being burned or consumed by fire, at least an ordinary fire.
income tax	a government tax charged against a designated portion of earned income.
in common	shared together.
incom´/pe/tency	inefficiency; a lack of some requisite ability.
incom´/pe/tent ev´i/dence	evidence which is not admissible under the established rules of evidence.
incon/sis´/tent	repugnant; not in harmony or accord; contradictory.
incon/ven´/ience	disquiet; uneasiness; annoyance; incommode.
incor´/po/rate	to combine in one unit; to form a corporation.
in corpore (PRON. in kor´po-re)	in body; in substance.
incor/po´/real	having no physical existence; intangible.
incor´/ri/gi/ble	unmanageable.
in´cre/ment	an addition or increase; growth.
incrim´i/nate	to charge with a crime; inculpate.
incroach´/ment	anything taken by advancing beyond proper limits (same as encroachment).
incul´/pa/ble	free from guilt; blameless; innocent.
incul´/pate	to charge with fault; to blame; to accuse; to involve in a charge; to incriminate.

incum′/bent	imposed as a duty; obligatory; one holding an office.
incum′/brance	a lien or liability that is attached to property.
incur′/able	beyond the power and skill of medicine.
indebt′/ed/ness	the aggregate of a person's debts; the state of being obligated upon a debt or debts.
inde′/cency	impropriety; indelicacy or immodesty.
inde/feas′/ible	that which cannot be defeated, revoked, or made void; usually applied to an estate or right which cannot be defeated.
indem′/nify	secure against loss or damage; make reimbursement for loss.
indem′/nity	an agreement by which one person agrees to secure another against anticipated loss or damage.
indent′	to prepare a deed or an agreement in the form of an indenture; to enter into articles of apprenticeship.
inden′/ture	a deed executed by both grantor and grantee or all parties to the instrument.
inde/pend′/ent con′/trac/tor	one who does work for another without being his employee.
inde/pend′/ent exec′u/tor	the executor named to execute a will without administration in the probate court, thus avoiding the usual costs of regular administrations.
independent school district	a school district which has not been consolidated with any other school district.
inde/ter′/mi/nate	that which is uncertain.
index (PL., indexes or indices)	a sign, a token, or indication; a guiding principle.
indicia (PL.) (PRON. in dish′i a) (SING., indicium)	distinctive marks; signs; indications; symptoms; disclosures.
indict′	to charge one with the commission of a crime by an indictment.
indict′/able offense	a felony.
indic′/tion	proclamation made every 15 years in the later Roman Empire, fixing the valuation of property to be used as a basis for taxation; a tax based on such valuation.

indict´/ment	a written accusation, especially that presented by a grand jury, charging that a person therein mentioned is guilty of a public offense, punishable on indictment.
in´di/gence	poverty.
indig´e/nous	originating or thriving naturally in a particular environment; native to a region.
in´di/gent	lacking the necessaries of life; poor; needy.
indis/pen´/sa/ble	vital; essential; that which cannot be dispensed with.
indi/vis´/ible contract	a contract impossible of division so as to render a valid part enforceable pro tanto where another part is invalid.
induce´/ment	that which prevails on a person to promote an act or acts by him; for example, fraud inducing the making of a contract.
induct´	to lead or conduct; to place or install a person in an office.
ine´/bri/ate	to intoxicate mentally or emotionally; to make drunk; exhilarate.
ineq´/ui/ta/ble	unjust; not according to the principles of equity.
inev´i/ta/ble	that which cannot be avoided, evaded, or escaped; certain or necessary.
inex´o/ra/ble	unyielding; not to be moved by entreaty.
in´famy	disgrace; loss of reputation; the stigma which attaches to a person who has been convicted of an infamous crime.
in´fant	one who is legally a minor, not being of full age.
infec´/tious	capable of transmitting a feeling, particularly a feeling of gaiety; capable of causing an infection leading to a disease.
inflam´/ma/ble	capable of being set on fire; combustible.
infor/ma´/tion	a written statement for the purpose of accusing another before a court or a court officer.
in´fra	meaning "below" and used with a page number in a brief to indicate, "see footnotes"; occurring in subsequent matter [opposite of "supra" and "ante"].

infrac'/tion	a breach, infringement, or violation.
infringe'/ment	a violation of a right or privilege; an encroachment.
ingen'/ious	having inventive faculty; skillful in contriving or constructing.
ingen'u/ous	free from reserve, restraint, or dissimulation; artless; innocent.
inhab'/it/ant	one domiciled in or having a fixed residence in a given locality.
inhere'	to belong intrinsically.
inher'/ent	an inseparable quality or part of a thing or a person; intrinsic to a thing or a person.
inher'/it/ance	that which is derived from an ancestor or as a legacy or which is transmissible to an heir; ownership.
inhib'it	to restrain, hinder, arrest, or check an action, impulse, etc.; to prohibit; to forbid.
inhi/bi'/tion	a prohibition; a writ to prohibit a judge from proceeding further in a matter.
ini'/ti/a/tive	an introductory act or step; enterprise; readiness and ability in initiating action; the general right or ability to present a new bill or measure, as in a legislature.
injunc'/tion	an order issued by a court of equity forbidding or commanding the performance of a certain act.
injured party	a person wronged by the action of the other.
in lieu of	in substitution for or in place of; ordinarily implying the existence of something to be replaced.
in lim'/i nē	at the outset; on the threshold.
innu/en'do	an indirect intimation about a person or thing; a parenthetic explanation or specification in a pleading.
inoc'u/late	to inject a virus into the body for the purpose of causing a disease in a mild form, thereby building up an immunity.
inop'/era/tive pat'/ent	a patent for an invention which fails to secure to the inventor a monopoly of his actual invention.

in perpetuity	of endless duration.
in′quest	a legal or judicial inquiry, especially before a jury.
inquirendo	an authorization to institute an inquiry on behalf of the government.
inquisition	a church tribunal for the discovery and suppression of heresy; in law, an inquest.
insecurity clause	a provision in a chattel mortgage which gives the mortgagee a right to take possession of the mortgaged chattels whenever he deems himself insecure.
in severalty	the character of a holding of land by one person in his own right only, without any other person being joined or connected with him in point of interest during the continuance of his estate in the land.
insig′/nia (PL.) insigne (SING).	coats of arms; armorial bearings; emblems of rank; pins, badges, or ribbons worn by members.
insol′/vency	the state of being unable to pay one's debts.
instal′/ment or install′/ment	any of several parts into which a debt or other sum payable is divided for payment at successive fixed times.
in′stance	a request; a precedent; instigation; solicitation; an occasion.
in′sti/gate	to stimulate or incite to an action, especially a bad act.
in′sti/tute	to set up or establish; to set on foot; initiate; inaugurate.
in′stru/ment	a formal or legal document in writing, such as a contract, deed, will, bond, or lease.
insuf/fi′/cient funds	the want of sufficient funds in a bank account for the payment of a check drawn by the depositor.
insu/lar′/ity	narrowness or illiberality of opinion.
insu/la′/tion	material used to prevent the passage or leakage of electricity, heat, or sound.
insur′/able risk	a person has an insurable interest if he might be financially injured by the occurrence of the event insured against.

intan´/gi/ble assets	assets having a value but representing no material substance, such as patents, goodwill, discoveries, claims, copyrights, etc.
inte´/gra´/tion	the bringing together of people of all races, but particularly of the black and white races, in all the common concerns of men—educational, political, industrial, religious, and social—by removing all bars of discrimination based on race or color.
intel´/li/gence quo/tient (I.Q.)	a rating by number of the level of intelligence of a particular person.
intem´/per/ance	immoderate indulgence in alcoholic liquors; lack of moderation or due restraint, as in action or speech.
inten´/tion/ally	in an intentional manner; with design; of purpose.
inter/cep´/ted shipment	a shipment of goods by the seller which the buyer intercepts before it reaches its original destination, thereby actually and lawfully obtaining possession.
inter/ces´/sion	the act of interceding between parties with a view that differences be reconciled.
inter/change´/able	capable of being put or used in place of each other.
inter/dict´	a legal order issued as a remedy forbidding something to be done.
interest upon condition precedent	a contingent interest.
inter/fer´/ence	an obstruction or hindrance to use, such as the placing of railings or barriers in a highway; opposition; collision.
in´terim	meanwhile; in the meantime.
interlocking directorate	the relationship between two or more corporations who have directors or officers in common.
inter/loc´u/tory	provisional; not final.
in´ter/loper	person who goes into a matter to which he has no right, or who interferes wrongfully.
inter/me´/di/ary	one who negotiates a matter between two parties.
inter/me´/di/ate	occurring between two events; intervening; interlocutory.

| inter/mit´/tent | that which ceases for a time; alternately ceasing and beginning again. |

inter/na´/tional extra/di´/tion — the surrender by one nation of an individual accused or convicted of an offense outside of the territory of the former and within the territorial jurisdiction of the latter, which, being competent to try to punish him, demands the surrender.

intern´/ment — the detention of a resident enemy alien during the existence of a declared war between his country and the United States; the act of a neutral nation in detaining ships, sailors, soldiers, or property of a belligerent.

inter-office — functioning or communicating between the offices of an organization.

interplead — to go to trial with each other to determine a right on which the action of a third party depends.

interpleader — a proceeding to enable a person to compel parties making the same claim against him to litigate the matter between themselves.

inter´/po/late — to insert words in an instrument or manuscript; to alter a complete document.

inter/po/si´/tion — intervention; stepping in between parties in opposition; an interference.

inter´/pret — to set forth the meaning of; to explain or elucidate.

inter/pre/ta´/tion clause — a clause contained in many statutes which governs the construction of the statute, or which defines one or more terms of the statute.

interregnum — period during which the normal functions of government or control are suspended; a lapse or pause in a continuous series.

inter/rog´a/to/ries — a formal list of questions addressed to a person, especially a witness.

inter/rup´/tion of pos/ses´/sion — an interruption of the continuity of the possession of an adverse claimant; any substantial interruption in the possession of an adverse claimant.

interstate commerce — commerce between states; interstate transportation or work so closely related thereto as to be practically a part of it.

interurban bus — a bus running between cities or other centers of population.

intervener OR intervenor	person interposing with permission of court.
intes'/tacy	state of dying without a valid will.
intes'/tate	the status of having died without making a valid will.
in'/ti/macy	a friendly relationship; an illicit, improper, and degrading relationship; an illicit sexual relationship.
intol'/er/ance	bigotry; narrow-mindedness; an intrusion upon our traditional concept of religious liberty.
intra/mu'/ral	occurring or being within the limits or confines of a community, institution, or group.
intran'/si/gent OR intransigeant	uncompromising, especially in politics; irreconcilable.
intra-office	within the office of an organization.
intrastate commerce	commerce within the limits of one state.
intra-urban (use hyphen)	within the limits of a city.
intrin'/sic	inherent; belonging to a thing by its very nature.
inure	to accrue to the benefit of a person; to devolve upon a person.
invei'/gle	to draw by beguiling or artful inducements; to allure; to win; to seduce by beguiling.
in'ven/tory	a list of assets of the estate; a detailed list of articles with their estimated values.
inves'/ti/ture	the act of investing or clothing a person with actual possession.
investment trust	a company which pools money received from individual investors and invests it in a diversified group of securities.
invi'o/la/ble	immunity from being violated; immunity or exemption from violence; not to be violated.
invol'/un/tary trust	a trust founded on a contract supported by a consideration; a trust arising by operation of law.
in witness whereof	a formal expression commonly used at the beginning of the attestation clause of any signed document, making it clear that the persons signing are witnesses.
irref'/ra/ga/ble	that which cannot be refuted or disproved.
irre/fran'/gi/ble	incapable of being broken or violated.

irrel´e/vancy   want of pertinency, whether in a pleading or in evidence; redundant; not forming or tendering any material issue in the case.

irre/sist´/ible   a force incapable of being resisted, repelled, or overcome; an overwhelming force, such as that of a mob.

irrev´o/ca/ble   that which cannot be changed; unalterable.

ir´ri/tant clause   a clause in a deed or other instrument containing a condition, the happening of which will render the instrument void.

is´su/able   prepared and ready for issue, as bonds; capable of being raised as an issue.

issue   person(s) descended from a common ancestor; point to be adjudicated.

itin´/er/ant   traveling from place to place; wandering; a person who roams or travels from place to place.

itin´/er/ary   a line of travel; a route; an account of a journey; a record or plan of travel.

J

jack-knife   a large pocketknife.

jackknifing   a familiar cause of highway accidents, being a movement of a trailer contrary to the movement of the tractor, so that, joined together, they bend in the middle.

jackpot   a game of chance; the amount in a slot machine which may be released to a winner.

jar´/gon   unintelligible or meaningless talk or writing; a technical or specialized vocabulary used by members of a particular profession.

jejune´   dull; lacking interest or significance; lacking maturity.

jeop´/ardy   danger; peril; hazard or risk of loss or harm.

jet´sam   floating material which was thrown overboard from a ship in danger of being wrecked or capsized.

jet´/ti/son   the voluntary casting overboard of part of the cargo in order to relieve the ship in distress; a peril of the sea within the meaning of a marine insurance policy.

jocus	a game of chance.
John Doe	a fictitious name of a person which is often substituted in an action or proceeding for a party's real name until the latter can be ascertained.
joinder	acting jointly with one or more other persons; joining.
joinder in demurrer	the formal acceptance by the adverse party to an action of the issue of law which is tendered by a party's demurrer to such adverse party's pleading.
joint and several note	a note with two or more signers, each of whom would be liable for the performance of the pledge.
joint covenant	a covenant made with two or more covenantees who carry the burden or receive the benefit as one person.
joint executors	two or more persons acting jointly as executors in the administration of a decedent's estate.
jointly and severally	together and separately; persons who are jointly and severally in a bond or note may all be sued together, or the creditor may select any one or more as the object of a suit.
joint-stock company	association of persons holding capital in common, but with any member being able to transfer his holdings at will.
joint tenancy	ownership wherein two or more persons have identical interests in property—when one dies, the other takes his share free of any claim of the heirs or widow.
join'/ture	a provision made for a wife by way of a marriage settlement.
joint will	a single testamentary instrument which contains the wills of two or more persons, is executed jointly by them, and disposes of property owned jointly, in common, or in severalty by them.
journal	a formal record of court proceedings; a record to which original entries are transferred; a publication, such as a magazine.
journeyman	one who has become qualified at his trade or occupation.

judgment	the official and authentic decision of a court of justice upon the respective rights and claims of the parties to an action or suit therein litigated and submitted to its determination.
judgment-creditor	one who is entitled to enforce a judgment by execution; owner of an unsatisfied judgment.
judgment-debtor	a person against whom a judgment has been entered and which has not been satisfied.
judgment lien	security for the judgment debt.
judi'/cial	having to do with courts, judges, or the administration of justice.
judicial dictum	an expression of opinion by a court on a point not necessary to a decision but deliberately passed upon by the court.
judicial notice	a method by which the court accepts certain facts without requiring evidence.
judicial process	all the acts of the court from the beginning of an action or proceeding to the end.
jural (ju'ral)	relating to rights and obligations as subjects of jurisprudence.
jura'/tion	the taking of an oath; the administration of an oath by one authorized.
jure (ju're)	in right; in law; by right; by law.
juridic OR jurid'i/cal	of or pertaining to the administration of justice; pertaining to law or jurisprudence.
juris/dic'/tion	the legal authority of a court.
juris/dic'/tional dispute	conflicting claims by labor unions over representation of employees or over the right to do certain types of work.
juris/pru'/dence	the philosophy of law, or the science which treats of the principles of positive law and legal relations.
juror (jur'or)	one of a body of persons sworn to deliver a verdict in a case submitted to them.
jury	a certain number of people selected according to law and sworn to inquire of certain matters of fact and declare the truth upon the evidence available to them.
jury box	that portion of the court room in which the jury are seated during the trial of a case.

jus'/tice	righteousness; equitableness; a judicial officer; a judge or magistrate.
justice of the peace	a local magistrate who administers summary justice in minor cases, administers oaths, performs civil marriages, and the like.
jus/ti'/ci/able	proper to be examined in courts of justice.
jus'/ti/fi/able	defensible; that which can be shown to be, or can be defended as being, just or right.
just title	same as color of title; a title that is imperfect, but not so obviously that the imperfection is apparent to one not skilled in the law.
ju've/nile	a young person; one not of legal age as prescribed by law.
jux/ta/po/si'/tion	position side by side; a placing close together.

K

kan/ga/roo' court	a mock court or trial characterized by irresponsible, irregular, or unauthorized status or procedure in which the principles of law and justice are perverted or disregarded.
Keogh plan	a relatively new pension plan which offers self-employed business and professional people the chance to obtain for themselves advantages long enjoyed by employees of many businesses.
kickback	the practice of an employer, foreman, or person in a supervisory position of taking back a portion of the wages due to workers; the payment of money or property to an individual for causing his employer, client, patient, customer, or principal to buy from, to use the services of, or to deal otherwise with, the person making the payment.
kill	a channel, stream, or creek.
kiln (PRON. kil OR kiln)	a furnace or oven for burning, baking, or drying.
kin	a group of persons of common ancestry; related by blood.
kin'/dred	a body of persons related to another, or a family, tribe, or race.

kite	to secure the temporary use of money by issuing or negotiating worthless papers and then redeeming such paper with the proceeds of similar paper. The word is also used as a noun meaning the worthless papers thus employed.
kit and kin	friends and relatives.
klep/to/ma´/nia	an irresistible propensity to steal, without regard to personal needs.
knowingly and wilfully	a purposeful failure to obey the law, with knowledge of the facts; an essential term in an indictment where it constitutes a part of the statutory definition of the offense.
known equivalent	a patent law term; a known device used as a substitute which effects the same result.

L

labor ag´i/ta/tor	one actively engaged in promoting the interests of labor.
lac/era´/tion	rough, jagged tear; mangling of flesh.
laches	unconscionable, undue, unexcused, unexplained, or unreasonable delay in assertion of right.
land grant institutions	educational institutions which have received a land grant made by Congress for the support of education.
landlord and tenant	a phrase used to denote the familiar legal relation existing between lessor and lessee of real estate.
landmark	a natural or artificial object having sufficient permanency to serve as a monument or marker of a land boundary.
land patent	a conveyance by which title to public land is passed.
lands, tenements, and hereditaments	inheritable lands or interests therein amounting to freehold estates.
lapi/da´/tion	stoning to death; the execution of the death penalty by stoning the defendant.
lapse	a slip or slight error; the termination of a right or privilege through neglect to exercise it or through failure of some contingency.

lar'/ceny	felonious stealing, taking and carrying, leading, riding, or driving away another's personalty.
lar/gess' (ALSO largesse)	an innate generosity of mind or spirit; excessive gratuities.
las/civ'i/ous	loose; wanton; lewd; lustful; tending to produce voluptuous or lewd emotions.
laser	*Light Amplification by Stimulated Emission of Radiation* (an acronym).
last clear chance	a doctrine which states that an injured party may recover, even though negligent, if the defendant could have avoided the injury after discovering the peril.
last will and testament	instrument executed by the maker for the purpose of disposing of his estate after death.
la'tent	hidden; concealed; present, but not visible or apparent.
latent defect	a defect not observable on casual inspection.
lat'/eral	from or toward the side.
lateral support	support which adjoining land or the soil beneath gives one's own land.
lawbook	a book primarily for use by lawyers, such as a digest, law report, text, or a volume of an encyclopedic work such as American Jurisprudence or Corpus Juris.
lawful heirs	those persons upon whom the descent of real property is cast upon the death of the owner intestate.
layoff	a temporary suspension of employment of a person at the insistence of his employer.
layout	a sketch of a building to be constructed; the plan or scheme determining the style and arrangement of a printed page, a newspaper, or an advertisement.
lease	a written agreement or oral contract, granting the right to use property for a certain length of time, usually gained by paying rent.
leasehold	an estate in realty held under a lease; an estate for a fixed term of years.
lech'/er/ous	characterized by lewdness; lustful.

led′/ger	a book of accounts in which a business keeps a record of all money transactions.
leg′/acy	a bequest of property by will.
legal	conforming to the law; according to law; required or permitted by law; not forbidden or discountenanced by law.
legal capacity	the ability to make contracts, conveyances, mortgages, etc., which are binding and beyond nullification, for disability of the person arising from infancy, mental incompetency, etc.
legal entity	an organization or association recognized in law as an entity apart from the individual members.
legal intent	a presumed intent; for example, the intent to accomplish the natural and probable consequences of one's acts.
le′gal/ize	to authorize; to sanction.
legal notice	notice complying with the requirements of the law.
legal tender	that kind of coin which the law authorizes a debtor to offer and the creditor to receive in payment of a money obligation when offered by the debtor in the correct amount.
legal title	a title under rules of law as distinguished from a title recognized in equity according to equitable principles.
leg/a/tee′	one to whom property is left by will.
leg′/is/la/tive intent	the vital part, heart, soul, and essence of statutory law; the guiding star in the interpretation of a statute.
legit′i/macy	the matter of lawfulness; having a lawful parentage; that is, of having been born in lawful wedlock.
le′nient	mild, clement, or merciful, as in treatment, spirit, or tendency.
les/see′	tenant under a written lease.
les/sor′	one who has leased property to another.
le′thal weapon	a deadly weapon; a weapon capable of producing great bodily harm.
let′/ter agree′/ment	an understanding between parties set out in the form of a letter.
letter of attorney	power of attorney.

letter rog'a/tory	formal communication in writing, sent by a court in which action is pending to a court or judge in a foreign country requesting that testimony be taken of a witness resident in the latter jurisdiction and transmitted for use in the pending action.
let'/ters	commissions, patents, or written instruments containing or attesting the grant of some power, authority, or right.
letters of administration	formal instrument of authority and appointment granted to an administrator of an estate by a proper court to administer goods or estate of a deceased person.
letters patent	written grant from a government to a person in a form readily open for inspection by all.
letters testamentary	the formal instrument of authority and appointment given to an executor by the proper court, empowering him to enter upon the discharge of his office as executor; similar to letters of administration granted to an administrator.
letting contract	steps in the formation and execution of a contract, particularly a public contract, including an advertising for bids, the reception of bids, and the award of the contract to the lowest bidder, provided he appears to be a responsible bidder.
leu/ke'/mia	a disease characterized by excessive production of white blood cells, which are usually found in greatly increased numbers in the blood.
levee'	an artificial embankment constructed to contain the flood waters of a river.
levy	to assess; raise; execute; exact; collect; gather; take up; seize.
lewd'/ness	obscenity or indecency; gross indecency with respect to the sexual relation.
lex	a law; the law.
li'ai/son	connecting link; a go-between; an illicit intimacy.
li'bel	defamation through print, picture, typewritten or handwritten material, tending either to blacken the memory of one who is dead, or the reputation of one who is alive, and thus expose him to public hatred, contempt, or ridicule.

li´bel/ant (ALSO libellant)	the complaining party in an admiralty suit; person slandered (same as plaintiff).
li´/bel/ous (ALSO libellous)	defamatory; containing or constituting a libel.
lib´/er/tine	one free from constraint or control; a dissolute man.
libi´do	the innate actuating or impelling force in living beings; the vital impulse or urge.
Library of Congress	the Congressional Library, established in 1800 for use by the Congress, the services of which have been extended for benefit of governmental agencies, other libraries, students, and the public, such institution occupying buildings opposite the Capitol at Washington, D.C.
li´cense	a grant of authority or permission.
lic´it	lawful; permitted; legal.
lici/ta´/tion	a method of dividing property held in common; the offering for sale to the highest bidder.
lie detector	an instrument, sometimes called a pathometer, whose advocates claim for it that when attached to a witness, it will indicate whether he is testifying truthfully or not.
lien	the right of a creditor against certain property as security for a debt or claim.
lienee´	one whose property has a lien.
lienor´	the holder or owner of a lien upon the real or personal property of another.
life estate	a right held by one for the use of property during his lifetime.
life tenant	a person who has a life estate, such interest giving him the status of a freeholder.
LIFO	(Last-In, First-Out); a bookkeeping method of calculating inventory values and cost of sales.
light´/er/age	the transportation of goods by lighter or barge; the charge for such transportation.
limited jurisdiction	jurisdiction which does not extend to the general administration of justice; having reference to inferior courts.
limited partnership	partnership differing from a general partnership in that the partner's liability is limited to an amount equal to his investment in the company.

lin′/eage	the line of descendants of a particular ancestor; family, race.
lin′/eal	direct line of ancestry or descendants.
lineal heirs	persons entitled to the property of an intestate as heirs by lineal descent.
liquid assets	assets readily convertible into cash.
liq′/ui/date	to pay a debt; to wind up, as in reference to the affairs of a business.
liq′/ui/da/ted dam/ages	a sum of money, agreed upon in advance by the parties or fixed by a court.
liq/ui/da′/tion	the extinguishment of a debt by payment; termination of a business, its assets being converted into cash.
lis pendens	a pending suit; in law, the jurisdiction, power, or control that a court has, during the pendency of an action, over the property involved therein.
lit′/eral	accurate; precise; following the exact words of the original, as a translation.
lit′i/ga/ble	matter in which judicial process is indicated.
lit′i/gant	a party to a lawsuit; one engaged in litigation; usually used in connection with active parties, not nominal ones.
liti/ga′/tion	a contest in a court of justice for the purpose of enforcing a right; a suit at law.
liti′/gious	contentious; involved in a suit at law.
lit′/toral	pertaining to the shore of a lake, sea, or ocean.
liv′/ery	the keeping of horses and vehicles ready for hire; a private carrier, not a common carrier.
Lloyds	the bankers (do not use apostrophe).
Lloyd's	the association of underwriters (use apostrophe).
Lloyd's Register	a yearly register of the tonnage, build, condition, and character of ships.
loaded dice	dice which are weighted or carved so that, when thrown, one side will come up much more frequently than would be the case without such tampering therewith.

lob′/by/ing	services in attempting to obtain the passage of favored legislation; the practice of addressing or soliciting members of a legislative body, in the lobby off the chamber, or elsewhere, for the purpose of influencing their votes.
lobbying contract	any agreement which tends to introduce personal influence and solicitation as elements in procuring and influencing legislative action.
local court	a court, the jurisdiction and process of which are confined to a certain locality.
local government	municipal, as distinguished from the state or national government; the government of a county, city, town, or district.
lockout	the closing of a business or wholesale dismissal of employees by the employer because the employees refuse to accept his terms or because the employer refuses to operate on terms set by a union.
lockup	a place for the temporary and compulsory confinement and detention of persons under arrest.
log′/roll/ing	the combining of two or more persons to assist one of them, in consideration of like combined assistance in the interest of each of the others in return; the action of rolling logs to a particular place.
lot′/tery	a scheme or arrangement for raising money, as for some public, private, or charitable purpose, by the sale of a large number of tickets, certain among which, as determined by chance after the sale, entitle the holders to prizes.
lucid interval	a period of sanity intervening periods of insanity.
lu′/cra/tive	profitable; remunerative.
lurch	the position of one discomfited or in a helpless plight; a sudden and unexpected movement of an aircraft due to turbulent atmospheric conditions or other manifestations of nature; a sudden swaying or staggering movement.
lynch′/ing	putting a person to death by hanging, burning, or otherwise, by some concerted action without authority or process of law, for some offense known or imputed.

M

mac/ad′/am/ize	to construct a road by laying and rolling successive layers of broken stone.
mace proof	immune from arrest.
Machia/vel′/lian	treacherous; characterized by duplicity; crafty. (Niccolo di Bernardo Machiavelli—1469-1527—Italian statesman and writer on government.)
mael/strom	a violent whirlpool; a state of agitation; any destructive or wide-reaching noxious influence.
mag/is/te′/rial	of, pertaining to, or befitting a master; authoritative; domineering.
mag′/is/trate	a lower judicial officer, such as a justice of the peace, police judge, etc.; a mayor.
mag′/is/trate's certificate	a certificate required by the terms of some fire insurance policies to accompany proofs of loss, to be procured by the insured from the nearest magistrate, notary public, etc., stating that the loss was sustained without fraud.
Magistrate's Court	(use apostrophe).
Magna Charta	A charter of liberties, now found to be embodied in some form in every one of the American Constitutions; guaranteeing that every person shall be protected in the enjoyment of his life, liberty, and property, except as they may be declared to be forfeited by the judgment of his peers or the law of the land; issued by King John, at the demand of the barons, June 15, 1215, confirmed, with some changes.
maim	to cripple; to mutilate; to deprive of the use of some bodily member.
main′/te/nance	making repairs and keeping premises in good condition; an officious intermeddling in a suit in which the meddler has no interest, by assisting either party with means to prosecute or defend it.
major′/ity opin′/ion	an opinion prepared or approved by a majority of judges sitting in the case; the opinion of the court.
mal′a/prop/ism	humorous or absurd misuse of words.

mal'e/fac/tor	a criminal; an offender against the law.
mal/fea'/sance	the commission of some act which is unlawful; ill conduct that interferes with the performance of official duties.
mal'/ice aforethought	a predetermination to commit an act without legal justification or excuse.
mali'/cious	spiteful; showing active ill will.
malicious prosecution	a suit begun in malice without probable cause to believe the charges can be sustained.
malig'/nancy	a dangerous condition of the body, especially a cancerous condition; a condition of ill will or malevolence.
malin'/ger	to feign sickness or injury in order to avoid duty or work.
mal/prac'/tice	professional misconduct in performance of duties.
man/da'/mus	we command; a writ issued from a superior court directing an inferior court or person in authority to perform a specific duty.
man'/da/tary	one who acts under a mandate or order.
man'/da/tory	imperative; required to be done or performed; compulsory, not a matter of discretion.
ma/neu'/ver (ALSO ma/noeu'/vre	a planned action; an adroit move; artful proceeding.
ma'nia	violent insanity; an obsession or craze.
man'i/fest	evident; readily perceived by the eye or the understanding; to prove; document required by merchant vessels, containing an account of cargo and other particulars.
mani/fes'to	a statement by an organization or group of people of its policy or position with supporting reasons.
man'/slaugh/ter	the unlawful killing of another, without malice.
manus (PRON. mā'nus)	power over persons, as that of the husband over the wife; an oath; a hand.
mar'/ginal	situated on the border or edge; supplying goods at a rate merely covering the cost of production.

mari/jua′na	a substance derived from a hemp plant, generally classified as a narcotic.
mar′i/tal	of or pertaining to marriage.
mar′i/time law	body of laws relating to actions and rights on the seas or other navigable waters.
mar′ket value	The price for which an article is bought and sold in the ordinary course of business.
mar/quee′	canopy; an awning projecting from a building, especially a theatre, over the sidewalk at the main entrance, sometimes supported by columns.
mar′/quis	a nobleman.
mar′/shal	an official; a person charged with the arrangement or regulation of ceremonies.
mart	a trading center; a market.
mate′/rial	substance of which things are made; relating to the substance rather than form; pertaining to physical rather than spiritual; likely to influence the determination of a cause.
mate/riel′	equipment; military supplies.
mast′/head	the top or head of the mast of a ship or vessel; a statement printed in all issues of a newspaper, a magazine, etc., giving the name, owners, staff, etc.
ma′/tri/cide	the murder of a mother; one who has killed his mother.
matric/u/la′/tion	enrollment as a student in an educational institution, particularly a college or university.
ma′trix (PL., ma′tri/ces)	that which gives origin or form to a thing; a mold for casting type faces.
matu′/rity	ripeness; full development; the time when a note or bill of exchange becomes due.
mav′/er/ick	one who is unorthodox in his ideas or attitudes.
max′im	a precise expression developed over the years in elucidating a principle of law by reasoning.
may′/hem	the intentional maiming or disfiguring of a person.
may′or	the principal officer of a municipality; the chief magistrate of a city or borough.

mazu'ma	slang for money, especially money taken illegally or employed for an ulterior purpose.
mean	middle between two extremes; an instrumentality; a method; small-minded or ignoble; miserly or stingy.
mean'/der	to slowly follow a winding course.
mechan'/ics lien (no apostrophe)	lien on behalf of those who performed work or furnished material.
me'di/ate	to reconcile; to settle; to bring about peace between parties by acting as mediator.
medi/a'/tion	an attempt to effect a peaceful settlement between disputing parties through the friendly good offices of another party.
melan/cho'/lia	a disease of the brain which in simple form is characterized by deep depression, sorrow, grief, and yet by no impairment of the intellectual powers.
melio/ra'/tion	improvement; making or becoming better.
memo/ran'/dum (PL., dums or da)	an informal writing of short length and simple language used to record some information or to pass on some information or instruction.
memorandum bill of lading	a duplicate of a bill of lading.
memo'/rial	a legal abstract; something designed to preserve the memory of a person, event, etc.
memo'/ri/al/ize	to address or petition by a memorial; to commemorate.
men/da'/cious	given to deception or falsehood; lying or untruthful.
mens rea	a criminal intent; a guilty mind.
men'/tal cru'/elty	misconduct which impairs or threatens to impair physical or mental health of a person.
mer'/can/tile	commercial; pertaining to trade and commerce in merchandise.
mer'/chan/dise	goods; commodities; manufactured goods.
mer'/chant/able	of good quality and salable, but not necessarily the best.
mere right	mere right of property, without earlier possession or even the right of possession.

mere/tri'/cious	based on pretense or insincerity; specious; of or relating to a prostitute.
mesne (PRON. mēn)	intermediate; intervening; the middle between two extremes; proceedings in suit intervening between primary and final process.
merg'er	an absorption of one estate or interest in another, or of a minor in a greater offense; a unification of business enterprises by consolidation of their properties.
meta (PRON. mēta)	an object marking a boundary; a monument.
metes and bounds	boundary lines of land with their terminating points or angles; a means of description of land in a deed.
mien (PRON. mēn)	external appearance or bearing.
mi'/grant la'/borer	a laborer who travels from place to place, often with the seasons, for work, usually connected with the farm, particularly the cultivation and gathering of vegetables and the harvesting of fruit crops.
mile'/age	the aggregate number of miles made or traveled over in a given time.
milieu (PRON. mē'lyoo)	state of life; social surroundings; environment.
mili'/tia	a body of men enrolled for military service, called out periodically for drill and exercise but for actual service only in emergencies.
min'er	one who mines.
min'i/miz/a/tion of damages	the duty of the plaintiff to take reasonable action to avoid enhancing the damages caused by the defendant.
min'i/mus	the least; the smallest.
mi'/nis/cule OR minuscule	very small.
min/is/te'/rial act	one which a person performs in a given state of facts in a prescribed manner in obedience to the mandate of legal authority, without regard to or the exercise of his own judgment upon the propriety of the act being done.

min´or — under legal age; lesser, as in size, extent, or importance, as being the lesser of two.

minor´/ity — a group or class of persons other than the predominant race or religion in a group, community, state, or political division.

mi´nus — decreased; less by the subtraction of; lacking or without.

mis/al/lege´ — to state, cite, or quote erroneously.

mis/ce/ge/na´/tion — intermarriage or interbreeding of different races.

mis/de/mean´or — offense lower than a felony and generally punishable by fine or imprisonment otherwise than in the penitentiary.

mis/fea´/sance — improper performance of an act which a man may lawfully do.

mis/no´/mer — a misapplied name or designation; an error in naming a person or thing.

mis/state´/ment — a misleading or incorrect statement.

mis/tri´al — invalid or nugatory trial; the effect of prejudicial error which cannot be corrected or obviated by any action taken by the court.

mit´i/gate — to lessen in force or intensity; to moderate the severity of.

mit´i/gat/ing cir/cum/stan´/ces — damages that do not constitute a justification or excuse of the offense in question, but which may be considered as extenuating or reducing the degree of moral culpability.

miti/ga´/tion of dam´/ages — alleviation, abatement, extenuation, or reduction of amount of damages; a term relating only to exemplary damages and their reduction by extenuating circumstances such as provocation of malice.

mit´/ti/mus — writ used in sending a record from one court to another; warrant of commitment to prison.

modus operandi (SING.) modi operandi (PL.) — the method of operation; the way in which a thing or person works.

mogul (PRON. mō´gul) — an important person; dominant figure in a particular field; a steam locomotive, used for hauling heavy trains.

moi´/ety (PL. moieties) — one-half of anything; joint tenants are said to hold by moieties; a part; a fraction of anything.

moni´/tion	a legal summons or citation to appear and answer a default; a citation in a suit in admiralty.
mon´i/tor	something that serves to remind or give warning; a pupil appointed to assist in the conduct of a class; to listen to broadcasts for operating propaganda, analysis, etc.
mon´u/ment	something erected in memory of a person, event, etc.; a tombstone; a shaft or stone, not a building.
moot	unsettled; undecided; a subject for argument; a moot case is one which seeks to determine an abstract question which does not arise upon existing facts or rights; debatable.
moot question	a hypothetical question; an abstract or academic question.
mor´al tur´/pi/tude	baseness, vileness, or depravity in the private and social duties which a man owes to his fellowmen or to society in general.
mora/to´/rium	period of grace allowed a debtor, during which payments that would normally be made are in abeyance.
mor´/dant	caustic or sarcastic, as wit, a speaker, etc.; sharply critical in manner, style, or thought.
mor´/dent	musical embellishment.
mores (PRON. mōr´ēz)	folkways of central importance accepted without question and embodying the fundamental moral views of a group.
mor´i/bund	in a state of dying, extinction, or termination.
mo´ron	a person of arrested intelligence whose mentality is judged incapable of developing beyond that of a normal child of eight to 12 years of age.
mor´phine	a bitter crystalline alkaloid of opium; a narcotic.
mort´/gage	a document representing a claim on property in favor of a person who has lent money in case the money is not repaid when due; chattel mortgages are against personal property; real estate mortgages are against real estate.
mort´/gage/able prop´/erty	property that can be subject to a mortgage, used usually in reference to personal property and chattel mortgages.

mort′/gage bond	a bond that is secured by a mortgage.
mort′/gage deed	a deed of the nature of a mortgage.
mort/ga/gee′	one to whom property is mortgaged; the lender of the money.
mort/ga/gor′	one who gives a mortgage on his property.
mort′/main	the condition of lands or tenements; corporation's possession or tenure which, by reason of nature of corporations, may be perpetual.
mor′/tu/ary	a place to which dead bodies may be taken for keeping before burial or cremation.
mo′/tion	the means of presenting a proposition in a meeting conducted according to parliamentary procedure.
mot′/ley	composed of diverse and often incongruous elements; heterogeneous.
mov′/ables	personal property; property not fixed.
mo′vant OR mo′vent	a party who makes a motion; an applicant for a rule or order.
moving papers	the affidavits submitted in support of a motion.
mug′/ging	assault by throwing an arm around the neck of the victim, usually upon an approach from behind, the purpose being to overpower the victim so that he can be robbed.
multi/far′/ious	having many different parts, elements, forms, etc.; numerous and varied; manifold.
mul/ti/lat′/eral	participated in by more than two parties, or states; having many sides.
multi-market company	a corporate conglomerate.
mul′/ti/ple dwelling	an apartment house; a tenement; any structure for the accommodation of two or more families in separate living units.
mul/ti/ver′/sity	newly coined word for a university containing many schools, colleges, and departments, and attended by an overwhelming number of students.
munic′/i/pal	pertaining to a town or city having local self-government.
municipal law	in the narrow sense, the law pertaining to municipal corporations; in a general sense, the law of a municipality, a state, even the nation, as distinguished from international law.

mu′ni/ments	written proof enabling one to defend title to his estate.
muniments of title	a document evidencing title; a title deed or other original document which, taken with other documents, shows a claim of title.
murder in the first degree	murder with malice aforethought, the unique characteristic of which is deliberation or premeditation, a design or purpose to take life.
murder in the second degree	the killing of a person by intent but without premeditation or deliberation, or, as otherwise stated, without malice aforethought or express malice.
mute	speechless; dumb; cannot or will not speak.
mu′/ti/late	to deprive of a limb or other important part; to injure, disfigure, or make imperfect by irreparably damaging parts.
mu′tiny	revolt, or a revolt or rebellion, against constituted authority, especially by soldiers or seamen.
mu′/tual	reciprocal; the same on both sides of a transaction or relationship, whether it be a matter of affection, aversion, assistance, or advantage.
mutual fund	(same as open-end fund) fund giving one a share at a price determined by dividing the fund's assets by the number of shares outstanding.
myth/o/log′/i/cal name	a name taken from mythology, especially mythology of the ancient Greeks.

N

naïve′ (PRON. na-ēv)	marked by unaffected simplicity; showing lack of informed judgment.
naked power	a power of disposal accompanied by no interest or estate in the donee of the power.
nar/cot′/ics	substances which directly induce sleep, allay sensibility, and blunt the senses, and which, when taken in large quantities, produce narcoticism or complete insensibility.
narrow construction	rejecting the comprehensive sense, in favor of a narrow, contracted meaning, of words.
nasci/tu′/rus	a person to be born in the future.
natu/ral/iza′/tion	investing an alien with the rights and privileges of a subject or citizen.

nat´u/ral law	an abstract concept of law in accord with the nature of man; a rule which so necessarily agrees with the nature and state of man that, without observing its maxims, the peace and happiness of society can never be preserved.
nat´u/ral per´/son	a private person, as distinguished from a corporation.
na´val	pertaining to ships, especially ships of war.
neb´u/lous	hazy, vague, indistinct, or confused; cloudy or cloudlike.
nec´/es/sar/ies	that which cannot be dispensed with; food, clothing, etc. required by a dependent or incompetent and varying with his social or economic position or that of the person upon whom he is dependent.
neces´/si/tous	destitute; needy; indigent.
nefas (PRON. nē´fas)	a wrongful, sinful, wicked, unlawful, or criminal act.
negate´	to nullify; deny; declare nonexistent.
neg´a/tive (v.)	to refuse to entertain.
(adj.)	expressing denial; expressing refusal to do something.
neg´/li/gence	the failure to exercise that degree of care which, under the circumstances, the law requires of ordinarily prudent persons.
nego/tia/bil´/ity	a technical term derived from the usage of merchants and bankers in transferring bills of exchange and promissory notes.
nego´/tia/ble	having the quality and requisites of negotiability.
negotiable instrument	document which upon delivery effects a transfer of property secured by it.
nego´/tia/tor	one who arranges for or brings about by discussion a settlement of terms; a person who disposes of by sale or transfer.
nemo (PRON. nē´mō)	no man; no one; nobody.
nep´o/tism	patronage bestowed in consideration of family relationship and not of merit.
net	that which remains after the deduction of all charges and outlays.

neur/as/the′/nia	nervous debility or exhaustion, as from overwork or prolonged mental strain, characterized by depression, worry, and pains having no apparent cause.
neu/ro′/sis	a mental affliction without serious derangement but which may constitute total disability.
newsstand	a small structure located in a place accessible to the public, at which newspapers, magazines, etc. are sold.
nexus	interconnection or link.
ni′hil (same meaning as nil—contraction for nihil)	nothing.
noi′/some	offensive or disgusting, often as to odor.
no-load fund	investment fund company that does not make a sales charge.
nolle (PRON. nol′e)	to be unwilling.
nom′i/nal	being such in name only; without any actual existence.
nominal damages	a trifling sum given for the violation of a right where no actual loss has resulted.
nomi/nee′	one nominated, as to fill an office or stand for election.
non′/age	a period of youth; legal minority.
non/com/mit′/tal	avoiding a definite statement or point of view.
non/cu′/mu/la/tive div′/i/dends	dividends on noncumulative preferred stock, once passed or omitted, are dead; can never be made up.
non/fea′/sance	the total omission or failure of an agent to enter upon the performance of some distinct duty or obligation which he has agreed with his principal to do; the failure to act where duty requires an act.
non/join′/der	omission to join, as of one who should have been a party to an action.
non/ne/go′/ti/a/ble in′stru/ment	an instrument which meets all requirements as to form of a negotiable instrument except that it is not payable to order or bearer.

non sequitur	illogical inference; that which does not follow.
nonsuit	failure to establish a case; a judgment given against a plaintiff for failure to prosecute his case.
non/sup/port′	offense of a husband who neglects or fails to provide his wife and children, or either, with the necessaries of life.
no par value stock	ordinary capital stock which has no face value.
no protest	note written on a check, note, etc., to indicate to the one who cashes it that in case of nonpayment it is to be returned to the creditor and not protested.
notar′/ial	pertaining or relating to the office or functions of a notary.
notary public	a public officer who administers oaths, attests or certifies deeds, takes affidavits, and the like.
nota′/tion	system of markings and symbols.
note	a written promise to pay a certain sum of money at a given date to a specified person, order, or bearer.
nothus	spurious; not genuine; illegitimate; a bastard.
nova′/tion	the substitution of a new obligation for an old one, which is thereby cancelled.
nox′/ious	hurtful; offensive.
nuclear explosion	an explosion resulting from the development of energy by nuclear fission or nuclear fusion.
nu′ga/tory	futile; ineffectual; of no real value.
nui′/sance	something offensive or annoying to individuals or to the community, to the prejudice of their legal rights.
nuisance per se	an act, thing, omission, or use of the property which in and of itself is a nuisance, and hence is not permissible or excusable under any circumstances.
null and void	that which is of no effect and binding on no one.
nul′/lify	to cause to be of no legal effect.
nul′/lity	legal invalidity; that which has no legal effect.
nunc pro tunc	now for then; acts permitted after the time they should have been done, with retroactive

	effect; i.e., with the same effect as if regularly done.
nun'/cu/pate	to make a verbal will.
nup'/tial	of or pertaining to marriage or the marriage ceremony.
nym/pho/ma'/nia	a morbid, uncontrollable sexual desire, but not insanity.

O

oath	a form of attestation by which a person signifies that he is bound in conscience to perform an act faithfully and truthfully.
ob'li/ga/tory	compulsory or incumbent; binding.
obli/gee'	person in whose favor an obligation is contracted.
obli/gor'	person incurring a contracted obligation.
ob'lo/quy	blame; reprehension; censure; reproach.
obscene'	offensive to purity of thought or to modesty.
obsig/na're	to affix a seal to a will or other document; to sign and seal an instrument.
obso/les'/cence	the condition of a thing which has passed out of general use, is outmoded, and out of fashion.
obstan'te	opposing; obstructing.
obstruct'	to make difficult of passage; to interpose obstacles or impediments.
occa'/sion	a particular time; a special or important event or function; opportunity; an incident.
oc'cu/pancy	possession in fact; the use of premises; exercise of dominion over a thing which has no owner so as to become the legal owner.
occur'/rence	an event; a happening; an incident.
o'dium	hatred or dislike, applied in law particularly to hatred or dislike of a party to an action or of his cause of action or defense.
of counsel	attorney or attorneys associated with those regularly retained; assisting counsel.
offense	a crime or misdemeanor; a transgression; attack or assault.
offi'/cial	in the capacity of an officer, especially a public officer; formal or ceremonious.

offset (adj.) (n.)	a printing process; a balancing or compensating factor; a counterclaim.
(v.)	to balance by something else as an equivalent.
ogive (PRON. ō′jiv OR ō′jaiv)	in statistics, a graphic curve commonly referred to as a growth curve; a pointed arch; a rib of a vault.
ohm (PRON. ōm)	the unit of electrical resistance; the resistance to a force of 1 volt in a current of 1 ampere.
O.K.	all right; correct. An abbreviation frequently used in the business world signifying the signer's approval of the instrument on which he endorses it.
Old-Age and Survivors' Insurance	The system whereby employees and employers are taxed to provide for the payment of benefits to workers and their wives upon their reaching a stated age or suffering disability, popularly known as social security.
ol′o/graph	a person's handwritten instrument.
olo/graph′ic will (same as holographic will)	a will wholly and entirely written by the hand of the testator.
omis′/sion	the state of being neglected or left undone; the failure to do something which ought to be done.
omit′/ted prop′/erty	property which has escaped taxation; property of a decedent omitted in the assessment of inheritance tax.
om′ni/bus	a bus; relating to or providing for many things or classes at the same time.
omni/bus bill	a legislative bill covering various and miscellaneous subjects; a bill purporting to amend many sections of a code.
on account	in partial payment.
on all fours	precisely in point; a case to be on all fours must be identical.
on′an/ism	withdrawal before occurrence of orgasm; masturbation.
once in jeopardy	essentially the same as the defense of prior jeopardy, although a distinction is recognized by some authorities; a plea setting up a former jeopardy of the defendant who is now charged with the same offense.

on demand	on an actual call or demand for payment.
on'er/ous	imposing or constituting a legal burden; oppressive or troublesome.
on information and belief	allegations of a verified pleading made on information and belief of pleader when he does not have positive knowledge of the facts.
onstand'	the payment of rent by an outgoing tenant to an incoming tenant for use and occupation during the harvesting of the outgoing tenant's crop.
onus'	responsibility; burden; obligation.
opaque'	not transparent; not clear; not letting light through.
open account	an account, the balance of which has not been ascertained; an account which has not been settled, paid, or adjusted by agreement of the parties.
open contract	oral or written contract between two or more parties, terms or duration of which remain unfulfilled.
open-end	mutual fund; fund giving one a share at a price determined by dividing the fund's assets by the number of shares outstanding.
operarius (ope/ra'/rius)	a feudal tenant who held his land by manual labor for the lord of the manor.
op'era/tive	having force, or being in effect or operation; effective; operating or exerting force or influence.
o'pi/ate	a narcotic drug containing opium or a derivative of opium; any substance which tends to soothe.
opin'/ion	an inference or conclusion of fact which a person has drawn from facts which he has observed.
opposing papers	affidavits offered in resistance to a motion.
oppro'/brium	infamy; disgrace or reproach incurred by conduct considered shameful; ignominy.
op'ti/mum	best or most favorable quantity, degree, etc.
op'tion	power or liberty of choosing; right of freedom of choice; a continuing offer to sell at a price stipulated.
oral contract	a contract which relies for the most part on spoken words, but may be partly in writing.

oral defa/ma'/tion	defamation by spoken words; slander; orally injuring another's reputation without justification; calumny.
orde'al	a severe test or experience.
order	a written direction of a court or court officer that is not included in a judgment; a command or direction; a list of goods or merchandise to be supplied by a dealer.
or'di/nance	enactment by municipal government; statute.
orphans' court (use apostrophe)	a probate court; the name is suggested by the jurisdiction exercised in matters involving the care of orphans and their property.
oscil/la'/tion	a single swing, or movement in one direction, of an oscillating body; fluctuation between opinions, etc.
osten'/si/ble	outwardly appearing as such.
oust'er	an eviction; a forced dispossession of real estate; a disseisin.
outlawed	barred by the statute of limitations; deprived of the benefits and protection of the law.
out/ra'/geous bat'/tery	malicious acts akin to mayhem.
outstanding account	uncollected or unpaid accounts.
overcyted	found guilty; convicted.
overdraft	withdrawal of money from a bank by a depositor in excess of the amount of money he has on deposit there.
overplus	a balance left over; that which remains.
overreaching	fraudulent conduct in taking unfair advantage.
overrule	to refuse to grant; to deny, as where the court denies an objection by counsel; to annul.
o'vert	manifest; not hidden; open; public.
overt act	act from which criminality may be implied; an act carrying an intent into effect.
o'ver/ture	an opening; a proposal; an introductory part.
owel (PRON. ō'el)	equal.
ow'ing	due or owed.
oyer	to hear; the right to hear an instrument read.

oyer and terminer	commission directing judge to hear and determine.
oyez	Hear ye! A command used in court to secure silence.

P

pact	agreement that is not actionable; a stipulation; a contract.
pac'/tion	a treaty; a pact; a contract.
Pandora's box	a mythical box from which all human ills escaped when it was opened.
paper	a negotiable evidence of indebtedness.
par	an equality in value or standing; term used to delineate the original terms at which shares of stock are issued; face value.
par'/al/lel	having the same direction, course, or tendency; analogous; similar; corresponding.
par'a/noia	a mental disorder characterized by delusions or hallucinations, particularly delusions of grandeur or persecution.
par'/aph	an official signature; a flourish at end of signature.
para/pher/na'/lia	personal belongings; in equity and under statute, a separate property of the wife.
par'/cel	a part of a unit of land; lot and section are synonyms.
parent company	company that owns or controls one or more other companies.
paren'/ti/cide	homicide in the killing of a parent.
pari delicto	in equal fault.
pari-mutuel	a method of wagering at race tracks, whereby those who bet on the winning horse share the total stakes less a percentage to the management.
parish	a territorial division of the state corresponding to what is otherwise called a "county"; in the State of Louisiana.
par'/ity	equality as in amount, status, or character; equivalence.

par/lia/men´/tary rules	the rules adopted by an organization to control the conduct of its meetings, such as those applicable to the annual meeting of a literary society.
paro´/chial	some particular narrow district or field.
par of exchange	value of a unit of one country's currency expressed in that of another.
parol´	verbal; oral; spoken.
parole´	conditional release from prison; a promise made and confirmed by a pledge.
parole contract	contract made without a seal; a specialty contract.
parol evidence	the oral or verbal testimony of a witness.
parol evidence rule	the rule which excludes evidence of prior or contemporaneous oral agreements which would vary a written contract.
par/ri/cide´	the murder of one's parent.
parti´/tion	division of lands held by joint owners; an interior wall or barrier dividing a building or enclosure.
part´/ner/ship	an association of persons joined as partners to carry on as co-owners of a business for profit.
partnership in commendam	contribution of either money or property by one to a partnership in anticipation of sharing in profits or losses in proportion to the contribution.
party litigant	a person named as a party to an action or suit.
party wall	wall erected between two adjoining lots, belonging to different owners, and used in common by both.
par value	the face value of a bond; a device whereby a corporation's shares are given an arbitrary value.
parvenu (PL., parvenus; FEM., parvenue; FEM. PL., parvenues) (PRON. pār-ve-nyoo ALSO par-ve-noo)	one who has not yet secured the social position appropriate to newly attained wealth or power; an upstart.
passageway	a way for entrance or exit; a hallway.

passbook	a book carried by the customer of a bank in which the teller enters the amount and date of a deposit made.
pas'/sen/ger	one who travels by some form of conveyance; a person being carried in an elevator or riding on an escalator.
pat'ent (adj.)	manifest or evident.
(n.)	grant of privilege, property, or authority by the government to individuals.
pat'/entee	the one to whom a patent has been granted.
pater'/nity	the relationship of a father.
pathol'/ogy	the branch of medicine concerned with the nature of disease and the changes in body, bones, and tissues produced by a particular disease.
pat'/ri/cide	the crime of murdering one's own father.
pat'/ri/mony	a right or estate inherited from one's ancestors, particularly from direct male ancestors.
pau'/per	an indigent person; one receiving public aid; a poor person.
pavil'/ion	a more or less open structure for purposes of shelter, pleasure, etc.; a projecting element in the front or side of a building.
payee'	one in whose favor a check or note is drawn.
payer' OR payor'	one who makes payment.
payoff	a final consequence; a settlement.
pecu/la'/tion	stealing or misappropriating moneys entrusted to one's care.
pecu'/ni/ary	involving money or money's worth; financial.
pecuniary damages	monetary damages; damages paid or to be paid in money.
ped'i/gree	an ancestral line, or line of descent; lineage; derivation, as from a source.
peer	equal in rank and station.
pe'jo/ra/tive	disparaging.
pe'nal	pertaining to punishment; involving penalties; punitive institutions.

penal code	a division of the statutory law of a jurisdiction comprehensive of crimes and criminal proceedings.
pend′/ency of action	the status of an action or suit from the time it is commenced until its final determination by judgment or order.
pendente lite	during the actual progress of a suit.
peni/ten′/tiary	a place for imprisonment and reformatory discipline.
penul′/ti/mate	next to the last.
peon (PRON. pē′on)	a debtor who is compelled to work for his creditor until his debt is paid.
peonage	the practice of holding persons in servitude or partial slavery, as to work off a debt.
peram/bu/la′/tion	visitation for making an inspection.
per annum	by the year.
per capita	share and share alike by the descendants regardless of degree of relationship.
per diem	by the day.
per/emp′/tion	a nonsuit.
per/emp′/tory	imperative; leaving no opportunity for denial or refusal; decisive.
per/emp′/tory chal′/lenge	right of prosecution or defendant to challenge certain jurors without announcing the cause.
peren′/nial	enduring; lasting for an indefinitely long time.
perfect on appeal	bring to final form; matters necessary to an appeal being complied with.
per/form′/ance bond	a bond which guarantees that the contractor will perform the contract, and usually provides that if the contractor defaults and fails to complete the contract, the surety can itself complete the contract or pay damages up to the limit of the bond.
peri/od′/i/cal	publication issued at regularly recurring intervals.
per′/jury	giving false testimony under oath.
per′/ma/nent	to continue indefinitely; remaining unchanged.
per/mis′/sive	allowed; permitted.

per'/nan/cy	the taking or receipt of the rents, profits, or other advantages arising from an estate in real property.
per/pe/tu'/ity	an interest under which property is less than completely alienable for longer than the law allows; endless.
per'/qui/site	an incidental emolument, fee, or profit over and above fixed income, salary, or wages.
per'/si/flage	a frivolous style of treating a subject; light, bantering talk.
per/sist'/ent vi'o/la/tor	an habitual criminal.
per'/sonal chat'/tels	movable property.
per'/sonal effects	possessions having a close relationship to one's person.
per'/sonal prop'/erty	goods, chattels, things in action, evidences of debt, and money.
per'/son/alty	personal property or estate; chattels.
per stirpes (PRON. stir'/pēs)	per class; by representation; taking a share which a deceased ancestor would have taken had he survived the estate.
per/suade'	to prevail on a person by advice, urging, inducements, reason, etc. to do something.
per'/ti/nent	relevant; relating to the matter at hand.
peti'/tion	formal written application to court requesting judicial action upon matter therein set forth.
peti'/tioner	one seeking relief by a petition.
petit larceny (pet'it lar'/ceny)	larceny in the taking of property of small value; a misdemeanor, rather than a felony under modern statutes.
petitory action	suit to try title; action for the recovery of real property.
petty cash	a sum of money kept on hand to pay small expenses.
philippic (phil/ip'/pic)	a bitter, denunciatory speech.
phi/lis'/tine	person guided by material rather than intellectual or artistic values.

physio´/ther/apy	the treatment of disease or bodily defects by physical remedies, such as massage, etc.
piercing the corporate veil	disregarding corporate entity and recognizing that effective control is in the hands of an individual or other entity.
pignus (pig´nus)	property held as security for a debt; the contract containing such a pledge.
pil´/fer/age	larceny or stealing something of small value; ruin by depredation.
pi´racy	robbery or illegal violence at sea or on the shores of the sea.
pla´/gi/a/rism	appropriation as one's own of the literary composition of another.
plain´/tiff	the party complaining in an action or proceeding; a person who brings a suit, action, or complaint.
plain´/tiff appel´/lant	a person who files an appeal.
plan´/gent	resounding; dashing noisily.
planned economy	economic system in which government seeks to counteract natural hazards.
plat	same as plot; a plot of ground, usually small.
plea	relief sought; that which is alleged or urged in defense or justification.
plead	to make an earnest entreaty; to use arguments or persuasions.
plead´/ings	formal written allegations of respective parties.
plea side	civil department of a court.
plebian (PRON. ple/bē´/ian)	of the common people; crude or course in manner or style; belonging or pertaining to the Roman plebs.
pleb´/i/scite	a popular vote on a proposed law or on any question submitted to the people.
pledgee	a person to whom personal property is pledged by a pledgor.
ple´/nary	full in all respects or requisites; complete; absolute; unqualified.
pleni/po/ten´/ti/ary	bestowing full power, as a commission; invested with authority, as a diplomatic agent.

plot	a small piece of ground; plotted map, chart, or plan.
plot'/t ge	area included in a plot of land; the added value that accrues to two or more lots under one ownership.
ploy	a tactic intended to embarrass or frustrate an opponent.
plu/ral'/ity	an excess of votes over those cast for an opposing candidate.
plu'/ries	a writ of attachment issued after other writs have been issued and proved ineffectual.
pole'/mic	an aggressive attack on, or refutation of, opinions or principles of another.
police precinct	a subdivision of the area of a municipality to which a part of the force of the city—officers and men—are assigned for duty, normally having a station house.
polit'/i/cal econ'/omy	government founded on the idea of regulating public affairs so as to conserve the interests of the public, and involving the production and distribution of wealth.
poll (n.)	an individual person; a register of persons who may vote in an election.
(v.)	to vote; to canvass the electorate for the purpose of forecasting the result of an election.
pol'y/an/dry	the state of a woman having more than one living husband.
polyg'/amy	the offense of marrying while still having a living legal spouse.
pop'u/lar action	an action to recover a penalty, the cause being given by law to the people in general.
pop'u/lous	full of people or inhabitants, as a region; well-populated.
posit (v.)	to state as fact; accept as real; to assume or affirm the existence of; to assume as a principle.
pos/sess'	to have as property; to hold or to occupy; to have as a faculty, quality, or the like.
pos/ses'/sory action	action to recover possession of personal property.

post (v.)	to transfer from a daybook or journal to the ledger.
post card (two words)	a card for mailing, privately produced and sold, usually containing a picture or words of greeting or congratulations on one side.
postdate	to date an instrument later than the day it was made.
pos/ter'/ity	succeeding generations collectively.
posthumous (post'/humous)	born after the death of the father; published after the death of the author; being or continued after death.
post'/ing	the process of transferring entries from a journal to a ledger.
post-mortem	expert examination of human body after death; autopsy.
post-obit	a bond payable upon death.
post office (two words)	a particular building or place for the receipt, handling, and delivery of mail matter, or the transaction of other business in connection with the postal service.
postoperative treatment	treatment of a patient after surgery.
post/pone'/ment	putting off to a later time; deferment.
postscript	an addition to a letter appearing after the signature; something added by the author at the end of a book or article.
pos'/ture	state or frame of mind; the position of the body and limbs as a whole; an affected or unnatural attitude.
poten'/tial	possible as opposed to actual; capable of being or becoming; latent.
potestas (PRON. pōtes'/tās)	power; authority; official authority; magistracy.
potestative condition	that which makes the execution of an agreement depend on an event which is in the power of either of the contracting parties to bring about or to hinder.
power of attorney	a written authorization to an agent to perform specific acts in behalf of his principal.
prac'/ti/ca/ble	feasible; capable of being done or effected, especially with the available means or with prudence or reason.

prac′/ti/cal	pertaining or relating to action or practice; connected with ordinary activities, business, or work of the world.
prac′/tice (n.) OR practise	habitual or customary performance; the form or manner of conducting legal suits.
(v.)	to carry out, perform, or do habitually or usually, or make a practice of; to follow or observe.
prac′/tic/ing law/yer	a lawyer who customarily and habitually holds himself out to the public as a lawyer and who demands compensation for his services rendered as such.
praecipe (PRON. prē′sipe)	an order; a command; a writ ordering the defendant to do a certain thing or to show reason why. An order to the clerk of the court, written out and signed, requesting him to issue a particular writ.
prai′/rie	an extensive level or slightly undulating treeless tract of land in the Mississippi valley, characterized by a highly fertile soil and originally covered with coarse grasses.
pre′/am/ble	an introductory statement.
pre/car′/i/ous	dependent on circumstances beyond one's control; uncertain; insecure; unstable.
precarious circumstances	a desperate financial condition; a financial condition approaching insolvency.
prec′/a/tory	a recommendation; in the nature of a prayer or entreaty; embodying an expression of a wish but not a positive command.
pre/ced′/ence	priority in rank, order, importance, etc.; priority in time; the order to be observed ceremonially by persons of different ranks.
prec′/e/dent (n.)	decision of a court considered as authority for a similar question of law; that which tends to serve as a guide or reason for a later course of action.
pre/ced′/ent (adj.)	going before; prior in time.
pre′/cept	a written mandate or command; an injunction as to moral conduct; a maxim.
pre/ci/′pi/tate	to throw down; to fall headlong; to hasten the occurrence of; to bring about in haste or suddenly.

pre/cip/i/ta´/tion	crisis unexpectedly; falling products of condensation in the atmosphere, as rain, snow, hail.
pre/clude´	shut out or prevent; make impossible.
pred´/a/tory	practicing plunder, pillage, or robbery; habitually preying upon other animals.
pre/dom´/i/nant	having ascendancy, power, influence, or authority over others.
pre/em´/i/nent	superior to or surpassing others; distinguished beyond others.
pre/empt´	to acquire (land) in order to establish a prior right to buy; to appropriate beforehand.
pre/emp´/tion	the right to purchase before or in preference to others.
preemptive OR pre-emptive	that which is subject to prior seizure or appropriation.
pre/emp´/tive rights	special privilege to buy land resulting from its prior occupancy.
pre/fab´/ri/ca/ted	constructed beforehand; manufactured in standardized parts or sections ready for rapid assembling and erection.
pref´/er/ence	the object of prior favor or choice; a practical advantage given to one over others.
pref/er/en´/tial pri´/mary	a form of primary election which, while not conclusive of nomination, gives the members of a political party, who are qualified to vote at the primary, an opportunity for expressing their choice, and gives a candidate a chance to test his appeal to the voters.
pre/ferred stock	stock which receives dividends before other capital stock, ownership of said stock making one a part owner of issuing company.
prej´/u/dice	an unfavorable opinion or feeling formed beforehand or without knowledge, thought, or reason; resulting injury or detriment.
prej/u/di´/cial	detrimental or derogatory to a party; probably or actually bringing about a wrong result.
pre/med´i/tate	to consider or plan beforehand.
prem´/ise	a tract of land; a proposition from which a conclusion is drawn; a basis, stated or assumed, on which reasoning proceeds.

prem'/i/ses	the grounds of an argument or dissertation; a building or part of a building, usually with its grounds or other appurtenances.
pre'/mium	a prize to be won in a competition; a reward or recompense for some act done; something given a purchaser of merchandise in addition to the article or commodity purchased.
pre/pon'/der/ance of evidence	evidence that carries the greater weight; does not refer to the greatest quantity but rather to the most total validity of evidence.
pre/req'/ui/site	required beforehand.
pre/rog'/a/tive	an exclusive or peculiar privilege; precedence; a prior right.
pre'/sci/ence	knowledge of things before they exist or happen; foresight.
pre/scribe'	to lay down, in writing or otherwise, as a rule or a course to be followed; to define authoritatively; to dictate or direct.
pre/scrip'/tive rights	rights to property which a possessor acquires by reason of continuance of possession for a time fixed by law.
pres'/ence	attendance; immediate vicinity; close proximity; the bearing or personality of a person.
pre/sent'/ment	notice taken by grand jury of an offense from their own observation and knowledge, without an indictment; an informal statement in writing by a grand jury as to a triable offense.
pre/serv'/ative	a chemical substance or preparation used to preserve foods, etc., from decomposition or fermentation.
pre/sump'/tion	an inference as to the existence of a fact not certainly known.
pre/sump'/tive title	a title appearing from nothing more than occupancy of the premises.
pret'/er/i/tion	the failure of a testator to mention in his will an heir who would be entitled to his estate or some portion of it in the absence of a will.
pre'/ter/mit	to neglect; to leave undone; to disregard; to pass by; to omit.

pretrial conference calendar	a court calendar, in addition to the trial calendar, listing the cases wherein a pretrial conference has been called and the time therefor.
price/earnings ratio	a yardstick for evaluating market price of stock by dividing the stock's quoted price by its earnings factor.
pri'/mary juris/dic'/tion	the power of a court to hear and adjudicate a case brought before it.
pri/mo/gen'/i/ture	right of succession by the first-born, especially inheritance of a family estate by the eldest son.
prin'/ci/pal	a person who has another person to act for him; first or highest in rank, importance, value, etc.; chief; foremost.
principal and agent	the combination of one (principal) who authorizes another (agent) to act for him.
prin'/ci/ple	rule; a fundamental, primary, or general truth, on which other truths depend; a fundamental doctrine or tenet.
pri/or'/ity	state of being earlier in time, or of preceding something else; precedence in order or rank; having certain rights before another.
priv'/i/lege	a right or immunity enjoyed by a person beyond the common advantages of others; a prerogative; an immunity existing under the law.
privileged communication	a confidence that may not be divulged, even in court.
privileges and immunities	rights which owe their existence to the laws of Federal Government.
priv'/ity	participation in the knowledge of something private or secret, esp. as implying concurrence or consent; the relation between knowledgeable parties.
privy	one connected with another by reason of their having a mutual interest in the same action or thing; admitted as one sharing in a secret.
privy verdict	a verdict delivered to the judge out of court, relieving the jury from their confinement in case of agreement after the judge has adjourned court, to be affirmed by an oral verdict given

publicly in court upon resumption of the session.

prob'/able cause | reasonable cause as shown by the circumstances of the case.

pro'/bate | legal and official proof, esp. of wills and testaments.

pro/ba'/tion | the testing or trial of a person's conduct, character, qualifications, etc.; a method of dealing with offenders, esp. young persons guilty of minor crimes or first offenses.

pro'/ba/tive | tending to prove or actually proving.

pro/ce'/dure | a particular course or mode of action; conduct; mode of conducting legal, parliamentary, or other business, litigation, or judicial proceedings.

proc'/ess | a systematic series of actions directed to some end; the summons, mandate, or writ by which a defendant or thing is brought before the court for litigation; a series of actions.

proc/la/ma'/tion | a public and official announcement.

pro/crus'/tean | tending to produce conformity by violent or arbitrary means.

proc'/tor | a person employed to manage another's cause in a court of civil or ecclesiastical law, or to collect tithes for the owner of them; an official charged with various duties, esp. with the maintenance of good order.

proc/u/ra'/tion | management for another; agency; a document whereby the authority is given.

pro/cur'er | a person who obtains anything by care, effort, or the use of special means; one who obtains for the gratification of lust.

pro/duc/tiv'/ity of land | cropping value; the ability to produce in terms of specified amounts, such as a stated number of bushes of grain per acre.

pro/fan'/ity | irreverence; vulgar conduct or language.

pro/fes'/sion | avowal; a declaration; a vocation requiring knowledge of some department of learning or science, esp. one of the three vocations of law, medicine, or teaching.

pro/fes'/sional serv'/ices	services rendered in a professional capacity.
pro forma	as a matter of form; provided in advance to prescribe form or describe items.
prog/no'/sis	a forecasting of the probable course and termination of a disease; a particular forecast made.
pro/le/gom'/e/non	a preliminary observation; prefatory remarks serving to introduce and interpret an extended work.
por/le/ta'/rius	a person who had no property to be taxed, but paid a tax only on account of his children.
prom/e/nade'	a walk in a public place for pleasure or display; a space on an upper deck of a passenger ship for the use of passengers.
prom/isee'	one to whom promise is made.
prom'/iser OR prom'/isor	one who undertakes to pay; one who promises.
prom'/is/sory note	a contract in writing for the payment of money, usually with the added feature of negotiability.
pro/mul'/gate	to make known by open declaration; to set forth or teach publicly.
prop/a/gan'da	the particular doctrines or principles propagated by an organization or concerted movement.
prop'/erty	that which one owns; a chattel or tract of land; something at the disposal of a person.
pro/pin'/quity	proximity; nearness in place; similarity; kindred.
pro/pone'	to make a motion; to proffer; to offer a will for probate.
pro/po'/nent	one who puts forth a proposal; a party who makes a motion.
pro/pos'al	an expression of intention.
pro/pound'	to put forward for consideration, adoption, or acceptance; to state formally for consideration.
pro/pri'/e/tary	pertaining to property or ownership; holding property.
pro/pri'/e/tary rights	rights which a property owner has by virtue of ownership.

pro rata	in proportion; according to a certain rate or exactly calculable factor.
pro/rate′	to make an arrangement on a basis of proportional distribution.
pro/ra′/tion	apportionment.
pro/ro/ga′/tion	prolonging or putting off till another day.
pro/scribed′	prohibited; condemned as harmful; denounced as dangerous.
pro se (PRON. prō sē)	for one's self; appearing for one's self in an action or criminal prosecution.
pros′e/cute	to institute legal proceedings against a person; to maintain rather than to commence or begin an action.
prosecuting attorney	a public officer elected or appointed, as provided by constitution or statute, to conduct suits, generally criminal, on behalf of the state in his jurisdiction.
prose/cu′/tion	the institution and carrying on of a suit or proceeding in a court of law or equity.
pro/spec′/tus	a proposal for a contract; a setting forth the nature and objects of an issue of securities created by the company or corporation; a printed statement distributed to describe and advertise a forthcoming literary work or a new enterprise.
pros/ti/tu′/tion	the selling of one's self or devoting to infamous purposes that which is in one's power.
pro tanto	to that extent; for so much.
pro′/tean	assuming different forms; variable; changeable.
pro/tec′/tor/ate	the relation of a strong state toward a weaker state or territory which it protects and partly controls.
pro′/tégé	one who is under the protection or friendly patronage of another.
pro tem	for the time being; temporary.
pro/ten′/sive	having lengthwise extent.
pro′/test (n.)	the formal expression of objection or disapproval.
pro/test′ (v.)	to make a remonstrance against; to object as disqualified, as an opponent or a player.

pro/thon'/o/tary	a principal clerk in some courts; one of a college of ecclesiastics of superior rank.
pro'/to/col	an agreement between states; ceremonial forms, particularly those governing conduct toward heads of state or their diplomatic representatives.
prov'/able debt	a debt susceptible of proof against a bankrupt estate.
prov'/e/nance OR provenience	the place of origin, as of a work of art, etc.
prov'/ince	an administrative division or unit of a country; a department or branch of learning or activity; the sphere or field of action of a person.
pro/vi'/sional	temporary in nature and subject to change, excluding the idea of permanency.
pro/vi'so	a clause in a statute, contract, or the like, by which a condition is introduced.
provo/ca'/tion	something that angers, incites, irritates, or instigates; words or conduct leading to a killing in hot passion and without deliberation.
prov'/ost	the head of certain colleges or churches; one appointed to superintend or preside.
prox'i/mate	closely adjacent; very near; fairly accurate; next in a chain of relation.
proximate cause	active cause that sets other causes in operation to produce a result; the cause most immediately connected.
proxy	the agency of a person deputed to act for another; a substitute; a document giving authorization as such.
pru'/ri/ent	morbidly uneasy, as desire or longing; wanton; lustful cravings; exciting to lasciviousness.
psy/chol'/ogy	the science of the mind and its perceptions; the mental states and processes of a person or of a number of persons, esp. as determining action.
psy/cho/path'ic	pertaining to or of the nature of, affected with, or engaged in treating mental disease or disorder.

pu´berty	sexual maturity; the age under common law at which a person may lawfully marry—12 for girls and 14 for boys.
pub´/lic	of, pertaining to, or affecting the people as a whole, or the community, state, or nation; open to all the people; maintained at public expense and under public control.
pueb´lo	communal house or group of houses, built of adobe or stone; an Indian village.
pu´is/sance	power, might, force, or authority.
pu´ni/tive	concerned with punishment; inflicting punishment or penalty.
punitive damages	damages in excess of actual damages awarded by a court to punish a defendant for a wrong.
purchase money mortgage	mortgage on property given to insure sale price.
pur/loin´	to take dishonestly or steal; to pilfer.
pur´/port (n.)	that which appears on the face of an instrument.
pur/port´ (v.)	to convey to the mind as the meaning or thing intended; to express; to imply.
pur/su´/ant to	acting or done in consequence or in prosecution of anything; agreeable; conformable; following.
pur/vey´or	one who provides or supplies; a royal officer who purchased articles for the king at his own price.
pu´/ta/tive	supposed; commonly regarded as such; assumed; believed.
pyr´a/mid/ing	building up to a peak; merging corporations in a complex form with a holding corporation at the top; controlling prices in a stock or commodity market by a series of operations.
pyro/ma´/nia	a mania for setting things on fire.
Pyrrhic victory	a victory gained at an excessive cost.

Q

qua	as; in what manner; in the character of; how; in the role of.

quaere (ABBR. q.)	query; it is a question (used to signify doubt or ask a question).
qual'i/fied endorse/ment	an endorsement with the inscription "without recourse."
qual'i/ta/tive rule of evidence	a rule by which the admissibility of evidence is determined.
quare	wherefore; because; on which account; why.
quar'/rel/ing	indulging by two or more persons in a brawl, dispute, or angry contest.
quash	abate; overthrow; annul.
quasi	having the character of; as if; as it were; term used to indicate that one thing resembles another to which it is compared in some characteristics but not in others.
quasi contract	an implied contract; contractual relation arising out of transactions between the parties which give them mutual rights and obligations.
quasi-entrepreneur	implied contractor.
quasi *in rem* action	an action in which the judgment deals with the status, ownership, or liability of particular property and operates only as between the particular parties to the proceeding.
quasi-judicial	the exercising of discretion of a judicial nature by public administrative officers under certain conditions.
quasi legal	having some legal implications but not genuinely legal.
quasi-lien	a lien not arising under contract or directly under statute, but existing by way of provisional relief obtained in an action, such as an attachment lien.
quay (PRON. kē)	a wharf; an artificial landing place, as of masonry, built along navigable water for vessels loading or unloading cargo.
quay'/age (PRON. kē aj)	a charge or toll exacted for the use of a quay or wharf.
quest (n.)	a search or pursuit made in order to find something.
(v.)	to search or seek for; to pursue.
quiet enjoyment	provision in a conveyance or lease promising grantee or tenant possession of premises without disturbance and in peace.

quitclaim	a deed in the words of "remise, release, and quitclaim," manifesting the intention of the grantor to convey his present interest, whatever it may be, to the grantee.
quitrent	rent paid by a tenant of a freehold, discharging him from other rent.
quit′/tance	discharge from debt or obligation; a release; an exoneration.
quo′/rum	the number of members of a body required to be present to transact business legally.

R

Rabelaisian (PRON. rab e lā′ /zien)	coarsely humorous; pertaining to or suggesting Francois Rabelais, whose work is characterized by broad, coarse humor and keen satire.
rack/et/eer′	using one's position to extort or obtain money by fraud; one engaged in an organized illegal activity such as extorting money by threat or violence from legitimate businessmen.
radar	an acronym derived from Radio Detection and Ranging; equipment possessed by police for measuring the speed of motor vehicles.
rad′i/cal/ism	the following of extreme views or principles.
radi/ca′/tion	taking root.
raison d'être (PRON. rā zon′dā′tr)	the reason or cause of being or existing.
rap/port′	harmonious or sympathetic relation; agreement.
ratable value	appraised or assessed value of property for purposes of taxation.
rati/fi/ca′/tion	sanction; confirmation; giving effect by approval.
rat′ing	credit standing of a firm or individual set by mercantile agencies.
ra′tio	proportional relation; the relation between two similar magnitudes in respect to the number of times the first contains the second.
ratio/ci/na′/tion	act of reasoning; deducing conclusions from premises.
ration/ale′	a reasoned exposition of principles, opinion, belief, or practice; an underlying reason.

rational intent	an intent founded on reason, as a faculty of the mind, and opposed to an irrational purpose.
reaction time	the time required for response to a stimulus, especially in an emergency.
readily accessible	available for immediate use in an emergency.
readmission	authorizing a foreign corporation to do business in the state after a withdrawal of the corporation from the state.
real	relating to land, as distinguished from personal property.
real estate	lands, tenements, and hereditaments—distinguished from personal property, chattels, and intangibles.
re'alty	real property.
rearage	linear extent of rear of property.
reargue	to repeat reasons for or against.
rear'/gu/ment	a rehearing of a motion; a rehearing in an appellate court.
rearraign'/ment	an arraignment of the accused after amendment of the accusatory pleading or the substitution of an indictment or information for one which has been lost.
rebut'/tal	contradiction or refutation; testimony addressed to evidence as reproduced by the opposite party; speech of a debater in refutation of the statements made by his opponent.
recant	to withdraw or disavow; to change one's testimony as given at a former trial because it is untruthful; to retract formally.
recap'i/tal/iza/tion	a form of reorganization in which outstanding capital stock may be replaced by a new issue.
receipt'	a written acknowledgment of having received money, goods, etc. specified; the acceptance of property upon delivery thereof.
receiv'/er/ship	an equitable remedy for the dissolution or reorganization of a corporation in financial distress.
reces'/sion	the act of ceding back; returning ownership to a former possessor; a temporary decline in business occurring during a period of generally increasing economic prosperity, esp. during a period of recovery after a depression.

recid′/i/vism	repeated or habitual relapse into crime.
recip′/ro/cal contract	a contract in which the consideration consists of an exchange of agreement between the parties.
recip′/ro/cal wills	wills in which the testators name each other as beneficiaries under similar testamentary plans.
reci/proc′/ity	mutual exchange; that relation or policy in commercial dealings between countries by which corresponding advantages or privileges are granted by each country to the citizens of the other.
reci′/sion	an invalidating or canceling.
recog′/ni/zance	a bond or obligation of record entered into before a court of record or a magistrate, binding a person to do a particular act, usually to appear and answer a criminal accusation.
rec′og/ni/zor	a person who binds himself by a recognizance.
recommendation for credit	a recommendation in commendation of another person's credit.
rec/om/men/da′/tion	representation in favor of a person or thing.
recom/mit′/ment	returning a convict to prison upon his breach of the terms or conditions of parole.
rec/on/cili/a′/tion	the process of making consistent or compatible.
recon/di′/tion	to restore to a good or satisfactory condition; to repair.
recon′/nais/sance	the act of inspecting, observing, or surveying the enemy or the enemy's strength or position, a region, etc. in order to gain information.
recon/ven′/tion	a counterclaim; a cross-demand.
recon/vey′/ance	a conveyance by the grantee under a former conveyance to the grantor in such conveyance.
recoup′/ment	compensation for; a cutting back; a deduction from a money claim whereby cross demands arising out of the same transaction are allowed to compensate one another, the balance only to be recovered.
recrimi/na′/tion	the act of bringing a countercharge against an accuser; accusing in return.
recur′/rent	appearing or occurring again either repeatedly or periodically.
redact′	to draft; to bring into presentable literary form; to revise; to edit.

red/den′/dum	a clause in a deed used to effect a reservation of an estate in the land granted.
red′/di/tus	a return or compensation for the possession of land; rent.
redemp′/tion	a repurchase; the buying back of one's property after it has been sold.
red herring	something to divert attention; a false clue; a preliminary prospectus circulated through the underwriters' offices during the "cooling-off" period—such document must contain a precautionary legend printed vertically on the left-hand front-face piece of the preliminary prospectus from top to bottom before final filing with the Securities and Exchange Commission.
rediscounting paper	a function of banks, particularly Federal reserve banks, in taking at a discount the discounted paper of other banks.
redoubt′/able	formidable—that is, to be feared; commanding respect.
re′dress (n.)	the setting right of what is wrong; means or possibility of seeking a remedy.
redress′ (v.)	to correct or reform abuses, evils, etc.
reduce to possession	to convert a claim to a tangible possession.
reductio ad absurdum	disproof of a premise by showing the absurdity to which it leads when carried to its logical conclusion.
redun′/dancy	a superfluity; excess, particularly in words; matter in a pleading not essential to the statement of cause of action or defense.
re-entry	coming or going into again; the retaking of possession under a right reserved in a prior conveyance.
ref/eree′	a person to whom a cause pending in a court is referred by the court to take testimony, hear the parties, and report thereon to the court.
ref/er/en′/dum	the principle or procedure of referring or submitting measures already passed on by the legislative body to the vote of the electorate for approval or rejection.

refu/gee′	one who flees for refuge or safety, esp. to a foreign country, as in time of political upheaval, war, etc.
re′gency	the office, jurisdiction, or control of one who exercises the ruling power in a kingdom during the minority or other disability of the sovereign.
regime′	a mode or system of rule or government; a ruling or prevailing system.
reg′/is/tered	enrolled; recorded; trade name, trade-mark, etc., filed and officially recorded in the U.S. Patent Office so that exclusive use is limited to the one submitting the name or mark for recordation.
reg′/is/trar	an official recorder of a transfer of corporate stock; the officer of a college, university, or other institution in charge of the enrollment of students.
registration of securities	preparation and filing with the Securities and Exchange Commission of a statement applying to securities being offered for public sale.
Registration Statement	a statement relative to securities being offered for public sale by an issuing company, the object being the disclosure of facts upon which investors may appraise the merits of such securities.
reha/bil′/i/ta/tion	restoring to a good condition; restoring to a former capacity, standing, rank, rights, or privileges lost or forfeited.
reim/burse′	to refund; to repay; to make repayment for loss or expense incurred.
rein/state′/ment	putting back or establishing again, as in a former position or state; restoration of a person or a thing to a position from which he or it has been removed.
rein/sur′/ance	insuring under a contract by which a first insurer relieves himself from a part or from all of the risk and devolves it upon another insurer.
rejoin′/der	the defendant's answer to the plaintiff's reply to defendant's original plea.

relat'or	a private person on whose suggestion or complaint an action or special proceeding in the name of the state is brought to try a question involving both public and private right.
release'	the relinquishment, concession, or giving up of a right, claim, or privilege, by the person in whom it exists or to whom it accrues, to the person against whom it might have been demanded or enforced.
relet'/ting	a definite letting of the same premises by the lessor under a prior lease upon the forfeiture of such lease or the failure of the lessee to take possession.
rel'e/vancy	applicability to the issue joined; the logical relation between evidence offered and a fact to be established.
rel'/ict	surviving spouse; widow or widower.
relief'	the objective of an action, proceeding, or motion; an award of damages or a judgment, decree, or order requiring an adversary to perform as directed or to refrain from specified conduct; help or assistance given, as to those in poverty or need.
relin'/quish/ment	an abandonment; surrender; a yielding up of all claim to a thing.
remain'/der	estate in expectancy, which becomes an estate in possession under certain qualifying circumstances.
remain'/der/man (PL., remaindermen)	one entitled to an estate in remainder.
remand'	to send back a case to a lower court from which it was appealed, with instructions as to what further proceedings should be had.
reme'/dial	affording remedy; providing a means of redress.
rem'/edy	the legal means of enforcing a right or redressing a wrong.
remise, release, and quitclaim	the formal words in a deed, sufficient to pass all rights to the estate on to another.
remis'/sion	pardon; the relinquishment of a payment, obligation, etc.; abatement or diminution, as of diligence, labor, intensity.

remit′	to transmit money to a person or place; to abate; to send back.
remit′/tance	money or its equivalent sent from one place to another.
remit′/ti/tur	a reducing of a verdict because of the excessiveness of the award, often required of a plaintiff as a condition of affirmance of the judgment entered upon the verdict.
rem′/nant	a fragment or scrap; a trace; vestige; remaining.
remon′/strance	a protest; an objection; an objection, for example, to the establishment of a highway.
renais/sance′ OR ren/ais/sance′	a new birth or revival.
Renaissance	the activity, spirit, or time of the great revival of art, letters, and learning in Europe during the 14th, 15th, and 16th centuries, marking the transition from the medieval to the modern world.
re/nas/cent′	being reborn; springing again into vigor or being.
ren′/dez/vous	an appointment or engagement made between two or more persons to meet at a fixed place and time; a place for meeting.
ren′e/gade	one who deserts a party or cause for another.
renewal of lease	a creation of a new lease rather than an extension of an old lease.
rent (n.)	compensation in money, provisions, chattels, or services, paid or given in exchange for the use and occupation of real estate.
(v.)	to obtain possession of premises under a lease.
renun/ci/a′/tion	the formal abandoning of a right, title, etc.; a sacrifice.
reo absente	defendant absent.
rep′a/ra/ble injury	an injury, the damage from which is merely in the nature of pecuniary loss, and can be repaired by compensation in money.
rep/a/ra′/tion	the redress of an injury; restoration to good condition; compensation by a defeated nation for damages to civilian population and property during war.

re/pa/tri/a'/tion	the restoration of a person to citizenship previously lost by expatriation; a return to the country of one's birth and citizenship of origin.
repen'/tance	regret for any past action.
replev'in	a personal action ex delicto brought to recover possession of goods unlawfully taken.
rep/li/ca'/tion	a reply made by plaintiff to defendant's plea or answer.
repos'i/tory	a receptacle or place where things are deposited, stored, or offered for sale; a person to whom something is entrusted or confided.
repos'it	to put back; replace; to lay up or store.
repost (ALSO ripost OR riposte)	a quick, sharp return; quick, clever reply.
rep/re/sen/ta'/tion	a statement made; the expression or designation by some term, character, symbol, or the like.
reprieve'	to relieve temporarily from any evil; to take back; the postponement of the execution of a sentence for a definite time, or to a day certain, not defeating the ultimate execution, merely delaying it temporarily.
rep'/ri/mand (n.)	a severe censure for wrongdoing.
(v.)	to reprove severely in a formal way.
repris'al	retaliation; the infliction of similar or severer injury on an enemy in retaliation for some injury.
repu/di/a'/tion	a denial of validity or of authority; refusal to recognize an obligation asserted as binding one; a denial of responsibility.
repug'/nancy	contradiction; hostility; inconsistency; objection, distate, or aversion.
rep'u/ta/ble	honorable; respectable; estimable.
req/ui/si'/tion	a demand made; a requirement or essential condition.
res (PRON. rās OR rēz)	the subject matter of the suit; the thing; any species of property.
res adjudicata (res judicata)	[See res judicata.]
rescind'	to annul; revoke; repeal; to invalidate by a later action or a higher authority.

rescis'/sion	cancellation; the act of cutting off.
re'script	any edict, decree, or official announcement; duplicate or copy; written order from court to clerk giving certain directions.
res'/cue	to liberate or take by forcible means from lawful custody; saving a person exposed to peril.
rescyt'	the receiving or harboring of a person who had committed a felony and had been convicted thereof.
resec'/tion	a cutting off or paring off.
res'i/ant	residing.
res'i/dence	a term of dual meaning, sometimes meaning a temporary, permanent, or transient character of abode; at other times meaning one's fixed abode or domicile.
resid'/ual	remaining; left over.
resid'/u/ary	pertaining to or of the nature of a residue; entitled to the residue of an estate.
residuary clause	the part of a will which disposes of property remaining after special devises have been made.
resid'/uum	the residue of an estate; the part which is left after deductions.
res judicata	the thing has been decided; controlling law; point already judicially decided.
respect'/able	worthy of esteem; of good social standing, reputable, etc.
respond'/ent	occupying the position of defendant; on an appeal, the party countering the appeal.
respondentia bond	a bond for a loan secured by the cargo of a ship.
respon'/si/ble	answerable or accountable, as for something within one's power, control, or management; having a capacity for moral decisions and therefore accountable.
res'/tau/rant	an establishment where meals are served to customers.
res/tau/ra/teur'	the keeper of a restaurant.
rest, residue, and remainder	phrase in will whereby testator bequeaths all his property not specifically devised by his will.

res/to/ra′/tion	act of renewal, revival, or reestablishment; a bringing back to a former, original, normal, or unimpaired condition.
restrain′/ing order	any injunction other than a mandatory injunction; a cease and desist order by an administrative agency.
restric′/tive endorse′/ment	an endorsement of a negotiable instrument which either prohibits the further negotiation of the instrument, or constitutes the endorsee the agent of the endorser, or vests the title in the endorsee in trust for or to the use of some other person.
resume′	a summary; abridgment.
retain′er	a fee paid to secure services, as of a lawyer.
retal/i/a′/tion	reprisal; an offensive rather than a defensive act.
reten′/tion	act or power of remembering things; continuing to hold in place or position.
retrax′it	a plaintiff's open and voluntary renunciation of his suit.
ret/ro/ac′/tive	operative with respect to past occurrences, as a statute.
ret/ro/ces′/sion	restitution of an old title to the true owner.
ret′/ro/spect	contemplation of the past; a survey of the past time, events, etc.
return′	a statement of financial condition; to give, as an official account, to a superior; the delivery of a legal order, as a writ, to the proper officer or court; an account or formal report.
return′/able	legally required to be returned.
rē′us	a defendant; a person who is guilty of a criminal offense; a party to a contract; a party to an action.
rev′e/nue	the collective items or amounts of income of a person, a state, etc.; the income of a government from taxation, excise duties, customs, or other sources, appropriated to the payment of the public expenses.
revers′/ible error	prejudicial error; error in the court below, which has injuriously affected the appellant or by which he has suffered a miscarriage of justice.

rever'/sion	act of turning something the reverse way; the returning of an estate to the grantor or his heirs after the interest granted expires.
revert'	to return to a former habit, practice, belief, condition, etc.; to go back in thought or discourse, as to a subject.
revest'	to vest again as with ownership or office; to reinstate.
reviv'al	restoration to life, consciousness, vigor, strength, etc.; restoration to a condition of activity.
rev'/o/ca/bil/ity	the quality of being subject to recall; the distinctive characteristic of a will; absent in a deed.
rev/o/ca'/tion	annulment; the nullification or withdrawal of an offer to contract.
rev/o/lu'/tion	a complete overthrow of an established government or political system; a complete or marked change in something; the action or fact of going round in an orbit.
ri'der	an additional clause, usually unrelated to the main body, attached to a legal document or a legislative bill, and considered to be a part thereof.
right'/ful	by right; proper; lawful; having a just claim as to some possession or position.
rigor mortis	the stiffening of the body after death.
ripar'/ian	belonging to the bank of a river, lake, or other natural body of water.
riparian rights	rights existing as natural and inherent incidents to ownership of land on the banks of a natural watercourse or body of water.
rit'/ual	a prescribed form for the conduct of a meeting of a lodge or fraternal benefit society.
Rockefeller Foundation	a trust chartered for the broad purpose of promoting the well-being of mankind throughout the world, the practical objectives being the advancement of knowledge and the application of knowledge to human interests and needs, particularly by studies in reference to the world's food supply, overpopulation, educational opportunities, and cultural activities.

rogues' gal'/lery	a collection of photographs of persons convicted of crime, preserved and exhibited in a police department or prison for the future identification of such persons.
roll'/ing stock	the wheeled vehicles of a railroad, including locomotives, cars, etc.; movable property belonging to a railroad company declared personal property for purposes of taxation.
rota'/tion	the turning of the earth daily on its own axis; regular and recurring succession.
roy'/alty	a payment made for the privilege of using a patented invention; a fixed portion of the proceeds from his work, paid to an author, composer, etc.; consideration paid to the lessor by the lessee under a gas or oil lease.
ru'bric	an established custom or rule; title of a statute or law; underlined with red or printed in red.
rules of evidence	principles which express the mode or manner of proving the facts and circumstances upon which a party relies to establish a fact in dispute.
ru'mor	unconfirmed gossip; popular report; a statement in current circulation without certainty as to facts.
run'/ning account	an open account; an account without interruption by settlement or adjustment.
run with the land	a covenant in a deed runs with the land when its legal effect is to bind subsequent transferees.
rut	a furrow or track in the ground; a fixed routine or course of practice; sexual excitement of the male deer, goat, or sheep at regular periods.

S

sab/bat'/i/cal leave	a term or a year of freedom from teaching, granted to a professor for study or travel, usually with pay.
sab'/o/tage	willful and malicious physical damage or injury to physical property.
sad'/ism	any morbid enjoyment in being cruel, or in hurting another; a species of mental disease in which the sexual instinct of the patient is abnormal or perverted.
sal'/able	suitable for sale.

sal'/vage	compensation given to those who rescue a ship or cargo from loss.
sal'/vian inter'/dict	(Roman law) a foreclosure of a pledge of the goods of a tenant given by him to secure the payment of his rent.
san'/gui/nary	characterized by bloodshed.
san'/guine	naturally cheerful and hopeful; confident; optimistic.
sans	without.
sanus	in a healthful state; whole; sound in mind or body.
satisfaction piece	a formal acknowledgment in writing that a judgment has been paid.
sat'/ur/nine	having a sluggish, gloomy temperament; taciturn; morose.
scan'/dal/mon/ger	one who spreads scandal maliciously.
scav'/age	a toll exacted of foreign merchants by town officers for showing or exposing goods for sale in the town.
sched'/ule in bank'/ruptcy	an inventory filed by the bankrupt in bankruptcy proceedings, containing a list of all his property and credits.
schism (PRON. siz'em)	division or disunion into mutually opposed parties.
schiz/o/phre'/nia	a mental disorder characterized by splitting of the personality, dissociation, emotional deterioration, or feelings of omnipotence and persecution.
scienter (sī-en'ter)	knowingly; in cases of fraud, signifying an assertion that the person making the representations knew that they were false at the time they were made.
scil'i/cet (PRON. sil'i sit)	to wit; that is to say. An introductory word to a statement of matters previously mentioned in general terms.
scin/til'la	a trace; a small particle; a spark.
scintilla juris	a spark of interest; a particle of right.
scintilla of evidence	the least particle of evidence; a mere trifle of evidence.
scrip	certificate for a fractional share of stock, or, in banking, representing a dividend still to be paid.

script	handwriting; the characters used in handwriting; an original written instrument as distinguished from a duplicate; manuscript of a play.
scrive′/ner	a professional or public writer; a clerk; a notary.
scru′/pu/lous	having or showing a strict regard for what is right; punctilious.
scru′/ta/tor	one who investigates.
s-curve (ALSO ogive)	in statistics, a graphic curve commonly referred to as a growth curve.
scur′/ril/ous	grossly or indecently abusive; vulgar.
seal	design stamped on to show ownership or authenticity; a scroll or other distinguishing mark placed upon an instrument as a seal.
se′ance (PRON. sā′ans)	a meeting of spiritualists seeking to receive communications from spirits.
seces′/sion	act of seceding; a withdrawal from membership in an organized group.
secondhand	not original; previously used or owned.
sec/tar′/ian	confined or devoted to a particular sect.
secured creditor	a creditor who is protected by a pledge of property or by a guarantee in the form of pledged securities.
securities acts	statutes controlling and regulating the issuance and sale of securities for the purpose of protecting the investing public.
sedi′/tion	incitement of discontent or rebellion against the government.
seg/re/ga′/tion	an enforced separation of races, particularly the white and black races, as under statutes and constitutions providing for the separate education of black and white children.
seised OR seized	having possession of a freehold estate.
seisin OR seizin (PRON. sē zin)	possession of premises with the intention of asserting a claim to a freehold estate therein, practically the same thing as ownership.
self-defense	a right founded upon the law of nature but deemed necessary even in organized society to personal safety and security and as not incompatible with the public good.

seman´/tic	pertaining to meaning or signification.
seman´/tics	the study of meaning and changes of meaning; the exploitation of ambiguity.
semiannual (ALSO biannual)	occurring every six months or twice a year.
senior´/ity	the principle in labor relations that length of employment determines the order of layoffs, rehirings, and advancements.
sen´/tence	a judicial statement or decree, esp. the determination of the punishment to be inflicted on a convicted criminal.
sen/ten´/tious	abounding in pithy sayings or maxims; given to excessive moralizing.
sep´a/ra/ble	capable of being divided into component parts.
se´quel	a literary work, complete in itself, but continuing a preceding work; subsequent course of affairs.
seques´/ter	to remove property temporarily from the possession of the owner; to seize and hold, as the property and income of a debtor, until legal claims are satisfied.
seques/tra´/tion	the confiscation or seizure of property by the court in order to assure obedience to a decree.
serial bonds	bonds issued by a public body payable at different times.
ser´/vi/ent	serving; subject to a service.
set off (v.)	to cross-demand or counterclaim.
setoff (n.)	a discharge or reduction of one demand by an opposite demand.
set´/tler	one who settles in a new country; a colonist.
set´/tlor	grantor or donor in a deed of settlement.
seven years' absence	absence from which there arises a presumption of death where it has continued as an unexplained absence of a person from his home or place of residence without any intelligence from or concerning him for the period of seven years.
sev´/er/a/bil/ity	the quality of being susceptible to division, leaving parts independent of each other.
severability of deposition	the quality upon which the right to use only a part of a deposition upon a trial is based.

sev′/er/alty	property held by one person; state of being separate.
sev′/er/ance	division; separation; breaking off, as of relations.
share	one of the equal parts into which the capital stock of a corporation is divided.
sharecropper	a tenant farmer who pays as rent a share of the crop.
shares	stock representing a share in its owner's extent of proprietorship in the issuing company.
sher′/iff	an officer having the dual character of a peace officer and a ministerial officer.
shib′/bo/leth	a peculiarity of pronunciation, or a habit, mode of dress, etc., which distinguishes a particular class or set of persons; a test word or pet phrase.
shipshape	in good order; well-arranged.
short exchange	bills of exchange payable at sight or in a few days.
shrie′/valty (PRON. shrē′ val-ti)	the period of a sheriff's term of office.
shy′/ster	a lawyer who uses unprofessional or questionable methods; one who gets along by petty, sharp practices.
sib′/ling	a brother or sister.
sic (adv.)	thus; so (often used parenthetically to show that something has been copied exactly from the original);
(v.)	to incite to attack (esp. of a dog).
sight	the date of acceptance of a bill of exchange.
sight draft	a draft that is due to be paid when presented.
sigil′/lum	a seal.
sig′/na/tory	a signer, or one of the signers, of a document.
sig′/na/ture	the name of a person written by himself and retaining his distinctive form of signing his name.
signed, sealed, and delivered	executed; an expression in a certificate of acknowledgment which states, in effect, the execution of the instrument.

silent partner	person who supplies capital or other acceptable asset but who is not openly declared to be a partner in an enterprise—he is equally responsible for all debts.
si/mil'/i/ter	a formal statement in writing whereby a party expresses his acceptance of an issue tendered by the pleading of his adversary; the like.
simon-pure	authentic; of untainted purity or integrity.
simple interest	interest which is computed on the original principal only.
si'ne/cure (PRON. sī ne cure)	an office requiring little or no work, esp. one yielding profitable returns.
sine qua non	something essential; an indispensable condition.
sinking fund	fund set aside in the form of cash or securities to retire a debt or part of it.
situs (SING. or PL.) (PRON. sī'tus)	position; situation; site; location.
slan'/der	defamation by oral utterance rather than by writing.
slander of title	words, written, printed, or uttered, which bring or tend to bring in question the right or title of another to real or personal property.
slough (PRON. sluf)	arm of stream which separates islands from one another and from the mainland; swampy area; a condition of degradation, embarrassment, or helplessness.
smart money	punitive damages awarded for gross misconduct; money ventured by one having inside information.
smog	a mixture of smoke and fog; any mixture in the air which impairs vision or is discomforting to a person in his breathing.
smug'/gling	importing prohibited articles, or defrauding the revenue by the introduction of articles into consumption, without paying the duties chargeable upon them.
snafu'	chaotic; out of control; in disorder; an acronym derived from *Situation Normal—All Fouled Up.*

Social Security	the welfare of the people with ample means of subsistence and enjoyment of life under the protection of the Government; the system which provides old-age and survivors' insurance benefits.
socii (PRON. so'shē i)	partners; associates; members of a partnership.
sod'/omy	unnatural sexual intercourse, as between persons of the same sex, or with beasts, or between persons of different sex but in an unnatural manner.
so'journ OR sojourn' OR sojourne (PRON. sō'jern)	to make a temporary stay in a place.
sola'/tium (PRON. sō lā'shi um)	compensation or damages for sorrow, mental anguish, or wounded feelings.
solic'/i/tor	person admitted to practice law and conduct litigation in the inferior courts of Great Britain.
sol'/vent	able to pay all that is owed.
som/nam'/bu/lism	sleepwalking; habit of walking about, and often of performing various other acts, while asleep.
sophis/ti/ca'/ted	artificial; worldly wise; changed from the natural character or simplicity.
sound and disposing mind and memory	the possession of sanity.
sound in tort	to have the nature or effect of a tort.
sov'/er/eignty	supreme and independent power or authority in government as possessed or claimed by a state or community.
spay'/ing	removing the ovaries of a female animal; sterilization of a female to prevent propagation.
spe'/cialty contract	a contract made under seal.
spe'/cie	coins or valued metal as opposed to paper money; coined money.
spec/i/fi/ca'/tion	a written enumeration and description of particulars; something specified as in a bill of particulars.
specific performance	actual accomplishment of a contract by the party bound to fulfill it.

spec′/u/la/tive dam′/ages	damages awarded in excess of actual loss suffered by injured party.
spendthrift trust	a trust created to provide a fund for the maintenance of the beneficiary which shall be secure against his improvidence or incapacity.
sper′/ma/to/zoa	seminal fluid.
spin-off	splitting of a corporation by apportioning all or part of its assets to another company in exchange for the latter's capital stock, such stock being distributed pro rata as a dividend to stockholders of the splitting company.
spo/lia′/tion	the destruction or material alteration of a bill of exchange, will, or the like.
spon/sa′/lia (PRON. spon-sā′lia)	mutual promises to marry.
spot′/ting	placing of cars for loading or unloading.
spouse	either member of a married pair in relation to the other.
spu′/ri/ous	counterfeit; not genuine.
squat′/ter	one who settles on another's land without complying with regulations.
sta/bi/liz/a′/tion of prices	various activities of the Federal government in the effort to keep prices of certain farm products stable, particularly in making payments to farmers for keeping land out of production of certain crops.
stake	the amount put up by way of wager or bet; a stock or post pointed at one end for driving into the ground as a boundary mark, a part of a fence, a support for a plant, etc.
stall′/age	the liberty of maintaining a market stall.
stare decisis (PRON. stā′re de-sī′sis)	the principle that decisions should stand as precedents for guidance in cases arising in the future.
statement of account	presentation of an account since the last payment.
statim (PRON. stā′/tim)	immediately.
stat′/ute	a law enacted by a legislative branch of a government.

statute law	a body of laws established by legislative enactment—opposite of common or unwritten law.
statute of frauds	a statute which requires certain classes of contracts to be in writing.
statute of limitations	statute defining the period within which a claim may be prosecuted.
stat'/u/tory	prescribed or authorized by statute.
stay of execution	an order issued by the court, upon cause shown, against the issuance or the enforcement of an execution.
stealth	secret, clandestine, or surreptitious procedure.
stellionate	fraud committed in entering into a contract for the sale of property which the vendor has previously sold.
ste'/ve/dore	a firm or individual engaged in the loading or unloading of a vessel.
sti/pen'/di/ary	a person who receives a remittance regularly; performing services for regular pay.
stip/u/la'/tion	an important article in an agreement; an undertaking in writing to do a certain act; an agreement between opposing counsel in a pending action.
stir'/pes (PRON. stir'pē z)	the person from whom a family or branch of a family is descended; a branch of a family.
Stock Clearing Corporation	a subsidiary of the New York Stock Exchange which clears securities transactions for member firms.
stockholder's derivative action	action by a stockholder in the name of the corporation and for the benefit of the corporation to recover damages for an injury done to the corporation.
stop'/page	cessation of activity; an obstruction or hindrance to the doing of a particular thing.
straiten	to narrow or restrict; to put into difficulties, esp. financial ones; in straitened circumstances.
stran/gu/la'/tion	causing death by cutting off the breath, as by squeezing the throat with hands or a cord.
strat'/a/gem	a deception by words or actions to obtain an advantage; any artifice, ruse, or trick.

street certificates	shares registered in brokers' names that are used for borrowings or clearances, being the floating stock representing the certificates in margin accounts of customers utilizing brokers' loans.
street name	certificates in brokers' names but held for clients' or brokers' accounts are in "street name."
strife	conflict, discord, or variance.
strip mining	a method of mining coal by uncovering the vein instead of reaching it by shaft and laterals.
struc'/tural defect	a condition in the structure itself which renders it not reasonably safe for the use for which it was intended.
stub	a short projecting part; a part of an instrument, especially the statement of an account, torn off and retained as a memorandum.
sub/merged lands	lands, particularly privately owned lands, covered by waters.
sub/or/na'/tion of per'/jury	the offense of procuring another to take false oath.
sub/pe'na OR sub/poe'na	the usual writ process for the summoning of witnesses.
subpena duces tecum	a subpena ordering the witness to bring with him books, papers, records, documents, or other evidence described in the subpena.
sub/pe'/naed	served or summoned by a subpena.
sub/ro/ga'/tion	substitution of parties; the right to take over the position of another; putting one thing in place of another.
sub rosa	privately; confidentially. (Under the rose; the rose being the symbol of the Egyptian god Horus, identified by the Greeks with Harpocrates, god of silence.)
sub/scrip'/tion	a signature at the end of an instrument; an application for a share or shares of a business trust.
subscription warrant	certificate granting stockholders of record the right to subscribe to certain securities.
sub'/se/quent	following in order or succession; occurring after or later.

sub/sid´/ence	the sinking or cracking of surface of land following a disturbance below the surface.
sub/sid´/iary com/pany	a company whose controlling interest is held by another.
sub/sist´/ence	the providing of sustenance or support; means of supporting life; existence; continuance.
sub/stan´/tial error	an error which upon the trial works harm and from which a party sustains substantial injury.
sub´/stan/tive	pertaining to the essential part or principle; substantial; independent and not derivative.
sub´/stan/tive law	that part of law which creates, defines, and regulates rights, as distinguished from rules of procedure.
sub´/stan/tive right	a right held to exist for its own sake and to constitute part of the normal legal order of society.
sub´/sti/tu/ted serv´/ice	service of process by leaving a copy of the summons or writ with a suitable person at the residence, dwelling house, or place of abode of the party to be served.
sub/sume´	to take up into or include in a larger or higher class or the like; to bring under another; to bring under a rule.
sub´/ter/fuge	an artifice or expedient employed to escape the force of an argument, to evade unfavorable consequences, etc.
sub/ven´/tion	the furnishing of aid or relief.
sub/ver´/sive	an organization that teaches and advocates the overthrow of government by force or violence.
suc/ces´/sion	the coming of one after another in order, sequence, or the course of events; sequence.
sue	to institute process in law against, or bring a civil action against; to make petition or appeal.
suf´/fer/ance	tolerance, as of a person or thing; tacit allowance; capacity to endure pain, hardship, etc.
suf´/frage	the right of voting, as in political affairs; a vote given in favor of a proposed measure, a candidate, or the like.
sum´/mary	done without any delay or formality.
sum´/mary pro/ceed´/ings	short and informal proceedings.

sum'/mons	an authoritative command, message, or signal by which one is summoned; a call or citation by authority to appear before a court or a judicial officer or the writ by which the call is made.
sump'/tu/ary laws	statutes restraining luxury and extravagant expense in dress, diet, and the like.
supercargo	person in charge of cargo in transit.
super/er/o/ga'/tion	the act of performing more than is required by duty, obligation, or need.
super/fi/cies'	outward appearance as distinguished from the inner nature.
supe'/rior lien	a prior lien.
super/sede'	to displace in office or promotion by another.
super/sed'/eas	a writ by which proceedings are stayed.
super/sti'/tious	characterized by a belief or notion, regardless of reason or knowledge, of the ominous significance of a thing or occurrence.
sup/ple/men'/tal brief	an additional brief on appeal filed by consent of court or pursuant to rules of court.
sup/ple/men'/tary pro/ceed'/ing	proceeding after judgment has been entered, looking toward the enforcement of the judgment against the property of the judgment-debtor.
sup/posi/ti'/tious	fraudulently substituted or pretended; spurious; not genuine; hypothetical.
su'pra	above; used in making reference to parts of a text.
suprem'/acy clause	the provision in Article VI, Clause 2, of the United States Constitution that "this Constitution and the laws of the United States which shall be made in pursuance thereof and all treaties made, or which shall be made, under the authority of the United States, shall be the supreme law of the land, and the judges in every state shall be bound thereby, anything in the Constitution or laws of any state to the contrary notwithstanding."
Supreme Court	in some jurisdictions, the highest appellate court; in other jurisdictions, a court of general jurisdiction.

sure'ty	one who binds himself to pay money in case another fails to pay, fill a contract, or serve with integrity; pledge or other formal engagement given for the fulfillment of an undertaking.
sure'ty bond	bond guaranteeing performance of a contract or obligation.
sur'/plus earn'/ings	an amount owned by a corporation, over and above its capital and actual liabilities.
sur/re/but'/tal	the giving of evidence to meet a defendant's rebuttal.
sur/re/but'/ter	a plaintiff's pleading in response to a defendant's rebutter.
sur/ren'/der by bail	the turning over or delivery of a tenant who had been released on bail to the custody of the law, by his bondsmen or sureties.
sur'/ro/gate	a judge who presides in a probate court in certain states of the Union and who has jurisdiction over the probate of wills, the administration of estates, etc.
Sur'/ro/gate's Court	a probate court.
sur/veil'/lance	watch kept over a person, etc., esp. over a suspect, a prisoner, or the like.
sur/vey'or	an overseer or supervisor; one whose business it is to survey land.
sur/viv'al acts	statutes which provide for the survival of a cause of action, notwithstanding the death of a party.
sur/vi'/vor	that one of two or more designated persons, as joint tenants or others having a joint interest, who outlives the other or others.
sus/cep'/ti/ble	readily impressed; capable of being affected easily.
sus/pen'/sion	a termination of an employee's service by the employer, usually for the purpose of an investigation to determine whether or not the employee should be retained in service.
sus'/te/nance	means of sustaining life; nourishment; means of livelihood.
su'ze/rain	dominant state controlling foreign relations of a dependent state.

sworn copy	a copy proved by oral testimony to have been examined with the original document and corresponding therewith; verified copy.
syb/a/ri´/tic	given to voluptuous, pleasurable, or luxurious living.
syl´/la/bus (PL., /buses or /bi)	a brief statement of the main points of a written article; brief statement of the rulings of a court upon the point or points decided in the case.
syl´/lo/gism	an argument, in logic, containing a major premise, a minor premise, and a conclusion.
sym´/bol	a mark, object, or letter that stands for something, such as a ditto mark indicating a repetition.
sym´/me/try	the proper or due proportion of the parts of a body or whole to one another with regard to size and form; excellence of proportion.
syn´/di/cate	a combination of persons or companies to carry out some undertaking, especially one requiring a large investment of capital.
syn/di/ca´/tion	period that precedes direct public sale of a stock offering in which brokers cannot make a firm public offering until such time as the securities come out of syndication.
syn/er/gis´/tic	working together; the capacity of two elements to act so that their combined action is greater than the sum of each if used independently.
syn´od	any council.
syn/op´/sis (PL., /ses)	a brief statement giving a general view of some subject; summary.
syn/op´/tic	affording a general view of a whole.
syph´/i/lis test	a test of the blood or other content of the body by chemical analysis to determine the existence of syphilitic infection.

T

tac´it law	that law which arises out of the silent consent and the custom and usages of the people without legislative enactment.
tail´/age	burdens, charges, or impositions, put or set upon persons or property for public uses.

take-off	the amount taken out of money in play by the person conducting the game; an imitation of a public character for comic effect.
tales juror (ALSO talesman)	juror summoned to fill vacancy in regular panel of jurors.
tan′/gi/ble assets	resources consisting of buildings, land, machinery, cash, inventories, etc.
tare	the difference between gross and net weight of shipment; an allowance for the weight of a container.
tare weight	weight of container or car, exclusive of contents; allowance for weight of crates or other containers.
tar′/get	the object of an attack; a definite goal, an objective, as such an amount of machines to be produced in a month.
tar′/iff	a schedule of charges made by a transportation company, containing the provisions governing their application; a list of duties which are payable on imports.
tau/tol′/ogy	redundancy consisting of needless repetition of meaning in different language.
tax′/able	liable to taxation; subject to a tax.
tax deed	a deed evidencing a sale of property for taxes.
tax eva′/sion	fraud in representation or concealment in attempting to avoid payment of a tax legally due, as in the case of an income tax; the filing of a return fraudulently understated in a willful attempt to evade payment.
tax lien	a privilege on property established in favor of state or municipality for unpaid taxes.
tax′/payer	one who pays taxes regularly.
tea′/zer	railroad operated at a loss.
tech′/ni/cal error	immaterial error; an error committed in the course of a trial, but without prejudice to a party.
teleph′/ony	the art or process of reproducing sounds at a distance, as by telephone.
ten′/ancy	a holding, or a mode of holding an estate; the period of a tenant's occupancy or possession.

tenancy by the entirety	joint ownership of real property by husband and wife, survivor to become sole owner.
ten'/ancy in common	joint ownership (not necessarily by husband and wife) but survivor does not take the whole; the holding of the same property together by several and distinct titles, but by writ of possession, in which grantees are to take in distinct shares.
ten'/ant in fee-simple	he who has lands, tenements, or hereditaments, to hold to him and his heirs forever, generally, absolutely, and simply.
ten'/ants in com'/mon	two or more owners of property who hold under a tenancy in common, whereby they are entitled to land in such manner that they have an undivided possession, but several freeholds or interests.
ten/den'/tious	having or showing a definite tendency, bias, or purpose.
ten'/der (n.)	an offer or proposal made for acceptance;
(v.)	to offer, as money or goods, in payment of a debt or other obligation, in accordance with the terms of the law and of the obligation.
ten'e/ment	that which may be held, such as lands, rents, franchises, etc.
ten'or	continuous course, progress, or movement; the exact words; a copy of an instrument setting forth the very words and figures.
ten'/ta/tive allow'/ance	a provisional allowance; an allowance not to be accepted as final.
ten'u/ous	having little substance or strength; delicate; thin.
ten'/ure	act or right of holding property; the right of certain public officers and public employees to be retained in employment, subject only to removal for certain enumerated causes and in a prescribed manner.
term insur'/ance	a policy of insurance under which the insurance contracted for covers only losses occurring before the expiration of a term stated in the policy.
ter'/mi/ne	to determine.

ter´/mi/nus	a term; an estate for years; an estate the duration of which is limited and determined.
ter´/mite	a wood-boring insect capable of causing much damage to wooden structures and furniture.
term´or	one who has an estate for a term of years or for life.
ter/ri/to´/rial waters	waters under state jurisdiction.
tes´/ta/ble	the state or condition of a person who is possessed of testamentary capacity.
tes´/tacy	state or circumstances of person who dies leaving a valid will.
tes´/ta/ment	a disposition of personal property to take place after owner's decease; synonymous with last will.
tes/ta/men´/tary	that which provides for the disposition of one's property, to take effect after death.
tes´tate	the status of having made and left a valid will.
tes/ta´/tor	one who leaves a will or testament in force at time of his death.
tes/ta´/trix	feminine of testator (see previous word).
teste	the witnessing or concluding clause of a writ or other precept.
tes/ti/mo´/nium clause	in conveyancing, the "in witness whereof" clause, stating that parties sign in testimony of document's contents.
tes´/ti/mony	statements of a witness under oath that are intended for use as evidence or proof.
tet´a/nus	an infectious disease characterized by contractions of muscles, especially the muscles of the jaw, so that the disease is often known as lockjaw.
tete-a-tete´ (PRON. tā t-ah-tā t)	face to face; a private conversation or interview between two persons.
text-writer	the author of a textbook or treatise upon some branch of the law or scientific subject.
the´o/rem	an idea accepted or proposed as a demonstrable truth, often as a part of a general theory.
the/o/ret´/i/cal inch	a term referred to in discussions of measurement of water.

the′o/rem	general statement proposed for testing as to its validity.
thereafter clause	a clause in an oil or gas lease intended to establish rights in the lessee, notwithstanding termination of the primary term of the lease, where production is maintained.
thereunto	an elliptical form of expression for the phrase "to do that."
the′/sis (PL., theses)	a proposition to be proven or one advanced without proof.
thor′/ough/fare	a passage through; a street or way open at both ends and free from any obstruction.
throe	a sharp attack of emotion; a violent spasm or pang.
tidelands	lands over which the tide ebbs and flows.
tidewater (tidal waters)	water coming in from the sea because of the rising tide; water in which the tide ebbs and flows.
tight money	the condition which exists when interest rates are high and credit is stringent.
tim′/ber/land	U.S. land covered with timber-producing forests.
time is of the essence	the condition of performance of a contract within the time limited for performance by the terms of the contract.
title	means by which right to possession is established.
title in fee simple	full and unconditional ownership.
title by oc′cu/pancy	ownership acquired through entering upon unclaimed land and taking possession.
title by pos/ses′/sion	the right of possession which in most of the states within the United States becomes established after 20 years of adverse or unchallenged possession.
title by pre/scrip′/tion	a title which may be acquired by use and time.
title of prop′/erty	rightful ownership and the evidence of such ownership.
title search	an abstract of title; an examination of the abstract of title to premises and of records of title and judicial records pertinent to the property made by the attorney for a purchaser prior to the closing of the deal.

tobog´/gan	a sled without runners, coasting or being towed on the boards or other material which makes its bottom.
to have and to hold	formal phrase used in habendum clause of deed.
toll (n.)	a payment exacted by the state, the local authorities, etc. for some right or privilege, as for passage along a road or over a bridge.
(v.)	to bar; defeat; take away; to summon or dismiss by tolling.
toll´/age	the payment of toll.
tolled	having run its full course.
toll gate	a gate erected upon a turnpike or toll road at which toll is collected from passing travelers.
ton´/nage	the capacity of a vessel in respect of the amount of cargo which it can carry; any measure in tons.
tor/na´do	a destructive rotatory storm, usually appearing as a whirling, advancing funnel pendent from a mass of black cloud.
Torrens system	a system used in many states whereby land titles are registered and certificates of title are granted; the system was named for its founder, Sir Robert Torrens who drew the first Registration Act, which was adopted in South Australia in 1858.
tort	a legal wrong against a personal right vested in the person or entity by law.
tort-feasor OR tortfeasor	a person who commits a tort; a wrongdoer.
tor´/tious	wrongful; of the nature of a tort.
tor´/tu/ous	full of twists, turns, or bends; not direct or straightforward, as in a course of procedure, thought, speech, or writing.
total loss	the complete destruction of the property covered by an insurance policy.
totem	an object or thing in nature, often an animal, assumed as the token or emblem of a clan, family, or related group.
totum	the whole.
tow (n.)	the coarse and broken parts of flax or hemp separated from the finer parts in hackling.

(v.)	to draw something along a course, particularly a vessel; to drag or pull by means of a rope or chain.
to wit	namely; that is to say.
township	an administrative division of a county; in U.S. surveys of public land, a region or district of 6 square miles.
trackage	the tracks of a railroad or railroad system, considered in their entirety.
trade accept'/ance	a bill of exchange drawn by the seller on the purchaser of goods sold, and accepted by such purchaser.
trade discount	percentage off from list price allowed a dealer as his profit on resale.
trade duty	tax imposed on goods for passing through a country.
trade-mark OR trademark	a sign, device, or mark by which the articles produced or dealt in by a particular person or organization are distinguished or distinguishable from those produced or dealt in by the others.
trade name OR tradename	the designation under which a person, partnership, or corporation does business.
trader	a member of an exchange trading for his own benefit and not for customers.
trade sale	an auction by and for the trade.
tram	a wheeled truck or car on which loads are transported in mines; correct position or adjustment; the word in Great Britain for streetcar.
tran/quil'/ity	peacefulness, quiet, calmness.
tran'/script	an official copy of the original proceedings in a court; any copy of a writing.
trans'/fer (n.)	a conveyance, by sale, gift, or otherwise, of real or personal property, to another.
(v.)	to make over the control or possession of; to transfer a title of land.
trans'/fer agent	an outside, individual trust company, or bank entrusted with issuing original certificates, canceling old ones, keeping stock certificates and stock ledgers of a corporation, etc.
trans/feree'	one to whom a transfer is made.

trans'/fer of title — the changing of ownership rights to property from one person to another.

trans'/feror — one who makes a transfer.

tran'/sient — a person passing through a place or staying there only temporarily.

tran'/si/tory
sei'/sin
(PRON. sē'zin) — seisin for the instant or for the moment, as where the person seised is a mere conduit of title for passing an estate.

trans/mu/ta'/tion — change into another nature, substance, form, or condition.

trans/ship'/ment — moving cargo from one vessel to another.

trau'ma — any injury to the body caused by external violence; a startling experience which has a lasting effect on mental life; a shock.

trau/ma'/tic — originating in a violent application of force to the body.

trav'/eler — one who travels in any way, even for a short distance.

trav'/erse   (n.) — a denial or contradiction.

tra/verse'   (v.) — to deny formally allegations contained in a previous pleading.

trea'/son — a violation by a subject of his allegiance to his sovereign or to the state.

treas'/ury note — note or bill issued by the Department of the Treasury which circulates as money.

tre'/ble dam'/ages — multiple damages awarded under statutory authority for certain classes of wrongs.

tres'/pass — an unauthorized encroachment on another's rights; every unauthorized entry on another's property.

tres'/tle — a support of a bridge; a frame used as a support, consisting typically of a horizontal beam or bar fixed at each end to a pair of spreading legs.

trial counsel — attorney who handles the actual litigation proceedings of a case.

trial de novo
(PRON. dē nō'vō) — a new trial or retrial had in an appellate court in which the whole case is gone into as if no trial whatever had been had in the court below.

trial exam'/i/ner — a hearing officer of an administrative agency, comparable to an auditor or special master of a court.

tri/bu´/nal	a place or seat of judgment; a court of justice.
trib´/u/tary	one who pays tribute; a stream contributing its flow to a larger stream or other body of water.
tri´/fling (adj.)	of little value; trivial.
(v.)	making play of another's affections.
trin´/ket	any small fancy article, bit of jewelry, or the like.
tri/par´/tite	divided into three parts.
triv´ia (PL.) triv´/ium (SING.)	trifles; inessential or inconsequential things; trivium—during the Middle Ages, the lower division of the seven liberal arts, comprising grammar, rhetoric, and logic.
tro´/ver	an action to recover the value of goods wrongfully converted by another to his own use.
truce	an agreement made between belligerent parties that they will temporarily cease hostilities.
trust	a nominal owner of property who holds, uses, or disposes of it for the benefit of another.
trust company	a corporation, usually engaged in a general banking business, and in particular as a compensated trustee of funds or property; a bank for purposes of regulation.
trust deed	a species of deed in the nature of a mortgage, being a conveyance in trust for the purpose of securing a debt.
trus/tee´	one appointed to execute a trust; one who holds property for the benefit of another.
trust inden´/ture	an instrument which states the terms and conditions of a trust, such as a pension trust or a trust created by way of security for a bond issue.
trus´/tor	the grantor, maker, creator, or settler of a trust.
trust *res*	article of trust.
tugboat	a strongly built, heavily powered vessel for towing other vessels.
tumul´/tu/ous	disorderly or noisy; disturbed or agitated; full of or marked by tumult or uproar.
tunc	then; at that time.
tur´/bu/lence	irregular motion of the atmosphere, as that indicated by gusts and lulls in the wind.

turnpike	generally, a toll highway.
turnstile	device set up in an entrance to bar passage until a charge is paid, to record the number of persons passing through.
tur'/pi/tude	things done contrary to honesty, justice, or good morals.
tutor (mas.) tutrix (fem.)	one having the guardianship, tutelage, care, and guidance of another.
tutorship	the position, duties, and authority of a tutor or tutrix.
typographical error	the error of a printer in setting type, or of a typist in operating the typewriter.
tyr'/anny	the rule of a despot or tyrant; absolutism.

U

ubiq'/uity	state or capacity of being everywhere at the same time; omnipresent.
ulti/ma'/tum	a final proposition; a final offer; a final statement of terms in diplomatic negotiations for the settlement of a dispute.
ul'tra	beyond; excessive; extreme; going beyond what is usual or ordinary.
ultra virez (ul'tra vī'rēz)	beyond the powers; beyond the scope or in excess of legal power or authority.
um'pire	a person selected to rule on the plays in a game.
unan'i/mous	in complete accord; of one mind; agreed.
unclean hands	not coming into court with a clear conscience.
uncon/di'/tional	without reservation; absolute.
uncon'/scion/able agree'/ment	an agreement, usually made when one of the parties was in a position of disadvantage, which is oppressive, especially one which unreasonably restricts the liberty of a party to exercise his calling or earn his living, or imposes an extortionate rate of interest.
uncon'/scious pla'/gi/a/rism	using the literary work of another in one's own work without realizing that it is actually the work of another, the ideas and concepts used having been implanted in the mind by a previous and forgotten study made of the work of the other person.

uncon/trol'/la/ble	irresistible; not subject to control.
undertaking	an engagement, stipulation, promise, or guaranty.
underwriter	one who underwrites policies of insurance, or carries on insurance as a business; one who underwrites shares or bonds.
undi/vi'/ded	that which may be owned by one of two or more tenants in common, or joint tenants before partition.
unearned income	income from property or an investment, as distinguished from income received from a trade, profession, or employment.
unearned in'cre/ment	value to property due to natural causes making for an increased demand.
une/quiv'/o/cal	clear; plain; not ambiguous.
uni/cam'/eral	consisting of a single chamber, as a legislative assembly.
Uniform Sales Act	a statute prepared by a commission for the purpose of securing uniformity in the rules and principles applicable to sales in the United States, and has been adopted by a majority of the state legislatures.
uni/lat'/eral	one-sided; having relation only to one of two or more persons or things; concerned with only one side of a question.
uni/lat'/eral con'/tract	a contract in which there is a promise on one side only, the consideration therefor being an act or something other than another promise.
uni/lat'/eral leg'/acy	a gift through will of a decedent's entire property.
uni/lat'/eral mis/take	a mistake on the part of only one of the parties to a transaction.
uni/lat'/eral rescis'/sion	a rescission of a contract by one party for cause.
un'ion/iz/ing	inducing the employees of a particular shop or business to join a labor union.
un/is'/sued stock	corporate stock which has been authorized but is not outstanding.
uni/ver'/sal	general; characteristic of all or the whole; relating or applicable to all the members of a class or genus.

unlaw'/ful detain'er	the unlawful withholding or detention of real property after the acquisition of a peaceable and actual, but unlawful, possession.
unliq'/ui/da/ted	remaining unassessed or unsettled; not ascertained in amount.
unnec'/es/sary expo'/sure	the failure to use ordinary care for one's own safety; that is, contributory negligence.
untime'ly	ill-timed or inopportune; not occurring at a suitable time or season.
upset price	lowest price owner is willing to take at an auction sale of his property; minimum price at which courts permit property to be sold at receivership sale following foreclosure.
ur'ban	pertaining to city; situated or dwelling in a city.
urbane'	suave; courteous; polite in a refined or elegant way.
ur'gency	imperativeness; insistence; a special condition calling for immediate action or relief.
us'age	established custom or practice.
us'ance	the time allowed by custom for payment of a bill of exchange in foreign commerce.
usu/a'/rius OR usu'/ri/ous	taking exorbitant interest for the use of money.
u'su/fruct	the right of using and enjoying the fruits or profits of something possessed by another, without impairing the substance.
usur/pa'/tion	unlawful assumption of the use of property belonging to another.
u'sury	a charge for the use of money beyond the rate of interest set by law.
u'ter/ine	born of the same mother, but by a different father.
uti/li/za'/tion facil'/ity	any equipment or device, except an atomic weapon, determined by rule of the Atomic Energy Commission to be capable of making use of special nuclear material in such quantity as to be significant to the common defense and security of the public.
utmost care	the highest degree of care to be exercised in a particular situation, consistent with the nature of the undertaking and the circumstances of the case.

ut'terly	to the full extent; totally.
uxor (ABBR., ux.)	wife.
uxo'/ri/cide	the killing of a woman by her husband.

V

va'cancy	unoccupied state; a gap or opening.
va'cate	to render inoperative; to leave; to quit; to annul.
vaca'/tur	a rule or order by which a proceeding is vacated.
vag'a/bond	an idle person; a wanderer; a nomad.
va'grancy	the wandering or going about from place to place by an idle person without visible means of support, who, though able to work, refuses to do so, and subsists on charity.
vagrant waters	flood waters, sometimes known as enemy waters.
vague'/ness	uncertainty; indefiniteness in statement or meaning.
vali/da'/tion	rendering legal that which was previously illegal.
valid'/ity	legal soundness or force; effectiveness.
val'u/able con/sid/er/a'/tion	a consideration in money or in something having monetary value.
van'/dal/ism	willful or ignorant destruction of artistic or literary treasures.
var'i/ance	divergence or discrepancy; a difference or discrepancy as between two statements or documents in law which should agree.
ve'hi/cle	any receptacle, or means of transport, in which something is carried or conveyed, or travels.
ve'nal	something that is bought; offered for sale; mercenary; corrupt.
vend	to sell; to transfer ownership for a price in money.
ven/dee'	purchaser or buyer.
ven'/der OR ven'/dor	one who sells or negotiates a sale.
ven/det'ta	a state of private war in which a murdered man's relatives execute vengeance on the slayer or his relatives.

| vend'/ing | selling goods; giving expression to one's opinions. |

| ven/due' | a sale; a sale at public auction. |

| ve'nial | forgivable; trivial; excusable; not seriously wrong. |

| veni're
(PRON. vē nī' rē) | panel from which a jury is drawn. |

| veniremen
(PRON.
vē nī' rē men) | persons whose names are drawn from the jury wheel for a venire or special venire and who are summoned by a writ of venire and are thereby upon the jury panel for a term of court, a part of a term, or for choosing jurors for a particular case. |

| ven'ue | the place or county in which a case is to be tried. |

| ver'/bal | of or pertaining to words; consisting of or in the form of words. |

| ver/ba'/tim | word for word, or in exactly the same words. |

| ver/bose' | wordy; characterized by the use of many or too many words. |

| ver'/dict | the answer of a jury given to the court concerning the matters of fact committed to their trial and examination. |

| veri/fi/ca'/tion | formal assertion of the truth of something; a short confirmatory affidavit at the end of a pleading or petition. |

| ver'i/fied
doc'u/ment | paper sworn to upon oath or formally affirmed. |

| ver'/ify | to prove to be true, as by evidence or testimony; to confirm or substantiate. |

| ver/nac'u/lar | native or originating in the place of its occurrence or use, as language or words; the native speech or language of a place. |

| ver'/sus
(ABBR., vs., v.) | against; the name of the plaintiff v. the name of the defendant. |

| ver'/tigo | a disordered condition in which an individual, or whatever is around him, seems to be whirling about; dizziness. |

| vest | to pass to a person, as where the title to property comes to the heir upon the death of the owner intestate; to accrue to; to take effect; to be fixed. |

ves'/ted	fixed in interest; indefeasible; accrued; settled.
vested right	a right that has become completely settled upon a legal person; an unconditional property right or a privilege granted by a government for service, as a franchise.
ves'/ti/bule	a passage, hall, or antechamber between the outer door and the interior parts of a house or building.
vest'/ing order	an order or decree of a court of equity transferring title to land.
ves'/ture	clothing; grass, grain, or other plants which cover the earth.
ve'to (PL., vetoes)	the power or right vested in one branch of a government to negate the determinations of another branch, especially the right of a chief executive to reject bills passed by the legislature.
via	by way of; by a route that passes through.
vi'able	capable of living; able to live and grow; alive.
vicar'i/ous	pertaining to or involving the substitution of one for another; acting or serving as a substitute.
vice	a fault, defect, or imperfection.
vice versa	conversely; the order being changed, from that of a preceding statement.
vicin'/ity	the region near a place; proximity; propinquity.
vi'cious	depraved; given or disposed to evil or bad; spiteful or malignant.
vict'uals (PRON. vit'ls)	articles of food prepared for use.
vidu'/ity	widowhood.
vin/dic'a/tive	exonerating; clearing from a charge, suspicion, or imputation.
vin/dic'/tive	revengeful.
vindictive damages	punitive damages in addition to actual damages.
vi'o/lence	rough force in action; any unjust or unwarranted exertion of force or power, as against rights, laws, etc.

vir´/tual   pos/ses´/sion — a kind of actual possession consisting of an occupancy in fact of a part of a tract claimed in the name of the whole.

visa — an endorsement made upon a passport of one country, testifying that it has been examined and found in order for passage to the country granting the visa.

vis-à-vis (PRON. vē´ze vē) — face to face; one face to face with, or situated opposite to, another.

vis´/count (PRON. vī´kount) — a nobleman next below an earl or count and next above a baron.

vis´i/ble con/tu´/sion — any injury to or morbid change in either the subcutaneous tissue or the skin, whether such results from external violence upon the exterior of the body or from internal injuries resulting from violence.

vi´ti/ate (PRON. vish´i ā t) — to make faulty; to mar; to contaminate; to corrupt; to make legally defective or invalid; to invalidate.

vit´/re/ous — glassy; resembling glass, as in transparency, brittleness, hardness, etc.

viva voce (PRON. vi´va vo´se) — the living voice; by word of mouth; testimony of a witness given in person, rather than by deposition or transcript of testimony given in former trial.

void´/able — capable of being adjudged or made void; not absolutely void, or void in itself.

vol´/un/tary bank´/ruptcy — bankruptcy instituted by an adjudication upon the petition of a debtor seeking such an adjudication.

voting trust — a trust holding corporate stock with authority to vote shares.

vouch´er — a written evidence of payment or a written permission to pay and have receipted.

vul/can/iz/a´/tion — the process by which crude rubber (India rubber) is converted to a form fit for use in the manufacture of tires and other products of industry.

W

wagering contract — an insurance policy not supported by an insurable interest on the part of the insured.

waiv´er	the intentional or voluntary relinquishment of a known right.
waiver of immunity	a means authorized by statute by which a witness, in advance of giving testimony or producing evidence, may renounce the fundamental right and privilege guaranteed to him by the Constitution, that no person shall be compelled in any criminal case to be a witness against himself.
want of issue	having no children.
wan´/ton	done, shown, or used maliciously or unjustifiably; lawless or unbridled with respect to sexual morality; loose; lascivious or lewd.
wanton negligence	an act or omission in complete absence of care for the safety of others, exhibiting indifference to consequences, but not necessarily ill will.
ward	a person under the care of a guardian or of a court.
warehouse	a place mainly used for the reception and storage of goods in bulk or in large quantities; a storage place used in connection with a wholesale business.
war´/rant	a writ from an authority in pursuance of law directing the doing of an act; an order authorizing a payment of money by another person to a third person.
war/ran/tee´ (PL., warrantees)	person to whom a warranty is made.
war´/ran/tor	one who makes a warranty.
war´/ranty (PL., warranties)	a promise that a proposition of fact is true.
wash sales	sham sales made to influence the stock market; a sale which is merely a bet upon the market.
Wasserman test	a test for syphilis which has been known to the medical world since about the year 1906, being a standard and well-recognized test.
wasteland	land permitted to go unused in the midst of a cultivated, settled region.
watercourse OR water course	a natural channel conveying water; a channel or canal made for the conveyance of water.
watered stock	stock issued by a corporation as fully paid up, when in fact the par value has not been fully paid in.

water pol/lu′/tion	the infection and contamination of a public water supply by dirt, bacteria, and coli, or any other infectious and contaminating material which render the water unfit for domestic use and unsafe and dangerous to individuals.
water ski′/ing	a sport in which the participant, being on skiis, is pulled across the water by a motorboat.
waterway	a navigable body of water.
waybill	description of goods sent by common carrier.
weir	an obstruction placed across a stream thereby causing the water to pass through a particular opening or notch, thus measuring the quantity flowing.
welfare	state of faring well; wellbeing; the good of the people; public relief for the poor, as provided under relief or welfare acts.
wetback	an alien who has gained an illegal entry into the United States by wading or swimming a stream on the border.
wharf′/age	money paid for privilege of landing goods at wharf or loading vessel while moored.
wharf′/in/ger	one who keeps a wharf for the purpose of receiving goods thereon for hire; owner or manager of a wharf.
whiplash	the lash of a whip; personal injury involving the neck, common in automobile accidents, the typical case occurring when the car in which the victim is riding is struck in the rear by another car or truck, the impact serving to throw his head back with violence.
wilful and mali′/cious injury (OR willful)	an injury to property inflicted intentionally and in disregard of duty.
wilful (OR willful) neg′/li/gence	an act done or omitted in such reckless disregard of the security and safety of another as to imply bad faith.
will	an instrument directing the disposition of one's property after death.
wiretapping	the illicit tapping of wires to learn the nature of messages passing over them.
with′/drawal of bid	the recalling of a bid made in the course of the letting of a public contract.

with/hold'/ing tax	the withholding of a portion of each salary or wage payment due an employee and turning it over to the government, the employee taking credit for the various amounts withheld in his tax return.
without day	without designation of day, as in an adjournment sine die.
without prej'u/dice	precluding any further assertion of a right of claim.
without recourse	a form of qualified endorsement, exonerating the endorser from liability as such.
wit'/tingly	with full knowledge and by design.
women's suffrage	the right of women to vote.
working capital	the difference between the current assets and the current liabilities.
workmen's compensation laws	the statutes that provide for a quick and definite indemnity to injured employees in the event of accidents.
wor'/sted	a specific kind of wool; cloth made from long-staple wool.
writ	a written command issued by a court of law, requiring the performance of an act, or giving authority and commission to have it done.
writ of certiorari (PRON. sur/shi/e/rar'i)	writ from superior to inferior court directing a certified record of certain proceedings be sent up for reviews.
writ of error	a commission by which the judges of one court are authorized to examine a record on which a judgment was given in another court, and to affirm or reverse that judgment according to law.
writ of habeas corpus	precept commanding one having custody of person to produce him.
writ of prohibition	writ issued by superior court to an inferior court commanding it to desist from proceeding in a matter not within its jurisdiction.
writ of replevin	process issued in an action of replevin authorizing an officer to seize the property involved in the action.
written law	statute law.
wrongdoer	one who commits a wrong against another.

wrongful commitment	commitment of a person to an institution for the insane upon proceedings in contravention of the constitutional rights of the person affected.
wrongfully	unjustly, unlawfully; contrary to sound moral principles.

X

X	symbol expressing the word "by"; symbol used by one who is unable to write his name for signature purposes; a symbol indicating place for a signature.
x-ray (n.)	an electromagnetic ray used in the diagnosis and treatment of certain bodily conditions of disease and injury because of its penetrating character.
(v.)	to examine by means of x-rays; to treat with x-rays.
x-ray technician	a person trained in the use of an x-ray machine, although not a radiologist.

Y

yacht basin	a place for the mooring of yachts and other pleasure craft.
year and a day	period of limitation in which the right to seize and sell land under a judgment must be exercised.
year-end bonus	a bonus paid to employees near the end of the calendar year.
year'/ling	an animal one year old or in the second year of its age.
year-to-year renewal	the option of the maker of a note for indefinite renewal.
yellow-dog contract	a contract between an employer and employee whereby the employee promises not to join a union.
yeo'/man	a petty officer in the navy, having chiefly clerical duties.
Yiddish	a dialect of the German language which includes words from other languages, particularly Hebrew.

yield (n.)	the action of yielding or producing; produce, harvest, fruit.
(v.)	to surrender or submit; to give forth or produce by a natural process or in return for cultivation.
yoke	a measure of land, being the area of land ploughable by an ox-team on one day; a symbol of bondage, deriving from the name of the wooden frame used in harnessing a pair of oxen for work.
youth rally	a meeting of young people called for discussion of a particular subject of interest.

Z

zealot	one who displays an excess of zeal.
zealous witness	a witness eager to be of service to the party calling him.
zig-zagging OR zigzagging	frequent sharp turns from side to side; veering back and forth across a highway.
zoning	dividing into zones, tracts, or areas, according to existing characteristics, or as distinguished for some purpose; dividing a city or town into areas subject to special restrictions as to buildings.
zoning commission	an administrative agency of a municipality to which the administration of zoning laws and regulations is entrusted.
zoo/log'i/cal	relating to or concerned with animals.
zymo'/sis	an infectious or contagious disease.
zymurgy (PRON. $\bar{zi}$'mur ji)	that branch of chemistry which deals with fermentation, distilling, the preparation of yeast, etc., particularly in the making of wine or the brewing of beer.

B.   Foreign Language Expressions and Definitions

A

ab ante (ab an'tē)	in advance; beforehand.
ab effectu	from that effect.
ab externo	from outside.
ab extra	from without; extrinsic; from outside.
ab initio (ab i-nish'i-ō)	from the beginning;

ab intra	from within.
ab invito (ab in-vī'tō)	unwillingly; against one's will.
absente reo (ab-sen'tē rē'ō)	defendant being absent.
absque (abz'kwē)	without.
absurdum	an absurdity.
a contrario	an argument based on contrast.
actio in rem (ak'she-o in rem) OR action in rem	action against the thing; a technical term applied to actions between parties where the object is to reach and dispose of property or interest owned by them.
actus	an act; a thing done.
ad absurdum	to what is absurd.
ad arbitrium	at will; arbitrarily.
addenda (PL.)	an appendix; something added or to be added.
addendum (SING.)	
ad finem (ad fī'nem)	to the end; finally
ad hoc (ad hōk)	for this special purpose; for this case only.
ad hom i-nem (ad hom'i-nem)	appealing to a person's feelings or prejudices rather than to his intellect.
ad idem (ad ī'dem)	same meeting of minds in making contracts.
ad infinitum (ad in-fi-nī'tum)	to infinity; endlessly.
ad inquirendum (ad in-qui-ren'dum)	for inquiry; a common law writ commanding an inquiry or investigation.
ad interim (ad'in'te-rim)	temporary; meanwhile; for the time.
ad judicium (ad jū-di'she-um)	to common sense; to the judgment.
ad libitum (ad lib'i-tum) (ABBR., ad lib.)	at pleasure; at will; to speak offhand, without notes.
ad litem (ad lī'tem)	during the pendency of the proceedings; for the suit or action.
ad nauseam (ad na'sē -am)	to disgust; to a disgusting extent.
ad quod damnum (ad kwod dam'num)	to what damage; used to designate that part of the writ stating the plaintiff's damage.
ad rem	to the thing or matter in hand; to the point.

ad valorem (ad va-lo′rem) (ABBR., ad val. OR a/v)	according to the value; proportional to the value.
adversus	in a hostile sense; aligned against.
a fortiori (a for-shi-o′ri)	with greater force; more conclusively; all the more.
agenda (a -jen′da)	things to be done, matters to be attended to, at a meeting.
aggregatio mentium (ag-re-ga′she-o men′she-um)	meeting of minds.
aide-de-camp (a d de-kamp′) (PL., aides-de-camp)	an officer of the armed forces serving as an assistant to an officer of higher rank.
alias (a′li-as)	another name; otherwise called; also known as; an assumed name.
alibi	in another place; elsewhere; statement by the accused that he was not at the site of the crime at the time of its occurrence.
alimony *pendente lite*	court-ordered allowance to either wife or husband while divorce action is pending.
aliunde (a -li-un′de)	from another source; independent of.
alma mater	fostering mother (a university, college, or other school where a person has been educated).
alter ego (al′ter e ′go)	another self; an exceptionally close friend.
alumna (PL., alumnae)	a female graduate of a school, college, university, or other institution of learning.
alumnus (PL., alumni)	a male graduate of a school, college, university, or other institution of learning.
amicus curiae (a-mi′kus ku′ri-e) (PL., amici curiae)	a friend of the court; one not legally a party to an action but interested in result and so joins action by permission of court.
animo et facto (an′i-mo et fac′to)	in intention and fact; the intent coupled with the fact, as in a change of domicile.
animo et fide	by or with courage and faith.
ante (an′te) (ALSO supra)	before; occurring in preceding matter.
ante litem (an′te li′tem)	before suit.
ante litem motam (an′te li′tem mo′tam)	before suit or controversy is instituted.

a posteriori
(ā pos-tē -ri-ō'rī)

reasoning which derives propositions from ob-servation or experience of facts; from a later or subsequent aspect or point of view.

a priori (ā prī-ō'rī)

reasoning derived from definitions formed or principles assumed; from the past; from what has previously transpired.

apropos (adj.)
(OR a propos)

to the purpose; pertinent to time, place, or occasion; poportune.

(adv.)

incidentally; by the way.

arguendo (ar gu en'dō)

for, in, or by arguing or reasoning; for purposes of argument.

au courant
(ō -koo-rau^n)

up to date; well-informed.

audita querela
(a-dī'ta kwe-rē' la)

a writ constituting initial process in action brought to obtain relief against consequences of judgment.

au fait

well-instructed; expert.

au fond (ō fon)

at the bottom; at the fount; substantially; essentially.

autre droit (ō'tre druä)

another's right.

autre vie (ō'tre vē)

the life of another.

avant-garde
(PRON. av-a^n-gard)

those who create new or experimental ideas, etc.; a group that is extremist; vanguard.

B

banc (bangk)

the full bench; all the judges of the court; a plenary session of a bench of judges.

beneficium
(be-ne-fi'shē-um)

a benefice; an advantage; a profit; a right; a privilege.

bête noire
(bāt-nwar)

a bugaboo; anything that is an object of hate, dread, or special aversion.

bona fide
(bō'na fīde)

in good faith; in reality.

bona fides
(bō'na fī'dēz)

good faith; integrity of dealing

bona vacantia
(bō'na vā-kan'she-a)

vacant, unclaimed, or stray goods; property without an owner; things in which nobody claims property right and which belong to the state by virtue of its prerogative.

C

caeteris (or ceteris) paribus (sē′te-ris pa′ri-bus)	other things being equal.
capias (kā′pi-as)	form of writ directing arrest.
capias ad satisfaciendum (kā′pi-as ad sa-tis-fā-she-en′dum)	you may take to satisfy; writ depriving person of liberty until he satisfies award.
caput (kap′ut)	head; chapter; a principal.
caput lupinum (kap′ut lū′pi-num)	(a wolf's head) a felon may be suspect because of past acts.
carte blanche (kart blonsh)	a signed paper to be filled in as the holder may please; unconditional permission or authority.
casus fortuitus (kā′sus for-tū′i-tus)	a loss happening in spite of all effort and sagacity.
causa causans (ka′za ka′zanz)	cause in action; the efficient cause.
causa proxima (ka′za pro′xi-ma)	the proximate cause; immediate cause.
causa sine qua non (ka′za si′ne quā non)	a condition which is indispensable; a cause without which the thing would not have happened; a cause which if it had not existed, the injury would not have been sustained.
cause célèbre (PL., causes célèbres)	a celebrated case; a legal case that excites widespread interest; a notorious incident.
caveat actor (kā′ve-at ak′tor)	let the doer beware.
caveat emptor (kā′ve-at emp′tor)	let the buyer beware, a maxim of the common law expressing the rule that the buyer purchases at his peril.
censo (sen′sō)	a ground rent; an annuity
cestui (ses′twē) (PL., cestuis)	he; the one; a short form for cestui que trust; the beneficiary of a trust.
cestui que (or qui) trust (ses′twē kē trust) (PL., cestuis que trust)	the beneficiary of a trust; the person for whose benefit property is held in trust by a trustee.
cestui que vie (ses twē kē vē)	he whose life is the measure of the duration of an estate.
ceteris paribus	other things being equal.

chargé d'affaires
(shär-zhā dä-fär)
(PL., chargés d'affaires)

subordinate diplomatic agent; an officer substituted in the place of the ambassador or minister to represent the nation during the latter's absence.

charta (kar'ta)

a charter, as a deed of land.

circa (ser'ka)
(ALSO circiter)
(ABBR., ca.)

about; around; in the neighborhood of; concerning; in respect to.

civiliter mortuuos
(si-vi'li-ter mor'tu-us)

civilly dead.

compos mentis

of a sound mind.

conditio sine qua non
(kon-dish'i-o si'ne kwa non)

a necessary condition; an indispensable condition.

confer
(ABBR., cf.)

compare

consortia
(PL.) (kon-sor'she-a)
consortium (SING.)

partnership

contra

against; opposite or contrary to.

contra bonos mores
(kon-tra bo'nos mo'rez)

against good morals; having pernicious consequences.

contra semble

it would appear to the contrary.

contretemps
(SING. and PL.)
(kan-tre-ta^n;
PL., kan-tre,ta^{n}z)

a mishap; an embarrassing or awkward occurrence.

conveyance *in pais*

transaction taking place on the land to be transferred.

coram nobis (ko'ram no'bis)

in our presence; before us; a writ used to obtain review of a judgment for the purpose of correcting errors of fact in criminal as well as in civil proceedings.

coram non judice
(ko'ram non jo'di-se)

before one who is not the proper judge; that is, before a court which has not jurisdiction of the matter.

coram vobis (ko'ram vo'bis)

a writ of error directed by a court to review to the court which tried cause, to correct an error in fact.

corpus (kor'pus)

the main body or corporeal substance of a thing; the principal of a fund or estate, as opposed to interest, income, dividends, or the like.

corpus delicti (kor′pus dē-lik′ti)	the body of the crime; the substance or foundation of the offense; the fact that a crime has actually been committed, that someone is criminally responsible.
corpus juris (kor′pus jū′ris)	a body of law; a comprehensive collection of the law of a country or jurisdiction.
coup (PL., coups)	sudden maneuver; an overthrowing of government.
coup de grace (kood-e-gras)	merciful blow; a finishing stroke.
coup de main	a sudden enterprise or effort
coup d'état (kood-e-ta)	a stroke of policy.
cui bono (kī bō′nō)	for whose benefit or welfare.
cul-de-sac (kul′de sak′) (PL., culs-de-sac)	a way, a street, or alley open only at one end; blind alley; a course which leads to nothing.
cum bona venia	with kind permission.
cum grano salis (kum grā′nō sā′lis)	with a grain of salt; with some allowance; with reservations.
cum onere (kum ō′ne-re)	with the burden; subject to the encumbrances or disadvantages that may be connected with the enjoyment of the right.
cum testamento annexo (c.t.a.) (kum tes-ta-men′tō an-neks′ō)	with the will annexed; used with reference to a person appointed administrator of a will where the testator appointed no executor.
cy-pres, cy pres, OR cypres (sē pra′)	as nearly as possible in conformity to the intentions of testator; rule for construction of instruments by which intention of party is carried out as near as possible.

D

damnosa haereditas OR damnosa heretas (dam-nō′sa hē-rē′di-tas)	a legacy involving a loss or hardship upon legatee.
damnum (dam′num)	harm, loss, detriment, either to character or property; a species of loss.
damnum absque injuria (dam′num abs′kwē in-jū′ ri-a)	a loss without an injury; damage without wrong, the sense of the expression being that there is no cause of action.
damnum fatale (dam′num fā-tā′le)	loss arising from inevitable accident or act of God.

damnum sine injuria
  (dam'num sī'ne in-jū'ri a)

a loss for which there is no remedy by process of law.

de bene esse
  (dē be'nē es'ē)

conditionally; provisionally; in anticipation of future need; of present, temporary validity; for what it is worth.

debitum (de'bi-tum)

a debt.

de bonis non (d.b.n.
  OR d/b/n)
  (dē bō'nis non)

of goods not yet administered.

de bonne grace

willingly; with good grace.

de bono et malo
  (dē bō'nō et ma'lō)

for good and evil.

decessit sine prole
  (d.s.p.)

died without issue.

de die in diem
  (dē dī'e in dī'em)

from day to day.

de facto (dē fak'tō)

from the fact; really; in fact, but without lawful title; without legal status.

de fide (dē fī'dē)

a matter of faith.

de gratia (dē gra'she-a)

by favor; by grace.

dehors (dē-horz')

without; out of; foreign; irrelevant; disconnected with; unrelated to.

de jure (dē jo'rē)

by lawful title; rightfully.

del credere
  (del kre'de-re)

a term of Italian origin signifying guaranty or warranty.

delictum (dē-lik'tum)

a delict, tort, wrong, or injury; a misdemeanor.

de minimis (dē mi'ni-mis)

trifles; concerning trifles.

de minimis non curat lex
  (dē mi'ni-mis non kū'rat leks)

the law does not concern itself with trifles.

de minis (de mi'nis)

a writ against threats; a writ to keep the peace.

de nouveau (dē nō'vō)
  OR de novo

afresh; anew; again; a second time.

de profundis

out of the depths.

descriptio personae
  (de-skrip'she-ō per-sō'nē)

description of the person; a word or phrase used for the purpose of identifying or pointing out a person.

desideratum
  (dē-sid-e-ra'tum)

that which is desired or called for.

de son tort (dē sōn tor)

by his own tort or wrong.

detente (dā-ta^{n}t)	a relaxation of strained relations or tensions, as between nations.
detinet (det-i′net)	action of debt, for the specific recovery of goods under a contract to deliver them.
de trop (de trō)	too many; superfluous; in the way; not wanted.
devastavit (dev-as-tā′vit)	misapplication or waste of deceased person's property.
dictum (dik′tum) (PL., dicta OR dictums)	a decision; a saying; an authoritative pronouncement; an expression of opinion contained in a court's decision upon a matter related to the subject of the decision, but not having the force of a decision.
dies non (dī′ēz non)	not a day for judicial business; a day on which judges do not sit.
dies non juridicus (dī′ēz non jū-ri′di-kus)	a day not for litigation. (see dies non.)
donatio (dō-nā′she-ō)	a donation; a gift; that which is given.
donatio mortis causa (dō-nā′she-ō ka′za mor′tis)	a gift in prospect of death (same as gift mortis causa).
duces tecum (dū′sēz tē′kum)	bring with you; a subpena.

E

ejusdem generis (ē-jus′dem je′ne-ris)	of the same kind.
elapso tempore	the time having elapsed.
emeritus (ē-mer′i-tus)	one retired from active official duties.
en banc (on bangk) (ALSO in banc)	in full court, or with full judicial authority; plenary session of a bench of judges.
en haut	on high; above.
en masse (on mas)	in a body; in one piece.
en passant (on pas-son′)	in passing; by the way; incidentally.
en rapport (ah^n-ra-por)	in a connection of mutual understanding or sympathy; in accord.
ensemble (on-som′bl)	all the parts taken together; all together.
eo nomine (e′ō no′mi-ne)	under that name; by that name or designation.
e pluribus unum (ē plo′ri-bus ū′num)	one composed of many; the motto of the United States government.

errare humanum est	to err is human.
esprit de corps	the animating spirit of a collective body.
esse (es'se)	to be; existence; being; to appear.
et al.	
et alia	and other things.
et aliae (FEM.)	and others.
et alii (MASC.)	and others.
et alibi	and elsewhere.
et alius	and another.
et ano.	abbreviation for "and another" in the listing of parties to an action in the action's title.
et cetera (etc., &c.)	and so forth; other things of a like kind.
et citatio (et cit.)	and citation.
et sequentes) (et seq.) et sequentia)	and what follows.
et sequitur (et seq.) et se'qui-ter)	and as follows.
et uxor (et ux.) (et u'xor)	and wife.
et vir	and husband.
ex cathedra (eks kath'e̅-dra OR eks ka-the̅'dra)	with high authority; from the chair.
ex contractu (eks kon-trak'tu)	upon or from a contract; arising out of a contract.
ex curia (eks ku̅'ri-a)	out of court; elsewhere than in court.
ex delicto (ex de-lik'to̅)	from or out of a wrongful act; from the crime.
ex demissione (ex dem.) (ex de-mi-she o̅'ne)	from or on the demise of.
ex dolo malo (ex do̅'lo̅ ma'lo̅)	from or out of fraud.
exempli gratia (e.g.) (eg-zem'pli̅ gra̅'she-a)	by way of example; for example.
ex facie (eks fa̅'shi-e̅)	on the face; on the face of an instrument.
ex gratia (ex gra̅'she-a)	of or by favor; not a matter of right, but resting in the exercise of a sound discretion to determine the demands of justice.

ex maleficio (ex ma-le-fi′she-o̅)	from an evil deed; out of illegal act; out of wrongdoing.
ex mero moto (ex me′ro mo̅′tu)	of his own accord; from mere impulse; a phrase occurring in grants, charters, etc.
ex necessitate legis (ex ne-ses-si-ta̅′te le̅′jis)	from legal necessity; by necessity of law.
ex officio (ex of-fi′she-o̅)	by virtue of his office; a right of privilege in an office arising from one's status as the holder of another office.
ex parte (ex par′te)	one side only; in the interest of one party only.
expediente (ex-pay-de-en′tay)	a file of documents pertinent to or necessary to a judicial proceeding.
explicatio (ex-pli-ka̅′she-o̅)	a pleading under the civil law which corresponded to the surrejoinder of the common law.
explicit (contraction for explicitus est) (ex′pli-sit)	end here; finished.
ex post facto (eks po̅st fak′to)	acting backward; an *ex post facto* law is one that can be applied to offenses charged as occurring before the law's enactment.
expressio unius (ex-pre′she-o̅ u̅′ni-us)	expression of one thing.
expressio unius est exclusio alterius (ex-pre′she-o̅ u̅′ni-us est ex-klu̅′she-o̅ al-te′ri-us)	the expression of one thing is the exclusion of the other.
ex relatione (ex rel.) (ex re̅-la̅-she-o̅′ne)	by or on the relation or information of; at the instance of.
ex tempore (ex tem′po-re)	without premeditation; for the time being; for the occasion; temporarily.

F

facsimile (fak-sim′i-le̅)	an exact reproduction or duplicate; make it like.
facta, non verba	deeds, not words.
facto (fak′to̅)	in or by the law; in fact; in deed.
fait accompli (fa-ta-ko^n-ple̅) (PL., faits accomplis) (fa̅-ta-ko̅^{n}-ple̅z)	accomplished fact; a thing done and not easily reversed.

falsus in uno, falsus in omnibus	false in one thing, false in all.
faux pas	blunder.
femme sole (fem sōl)	a woman unmarried.
fiat lux	let there be light.
fide et amore	by faith and love.
fide et fortitudine	with faith and fortitude.
fieri (fī´e-rī)	to be made up; to be done.
fieri facias	directing an execution to be levied on the goods of a debtor.
finis (fī´nis)	the end.
flagrante delicto (flā-gran´tē dē-lik´tō)	in the commission of the crime; (caught "red-handed").
folgende seiten (ff.)	following pages; and the following.
force majeure OR force majesture (fors ma-zur´)	an event or effect that cannot reasonably be anticipated or controlled, such as earthquake, storm, freezing, lightning, sunstroke, etc.
formaliter	formally; in form; to the formal cause.
forma pauperis (for´ma pa´pe-ris)	in the character or manner of a pauper; permission given a poor person to sue without liability for costs.
fortiter in re	with firmness in acting.
fugit hora	the hour flies.
functus officio (fungk´tus o-fish´i-ō)	having performed his office; legally defunct.

G

genius loci	the guardian of the place.
gradatim (grā-dā´tim)	gradually; step by step.
gratia placendi	the delight of pleasing.
guardian *ad litem*	guardian appointed by the court to represent a minor and protect his interests in a particular legal proceeding.

H

habeas corpus ad prosequendum (hā´be-as kor´pus ad prō-se-quen´dum)	writ which issues when necessary to remove prisoner in order to prosecute in proper jurisdiction.

habitatio (ha-bi-tā′she-ō)	a right in respect of an object, usually land owned by one person subject to use by another person.
hac lege	with this law or condition.
haec verba (PL.) haec verbum (SING.) (hēk ver′ba)	the same word; this word.
haeredes proximi (PL.) haeres proximus (SING.) (hē-rē′dēz prok′si-mī)	nearest or next heir; children or descendants of the decedent.
haeredes remotior (SING.) (hē-rē′dēz re-mō-she-ōr) haeredes remotiores (PL.) (hē-rē′dēz re-mō-she-ō′rēz)	a more remote heir; kinsman other than child or descendant.
hic et ubique	here and everywhere.
hoc anno	in this year.
hoc loco	in this place.
hoc tempore	at this time.
homo alieni	a man under the control of another.
homo sui juris (hō′mo su′ī ju′ris)	a man who is his own master.
hors de combat (or de kon-ba′)	out of the combat or struggle.
humanum est errare	to err is human.

I

ibidem (ib. or ibid.) (i-bī′dem)	in the same place; in the same book.
idem quod (i.q.) (ī′dem quod)	the same as.
id est (i.e.)	that is.
ignorantia facti excusat, ignorantia juris neminem excusat (ig-nō-ran′she-a fak′ti ex-kū′zat, ig-nō-ran′she-a ju′ris nem′ i/nem ex-kū′zat)	ignorance of fact excuses, ignorance of the law (which everyone is presumed to know) excuses no one.
implicite	by implication.
impos animi	of weak mind; imbecile.
imprimis (im-prī′mis)	in the first place; first in order.
in absentia (in ab-sen′she-a)	in absence.

in actu	in act or reality.
in aeternum	forever.
in alio loco (in a'li-ō lō'kō)	in another place.
in ambiguo (in am-bi'gu-ō)	in doubt.
in banc OR in banco (in bang) (in bang'kō)	on the bench; in bank—that is, when all of the judges of the court are sitting.
in camera (in kam'e-ra)	in chambers; in private; a trial in which the court excludes the public from the courtroom.
in contumaciam	in contempt of, or disobedience to, an order or summons of court.
in curia (in kū'ri-a)	in the court.
in custodia legis (in kus-tō'di-a lē'jis)	in custody or keeping of the law.
in dubiis (in du'bi-is)	in doubt.
in equilibrio	in equilibrium; equally balanced.
in esse (in es'ē)	in being.
in extenso (in eks-ten'sō)	at full length.
in extremis	in a terminal condition; in extremity.
in fieri (in fī'e-rī)	in course of completion.
infinito (in-fī-nī'to)	perpetually.
in flagrante delicto (in flā-gran'te dē-lik'tō)	in the act of committing the offense; ("red-handed").
in forma pauperis (in for'ma pa'pe-ris)	as a poor man; to sue *in forma pauperis* is to sue as a poor man, which relieves from cost.
infra (ALSO post)	below; beneath; after; occurring in subsequent matter.
infra dignitatem (in'fra dig-ni-tā'tem)	below one's dignity.
in futuro (in fū-tū'ro)	in the future; henceforth; for the future.
in hac parte (in hak par'tē)	on this side; in this behalf.
in haec verba (PL.) in haec verbum (SING.) (in hēc ver'bum)	in these words; in the same words.
in hoc (in hok)	in this respect.
in invitum (in in-vī'tum)	against the will; without consent.

in loco (in lō′kō)	in the place; in the proper or natural place.
in loco parentis (in lō′kō pa-ren′tis)	in the place of a parent.
in medias res (in mē′di-as rēz)	into the midst of things or affairs; into the meat of the matter.
in nomine (in nō′mi-ne)	in the name of.
in pace (in pa′se)	in peace.
in pais (in pā)	having taken place without legal proceedings.
in pari delicto (in pa′rī de-lik′tō)	equally at fault.
in pari materia (in pa′rī ma-te′ri-a)	in equal matters—things being equal.
in perpetuum (in per-pe′tu-am)	forever.
in persona (in per-sō′na)	in person.
in personam (in per-sō′nam)	remedy where the proceedings are against the person.
in pleno (in plē′nō)	in full.
in posse (in pos′e)	in possible existence.
in praesenti (in prē-zen′tī)	at the present time.
in propria persona (in prō′pri-a per-sō′na)	in one's own person or character.
in re (in rē)	in the matter of; concerning.
in rem (in rem)	against the thing or property.
in sano sensu	in a proper sense.
in se (in sē)	in itself.
in situ (in sī′tū)	in its original situation.
in solido (in sol′i-dō)	as or for the whole.
in statu quo (in sta′tū quō)	in the same state or condition in which it was formerly.
inter alia (in′ter ā′li-a)	among other things.
inter alios (in′ter ā′li-ōs)	among other persons.
interesse (in-ter-es′e)	a legal interest in property.
inter nos	between ourselves.

inter se (in'ter se̅) (ALSO inter sese)	among ourselves.
inter vivos (in'ter vi̅'vos)	between the living.
inter vivos trust (in'ter vi'vos trust)	trust between the living; from one living person to another.
in toto (in to̅'to̅)	completely; in entirety; as a body.
in transitu (in tran'si-tu̅)	during the passage; in transit; while passing from one person to another.
intra parietes (in'tra pa-ri-e̅'te̅z)	within walls, or in private.
intra vires (in'tra vi̅'re̅z)	within legal power or authority.
in vacuo (in vak'u̅-o̅)	without object; without concomitants or co-herence; in empty space or in a vacuum.
inverso ordine	in an inverse order.
ipse (ip'se̅)	he; himself.
ipse dixit (ip'se̅ dik'sit)	assertion made but not proved; he himself said it; that is, it was his own statement not made on the authority of any precedent.
ipso facto (ip'so̅ fak'to̅)	by the fact itself; by the act itself; in itself.
ipso jure (ip'so̅ ju're)	by the law itself.
ita est	it is so; it is thus.
iterum	again; once more; anew.
ius	right; law; (variation of "jus")

J

jacta est alea	the die is cast.
joie de vivre (zhwah-de-ve̅vr)	buoyant enjoyment of living.
judgment *non obstante* *veredicto* (n.o.v.) (juj'ment non ob-stan'te ve̅-re-dik'to̅)	judgment notwithstanding the verdict; a judg-ment entered for the plaintiff notwithstanding the verdict.
judicium	judgment.
jura (PL.) (ju̅'ra) jus (SING.)	rights.

jura in re (jū′ra in rē)	rights in a thing.
jure divino (jū′re di-vī′nō)	by divine law.
jure humano	by human law.
jus ad rem (jūs ad rem)	a right to a thing.
jus civile (jūs si′vi-le)	civil law.
jus commune (jūs kom-mū′ne)	common law.
jus disponendi (jūs dis-pō-nen′dī)	right of disposal.
jus gentium (jūs jen′she-um)	law of nations.

L

labore et honore	by labor and honor.
labor omnia vincit	labor conquers everything.
laisser-faire (ALSO laissez-faire)	let people do as they wish without governmental interference.
lapsus linguae (lap′sus ling′gwē)	a slip of the tongue; language differing from that which the speaker intended to say.
lapsus memoriae	a slip of memory.
latine dictum	spoken in Latin.
legem habere (lē′jem hā-bē′re)	to have the right to give testimony under oath; to have one's law.
lese-majeste (lēs lese-majesty maj′es-ti) leze-majesty	an offense against sovereign power; high treason.
lex (leks)	the law.
lex fori (leks fō′rī)	the law of the jurisdiction in which the litigation occurs, controlling all of that part of the litigation which is concerned merely with remedy.
lex generalis	a law of general application.
lex loci (leks lō′sī)	the law or custom of the place.
lex loci contractus (leks lō′sī kon-trak′tus)	the law of the place where the contract is made.

lex loci delictus (leks lō'sī de-lik'tis)	the law of the place of the crime, the wrong, the tort.
lex mercatoria lex mercatorum (leks mer-ka-tō'ri-a)	the law merchant.
lex non scripta (leks non skrip'ta)	the common law.
lex scripta (leks skrip'ta)	statute law.
lex terrae (leks ter're)	the law of the land.
liber (lī'ber)	a book of records; a book of deeds; a volume; one of the units of a published work.
liberum arbitrium	free will.
licet (lī'set)	that which is lawful.
lis pendens (lis pen'denz)	a pending suit; a notice filed in the County Clerk's office giving public notice that certain property is the subject of litigation and within the control of the court.
lis sub judice	a case not yet decided.
loco citatus (loc. cit. OR l.c.) (lō'kō si-ta'tō)	in the place cited.
loco parentis (lō'kō pā-ren'tis) in loco parentis locus parentis	in place of a parent.
locum tenens (lo'kum te'nenz)	holding the place; a person whose term of office has expired is locum tenens until he shall be superseded by some person authorized by law to be inducted into the office.
locus (lō'kus)	a place; a location; a piece of ground; a neighborhood; the place where a thing is done.
locus contractus (lō'kus kon-trak'tus)	the place of the contract; the place where the contract is entered into.
locus criminis (lō'kus kri'mi-nis)	the place of the crime; the place where the crime or tort was committed.
locus in quo (lō'kus in quō)	the place in which; the premises described in the writ.

locus sigilli (L.S.) (lō'kus si-jil'lĭ)	the place of the seal.
locus standi (lō'kus stan'dĭ)	a place to stand; a standing.
lucidus ordo	a clear arrangement.
lucri causa (lū'krĭ ka'za)	for the sake of gain or advantage

M

magister ceremoniarum	master of ceremonies.
magnum bonum	a great good.
magnum opus	a great work.
mala fide (mā'la fī'de)	with bad faith; treacherously; with intent to deceive.
mala fides (mā'la fī dēz)	bad faith.
mala in se (PL.) (má'la in sē)	act wrongful in itself; offense against conscience; act that is morally wrong; bad in itself.
malum in se (SING.) (ma'lum in sē)	
mala prohibita (PL.)	prohibited evil; acts wrongful because prohibited by law; evil because prohibited.
malum prohibitum (SING.) (ma'lum prō-hi'bi-tum)	
mal à propos	inappropriate.
mali exempli	of a bad example.
malo animo (má'lō ā'ni-mō)	with bad intent; with a wicked or evil heart.
malo modo	in a bad manner.
malus animus (ma'lus a'ni-mus)	evil or bad intent.
mandamus	writ issued by a superior court directing an inferior court or person in authority to perform a specific duty.
manu forti (ma'nū for'tĭ)	with a strong hand; an expression used to characterize an entry upon real estate as partaking of criminality due to its forcible or violent nature.
mea culpa	through or by my fault.

medium tenuere beati	happy are they who have kept the middle course.
me judice	I being judge; in my opinion.
memorabilia	things to be remembered.
mens (mēnz)	mind; meaning; intention; understanding; will.
mens legis (mēnz le'jis)	the purpose, spirit, or intention of a law or the law generally.
mens legislatoris (mēnz le-jis-la-tō'ris)	the intention of the lawmaker; the legislative intent.
mens rea (mēnz re'a)	an evil intent; a guilty mind.
mens sana in corpore sano	a sound mind in a sound body.
meo voto	by my desire, or according to my wish.
mesne (mēn)	intermediate; proceedings in suit intervening between primary and final process.
milieu (mē-lyer, mē'lē-er OR mē-lyoo)	state of life; social surroundings; environment.
minimus (min'i-mus)	the very least or smallest part.
mirabile dictu	wonderful to relate.
mirum in modum	in a wonderful manner.
mittimus (mit'i-mus)	we send; a writ to commit an offender to prison.
mobile perpetuum	perpetual motion; something in constant motion.
modo et forma (mō'dō et for'ma)	in the manner and form.
modus operandi (mō'dus o-pe-ran'dī)	the method of operation.
modus vivendi (mō'dus vī-ven'dī)	the mode of living.
more suo	in his own way.
motu proprio	of his own accord.
multum in parvo	much in little.
mutatis mutandis (mū-ta'tis mū-tan'dis)	with the appropriate changes in points of detail; changed according to circumstances; with the necessary changes.

mutato nomine (mū-tā'tō nō'mi-ne)	the name being changed.
mutuus consensus	mutual consent.

N

naïve (na-ēv)	marked by unaffected simplicity; showing lack of informed judgment.
naïvete'	the quality or state of being naive; a naive remark or action.
necessitas non habet legem (ne-ses'si-tās non hā'bet lē'jem)	necessity has no law.
nee (nē)	used in introducing the maiden name of a married woman.
ne exeat (nē ek'sē-at)	let him not go; a writ issued by a court of equity to restrain a person from going beyond the limits of the jurisdiction of the court, until he has satisfied the plaintiff's claim or has given bond for the satisfaction of the decree of the court.
nemine contradicente (nem'i-nē kon-tra-di-sen'tē)	without opposition; no one speaking in opposition.
nemine dissentiente	no one dissenting; without a dissenting voice.
nemo est heres viventis (nē'mō est hē'rez vī-ven'tis)	no one is the heir of a person who is alive.
nemo mortalium omnibus horis sapit	no one is wise at all times.
nemo plus juris in alium transferre potest quam ipse habet (nē'mō plus jū'ris in a'li-um trans-fer're po'test, quam ip'se hā'bet)	no one can confer a better right to another than he has himself.
nemo praesumitur malus (nē'mō prē-zu'mi-ter ma'lus)	no one is presumed to be bad or wicked.
nemo tenetur seipsum accusare (nē'mō te-nē'ter se-ip'sum a-ku-zā're)	no one is bound to accuse himself; i.e., cannot be compelled to incriminate himself.
ne plus ultra (nē plus ul'tra)	nothing further; the uttermost point.

ne varietur
(nē va-ri-ē´ter)

lest it be changed; a mark or annotation placed on an instrument by a notary public by way of identification of the instrument.

nihil (contraction=nil)
(nī´hil)

nothing; a thing of no account.

nil desperandum

never despair.

nil dicit
(nil di´sit)

he makes no answer; meaning that he has not pleaded; that he has failed to interpose a plea or answer to the plaintiff's declaration or complaint.

nisi prius
(nī´sī prī´us)

unless before; a trial before a single judge; the trial, as distinguished from the appellate court, where both have exercised jurisdiction in a cause.

noblesse oblige
(nō-bles´ō-blēzh)

noble rank imposes obligations; literally, those of the higher rank or better class will be compelled.

nolle prosequi
(nol. pros.)
(nol´e pros´e-kwī)

an agreement to proceed no further with the prosecution.

nolo contendere
(nō´lō kon-ten´de-rē)

will not contest; a plea of guilty; an implied confession; literally, "I do not wish to contend."

nom de plume

an assumed or literary title.

nominatim
(no-mi-nā´tim)

by name; expressly; each in turn; particularly; one by one.

non

by no means; not; no.

non assumpsit
(non a-sump´sit)

a plea of the general issue in an action of assumpsit, that "he did not undertake and promise," etc.

non compos mentis
(non kom´pos men´tis)

not in sound mind; destitute of memory and understanding.

non constat
(non kon´stat)

it is not certain; it does not appear.

non ens

nonentity.

non est

it is wanting; it is not.

non est inventus
(non est in-ven´tus)

he has not been found—words used in an officer's formal return upon his unsuccessful attempt to arrest a defendant under a capias.

non libet

it is not pleasing.

non licet (non lī´set)	it is not permitted or lawful.
non nobis solum	not merely for ourselves.
non obstante (non ob-stan´te)	notwithstanding.
non obstante veredicto (non ob-stan´te ve-re-dik´tō)	notwithstanding the verdict.
non sequitur (non sek´wi-ter)	it does not follow; an unwarranted conclusion.
non sui juris (non su´ī ju´ris)	legally incompetent to act for himself in making a contract or in appearing in a cause by himself or through an attorney; not his own master.
nota	note; take notice; observe.
nota bene (N.B.)	observe; note well.
notatu dignum	worthy of note.
novus homo (nō´vus hō´mo)	a new man; one who has raised himself from obscurity.
nudis verbis	in plain words.
nudum pactum (nū´dum pak´tum)	a mere agreement; a contract made without any consideration, and therefore void, unless under seal.
nugae	trifles.
nulli secundus	second to none.
nullius filius (nul´li-us fi´li-us)	the son of nobody; a bastard; the status of an illegitimate child.
nun aut nunquam	now or never.
nunc pro tunc (nunk prō tunk)	now for then; acts permitted after the time they should have been done, with retroactive effect—i.e., with the same effect as if regularly done.

O

obiit sine prole (o.s.p.) (ob´it si´ne prō´le)	died without issue.
obiter (ob´i-ter)	incidentally; in passing; by the way.
obiter dicta (PL.) (ob´i-ter dik´ta) obiter dictum (SING.)	an opinion expressed by the judge in his decision, but not necessary to the determination of the case.

observanda	things to be observed.
omen faustum	a favorable omen.
omnem movere lapidem	to turn every stone; to leave no stone unturned.
onus probandi (o'nus prō-ban'dī)	the burden of proving.
ope ete consilio (o'pe et kon-si'li-o)	by or with aid and counsel.
operae pretium est	it is worthwhile.
opere citato (op. cit.)	in the work quoted or cited.
opus novum (o'pus no'vum)	new work.
ora e sempre	now and always.
ore tenus (ō're̅ te̅'nus)	by word of mouth.
O tempora! O mores!	O times! O manners!
otia dant vitia	idleness tends to vice.
otium cum dignitate	ease with dignity; dignified leisure.
otium sine dignitate	ease without dignity.
oyer (ō'yr)	a hearing or inspection in open court; to hear; the right to hear an instrument read; a hearing at common law on a bail bond.
oyez (ō'yez)	hear ye.

P

pace tua	without your consent.
pacta conventa (pak'ta kon-ven'ta)	the conditions agreed upon.
par accord	by agreement; in harmony with.
parens patriae (pa'renz pa'tri-e̅)	denoting the legal position of the monarchs in England, or the state in the United States, as legal guardian of persons under disability; the parent of the country.
par example	for instance.
pari causa (pa'rī ka'za)	with equal right; on the same basis.
pari delicto (pa'rī de̅-lik'to̅)	in equal fault.
pari materia (pa'ri ma-te'ri-a)	on the same subject; of the same matter.

pari passu (pa´ri pas´u)	together; with equal pace; in equal degree; of the same grade.
par oneri (par o´ne-ri)	equal to the burden.
par pari refero	I return like for like.
pars adversa	the adverse party.
pars pro toto (parz pro to´to)	part for the whole.
particeps criminis (par´ti-seps crim´i-nis)	an accomplice in a crime.
passim (pas´im)	here and there; everywhere; indiscriminately.
pendente lite (pen-den´te li´te)	during the litigation; while the suit, action, or litigation is pending.
per ambages (per am-ba´jez)	indirectly or figuratively; by circuitous ways; by evasions.
per autre vie OR pur autre vie (per o´ter ve)	during another's life; estate enduring only for the duration of the life of a third party.
per capita (per ka´pi-ta)	for each individual; share and share alike; by the head or individual.
per contra (per kon´tra)	contrariwise; on the other hand.
per curiam (per ku´ri-am)	by the court; by the court as a whole.
per diem (per di´em)	by the day; the compensation of a public officer in the form of an allowance for days actually spent in the performance of official duty.
per gradus	step by step.
periculum (pe-rik´u-lum)	peril; danger; risk.
per interim	in the meantime.
per se ALSO per sese	of or by itself; inherently; for its own sake.
persona grata (SING.) personae gratae (PL.)	an acceptable person.
persona non grata (SING.) personae non gratae (PL.)	an unacceptable person.

per stirpes
(per ster'pēz)
method of dividing an estate whereby a group takes that which a deceased ancestor would have taken, the group's right being by representation and not as individuals; according to root or stock; per class, particularly distribution by class.

per viam
by the way of.

pessimi exempli
(pes'si-mī eg-zem'plī)
of the worst example.

petitio justitiae
(pe-ti'she-ō)
petition of right.

pièce de résistance
(PL., pièces)
(pē-es-de-re-zē-stants)
the main or outstanding item.

pleno jure
(plē'nō ju're)
with full right; with full authority.

post (ALSO infra)
occurring in subsequent matter.

postea (pōs'tē-a)
an endorsement on the record, made in the trial court, reciting all the proceedings had in the trial court after the cause was ready for trial.

post facto
(pōst fak'tō)
after the fact; after the commission of the crime; after the event.

post-factum
(post-fak'tum)
an after act; an act which is done afterward.

post hoc
(pōst hōk)
after this; in regard to an accident or other event, that which happened after the event.

post obitum
after death.

praecipe (prē-si-pe)
an original writ commanding to do the thing required; an order.

prima facie
(prī'ma fā'shi-e)
at first sight; on the face of it; in regard to evidence, adequate as it appears, without more.

prima facie evidence
(prī'ma fā'shi-e)
evidence which suffices for proof of a particular fact until contradicted or overcome by other evidence.

primo (prī'mō)
in the first place.

probatum est
it is proved.

pro bono publico
(prō bo'nō pub'li-kō)
for the public good or welfare.

procedendo
(prō-sē-den'dō)
a writ issuing out of a superior court to an inferior court authorizing or directing the inferior court to act upon certain matters, as in remitting a cause for trial.

pro confesso (prō kon-fes'ō)	as if conceded.
pro et con	for and against.
pro forma (prō for'ma)	for the sake of form; as a matter of form.
pro hac vice (prō hak vī'se)	for this turn or occasion.
pro nunc	for now.
pro se (prō sē)	for one's self; appearing for one's self in an action or criminal prosecution.
pro tanto (prō tan'tō)	for so much; to that extent.
pro tempore	temporarily; for the time being.
pur autre vie (por ō'tre vē) (ALSO per autre vie)	during another's life; an estate enduring only for the duration of the life of a third person.

Q

qua (kwa)	in the character of; in the capacity of.
quaere (ABBR., q.) (kwē'rē)	a query; inquiry; it is a question.
quanta (PL.) (adv.) (kwon'ta)	as much as.
quantum (SING.) (n.)	concrete quantity; a specified amount.
quantum meruit (kwon'tum me'ru-it)	as much as is deserved; as much as it is worth; a common count of general assumpsit.
quantum sufficit (kwon'tum su-fis'it)	a sufficient quantity.
quantum vis	as much as you will.
quare impedit (kwā're im'pe-dit)	the action itself; because he has hindered; a writ by which a common-law action for deciding a disputed right of presentation to a benefice was begun.
quasi (kwā'sī)	as if; in a manner; as it were; relating to or having the character of.
quasi ex contractu (quā'sī ex kon-trak'tu)	as if from or by contract.
quasi in rem (quā'sī in rem)	term applied to proceedings not being strictly in rem, being against defendant personally, the real object being to deal with particular property or subject property to the discharge of claims asserted.
quid faciendum	what is to be done?

quid pro quo (kwid prō kwō)	one thing for another; an equivalent; something in return.
qui non proficit, deficit	he who does not advance goes backward.
qui tacet consentit (quī ta′set kon-sen-tit)	he who is silent gives consent.
qui tam (quī tam)	who also share.
quoad (kwō′ad)	as far as; as long as; as to; until.
quoad hoc (kwō′ad hok)	as to this matter; up to this time.
quo animo (kuō an′i-mō)	with what mind or intention? with what intent?
quocunque nomine (quo-kun′kwe)	under whatever name.
quod erat demonstrandum (Q.E.D.)	which was to be proven or demonstrated.
quod erat faciendum	which was to be done.
quod lex non vetat permittit	what the law does not forbid, it permits.
quod vide (SING.) quae vide (PL.) (q.v.) (quod vī′dē)	which see.
quo jure (kwō jo′rē)	by what right; by which right.
quo warranto (kwō wo-ran′tō)	by what authority; a writ against one who claims or usurps an office, franchise, or liberty, to inquire by what authority claim is supported in order to determine the right.

R

raison d'etre (rā-zon′dā-tr)	reason for being; an excuse for existing.
rapprochement (rap-rōsh-maⁿ)	a state of harmony or reconciliation; a restoration of cordial relations.
ratio decidendi (rā′she-ō de-si-den′dī)	the point in a case which determines the judgment; the reason for deciding.
ratione contractus (rā-she-ō′ne kon-trak′tus)	by reason of the contract.
ratione loci (ra-she-ō′ne lō′sī)	by reason of the place.
ratione reisitae	by reason of the situation of the thing.
re (rē)	with regard to; in the matter of.
rebus (rē′bus) (PL. of res)	by things.

rectus in curia (rek'tus in kū'ri-a)	upright in the court; with clean hands; in good standing in the eyes of the court.
reductio ad absurdum (rē-duk'shi-ō ad ab-ser'dum)	an absurd conclusion; reducing a position to an absurdity.
remittitur (rē-mit'i-ter)	a remission or surrender; a sending back, as of a record, from a superior to an inferior court.
reo absente (re'ō ab-sen'te)	defendant absent.
res (rās OR rēz)	a particular thing; any species of property.
res adjudicata OR res judicata	which see; the thing has been decided, been adjudicated.
res alienae	things belonging to others.
res communes (rēz kom'mu-nēz)	things owned by no one and subject to use by all.
res completa	a complete thing.
res gestae (rās jes'tē)	exploits; things done; all the essential circumstances attending a given transaction.
res ingusta domi	narrow circumstances at home; poverty.
res ipsa loquitur (rēz ip'sa lo'qui-ter)	the thing speaks for itself.
res mobiles (rēz mō'bi-lēz)	movable things.
res nihili OR res nullius	a thing of naught; a nonentity.
res nova (rēz nō'va)	new matter; a point that has not been decided; a new case.
respice finem	look to the end.
respondeat superior (re-spon'de-at su-pe'ri or)	let the principal answer; the doctrine under which liability is imposed upon an employer for the acts of his employees committed in the course and scope of their employment.
respublica	the state; the government; the republic; the commonwealth.
reus (rē'us)	a defendant; a person who is guilty of a criminal offense; a party to an action.
re vera	in truth.

S

salvo jure (sal'vo jū're)	the right being safe.

sans (sanz)   without.

sauf erreur ou omission   errors or omissions excepted.
 (ABBR., s.e.o.o.)

savoir faire   social adroitness; tact.
 (sav-war-far)

savoir vivre   good breeding and manners.
 (sav-war-vē-vr)

scienter   knowingly; willfully; knowledge which charges
 (sī-en'ter)   with guilt or liability.

scilicet   permitted to know; to wit, namely.
 (sil'i-set)

scire facias   cause it to be known; a judicial writ founded
 (sī're fā'shi-as)   upon some matter of record and requiring the
                                     party proceeded against to show cause why the
                                     record should not be enforced, annulled, or
                                     vacated; also, the proceeding so instituted.

secundum   according to; in accordance with; in favor of;
 (sē-kun'dum)   following; coming close behind.

secundum allegata et   according to the pleadings and the proof;
 probata   according to what is alleged and proved.
 (se-kun'dum al-le-gā'ta
 et prō-bā'ta)

secundum legem   according to law.
 (se-kun'dum lē'jem)

secundum regulam   according to rule.
 (se-kun'dum re-gū'lam)

secus (se'kus)   otherwise; not so; an exception to a rule; a
                                     dissenting or divergent view of the rule.

se defendendo   in self-defense.
 (sē dē-fen-den'dō)

sed haec hactenus   so far, so much.

semel pro semper   once for all.

semper fidelis   always faithful.

semper paratus   always ready; always prepared.
 (sem'per pa-rā'tus)

sensu bono   in a good sense.

sensu malo   in a bad sense.

sequela (se-kwē'la)   a secondary result; aftereffect of injury or
 (PL., sequelae)   disease.

sequens (seq.)	the following.
sequente (SING.) (seq.)	and in what follows.
sequentes (PL.) (seqq.)	the following.
sequentia (PL.-neu.) (seqq.)	the following.
sequentibus (seqq.)	in the following places.
sequitur (seq.)	it follows.
seriatim (sē-ri-a'tim)	severally in order; serially; in succession.
sic (sik)	thus in the original; so; thus; simply; in this manner.
sic passem	so everywhere.
silentium altum	deep silence.
similiter (si-mi'li-ter)	in like manner; the like; a formal statement in writing whereby a party expresses his acceptance of an issue tendered by the pleading of his adversary.
simpliciter (sim-plis'i-ter)	absolutely; wholly; simply.
sine (sī'nē)	without.
sine cura (sī'nē kū'ra)	without charge or care; charged with no duty.

sine die
   (sī'nē dī'ē)
   (sin-ē dē'a)
	without day; finally; without any time set for further consideration; without a day appointed.

sine dubio	without doubt.
sine hoc (sī'nē hōk)	without this.
sine loco, anno, vel nomine	without place, date, or name.
sine mora	without delay.
sine praejudicio	without prejudice.
sine qua non (sī'nē kwā non)	an indispensable thing or condition; without which it is not.
sotto voce	in an undertone.
spectemur agendo	let us be judged by our actions.
stante matrimonio	while the marriage is in force.
stare decisis (stā're de-sī'sis)	the doctrine that decisions of the court should serve as precedents for future cases.

status quo
  (stā'tus kwō)
  (ALSO in statu quo)
the state in which anything is; as it is; in the former condition or position; the state of affairs before change or alteration.

status quo ante
the former state of affairs.

sua sponte
  (su'a spon'te)
of his or its own will or motion.
of one's own accord; voluntarily.

sub conditione
under the condition.

sub judice
  (sub jo'di-sē)
before the judge; under judicial consideration.

sub nomine
  (sub. nom.)
in the name of; under the title of.

subpoena ad testificandum
  (sub-pē'na ad
  tes-ti-fi-kan'dum)
an order to appear in court for the purpose of testifying, this being the form used by a court in summoning a witness to appear before it.

subpoena duces tecum
  (sub-pē'na dū'sēz tē'kum)
an order to appear in court and bring books or other prescribed articles desired as evidence.

sub rosa
  (sub rō'za)
privately; in strict confidence.

sub silentio
  (sub sī-len'she-ō)
in silence; silently.

sub voce (sub vō'se)
under the voice; under the word or title.

sui generis
  (su-i jen'e-ris)
of his, her, or its own kind.

sui juris
  (sū'ī jo'ris)
of full legal capacity; in his own right; capable of entering into a contract.

summa cum laude
with the highest distinction.

summum bonum
the chief good.

summum jus
  (sum'mum jūs)
the highest right; the strictest or most rigid law.

supersedeas
  (sū-per-sē'dē-as)
a writ by which proceedings are stayed.

suppressio veri
suppression of the truth.

supra (sū'pra)
occurring in preceding matter; above; before.

T

tempori parendum
one must yield to the times.

tempus fugit
time flies.

tempus omnia revelat
time reveals all things.

tenax propositi
tenacious of his purpose.

tenere (te-neˉ´re)	to have in possession.
totidem verbis (tot´i-dem ver´bis)	in so many words.
toties quoties (toˉ´shi-ēz kwoˉ´shi-ēz)	as often as occasion shall arise; as often as it shall happen.
totis viribus	with all one's might or power, very strenuously.
tour de force (PL., tours de force)	feat of strength, skill, or ingenuity.
tuum est	it is your own.

U

ubi jus ibi remedium (u´bi jūs i´bi (re-meˉ´di-um)	wherever the law gives a right, it also gives a remedy; there is no wrong without a remedy.
ubi supra (uˉ´biˉsuˉ´pra)	where abovementioned.
ultima ratio (ul´ti-ma raˉ´she-oˉ)	the last reason; the last resort; the last argument.
ultima thule	the utmost boundary or limit.
ultima voluntas (ul´ti-ma vo-lun´tāˉs)	a last will.
ultimatum (Sing.) ultimatums OR ultimata (Pl.)	a final proposition; a final offer; a final statement of terms.
ultimus haeres (ul´ti-mus heˉ´rēz)	the last heir; the lord; the king.
ultra (ul´tra)	in excess of; outside of; beyond; more than.
ultra licitum	beyond what is allowable.
ultra valorem	beyond the law.
ultra vires (ul´tra viˉ´rēz)	beyond power; beyond the scope or in excess of legal power or authority.
una voce (u´na voˉ´se)	with one voice; with one accord; unanimously; no dissent.
usus loquendi (uˉ´sus lo-quen´dīˉ)	the customary language; usage in speaking.
ut infra	as below.
ut supra (ut suˉp´raˉ)	as above; as above stated.
uxor et vir (ux.)	wife and husband.

V

valeat quantum valere potest (va'le-at quan'tum va-le're po'test)	let it pass for what it is worth; let it have effect to such extent as it can have effect.
verba generalia (ver'ba je-ne-ra'li-a)	general words or terms.
verbatim ac literatim	word for word and letter for letter.
verbis aut cantilenis (ver'bis at kant -i-len' is)	by words or in song.
verbum sat sapienti	a word is enough for a wise man.
veritas praevalebit	truth will prevail.
veritas vincit	truth conquers.
versus (v. or vs.)	against.
vexatae quaestiones (PL.) vexata quaestio (SING.)	moot questions; vexatious questions; a disputed question.
via (vi'a) (noun) (prep.)	a way of. by way of.
via amicabili (vi'a a-mi-ka'bi-li)	in a friendly way.
via facti	in a forcible way.
via media	a middle course.
vice versa (vi'se ver'sa)	the other way about; under a reversed position of the parties.
vide (v. or vid.) (vi'de)	see; refer to (used to direct attention).
videlicet (viz.) (vi-del'i-set)	to wit; namely; that is to say; in other words.
vincit omnia veritas	truth conquers all things.
vir et uxor	man and wife.
virtute cujus (vi-tu'te ku'jus)	by virtue of which.
virtute officii sui (vir-tu'te of-fi'she-i su'i)	by virtue of his office.
vis major (vis ma'jor)	a greater or superior force; an irresistible force.

viva voce (vī'va vo'se)	by oral testimony; by the living voice; by word of mouth.
voir dire (vwor der)	to speak the truth; an oath requiring one to speak the truth; an oath administered to one called as a witness or a juror prior to an examination of him in reference to his qualifications or disqualifications as witness or juror.
volente non fit injuria (vo-len'tī non fit in-jū'ri-a)	no injustice is done to the consenting person; he who consents cannot receive an injury; one is not legally injured if he has consented to the act complained of or was willing that it should occur.
volte-face (velte-fas)	a turning about; change of front.

Part II

PART II, "Abbreviations," includes both English and foreign abbreviations, as well as abbreviations used within citations and those used in citation reports. Commonly used medical abbreviations are also included.

The actual abbreviations are presented first and the explanatory words afterwards, because this is frequently the order in which such information is imparted to the secretary. It is important that the legal secretary be familiar with frequently used legal, medical, and standard abbreviations. A knowledge of these abbreviations can be useful in taking down the dictated material, as well as in the actual transcription of such abbreviations as frequently appear in a finished legal document. The list presented herein is by no means a complete list of all abbreviations used in legal work, but it is representative of the abbreviations most frequently used.

Since abbreviations used in citation reports are not standardized, the reader may find some variance between the abbreviations given in this chapter and those common to a particular locality. While the listing here is not intended to be a comprehensive list, it is quite substantial and may be used as a convenient guide.

Abbreviations

A. Frequently Used Abbreviations of English Words and Foreign Terms

a.	ampere
abs. re.	absente reo (the defendant being absent)
ad. lib.	ad libitum (to speak offhand, without notes)
ad. val. OR a/v	ad valorem (proportional to the value)
a.k.a. OR a/k/a	also known as
and ano. OR et ano.	and another
anon.	anonymous
arg.	arguendo
a/v OR ad val.	ad valorem (proportional to the value)
B/E	bill of exchange
b/l	bill of lading
B/P	bill of particulars
©	copyrighted
ca.	circa, circiter (about; in the neighborhood of)
ca. sa.	capias ad satisfaciendum (writ of execution for arrest and imprisonment until a claim could be satisfied)
C.E.	common era
cf.	conferre (compare)
c.i.f. OR c/i/f	cost, insurance, freight
c/o	care of
c.o.d.	cash on delivery
c.t.a.	cum testamento annexo (with the will annexed)
d.b.a. OR d/b/a	doing business as
d.b.e.	de bene esse (sufficient for the time being)
d.b.n. OR d/b/n	de bonis non (of goods not yet administered)
d.b.u. OR d/b/u	doing business under
dem.	demise
do.	ditto
d.s.p.	decessit sine prole (died without issue)
D.T.'s	delirium tremens (systemic disorder in alcoholics)
d.v.n.	devisavit vel non (issue of fact as to whether a will in question was made by the testator)
e.g.	exempli gratia (for example)
et al.	et aliae, et alii, et alibi, et alius (and others)
etc. OR &c	et cetera (and so forth)
et seq.	et sequentia (and as follows)
et ux.	et uxor (and wife)
ex dem.	ex demissione (upon the demise)
exr.	executor
ex rel.	ex relatione (on the relation of)
f.a.s. OR F.A.S.	free alongside
ff.	folgende seiten (following pages; and the following)
fi.fa.	fieri facias (writ of execution of property)
f.o.b. OR F.O.B.	free on board
f/u/b	for use and benefit
GNP	Gross National Product
ib. OR ibid.	ibidem (in the same place)
id.	idem (the same)
i.e.	id est (that is)
i.q.	idem quod (the same as)
in init.	in initio (in beginning)
in pro. per.	in propria persona (in one's own proper person)
loc. cit.	loco citato (in the place cited; in passage already quoted)
L.S.	locus sigilli (place of seal)
Ltd.	Limited
MS. or ms.	manuscript
MSS. or mss.	manuscripts
N.B.	nota bene (note well)
nem. con.	nemine contradicente (no one contradicting)
nem. diss.	nemine dissentiente (no one dissenting)
nol. pros. OR nol-pros	nolle prosequi (an agreement to proceed no further with the prosecution)
non seq.	non sequitur (it does not follow; illogical inference)
n.o.v.	non obstante veredicto (notwithstanding the verdict)
nth degree	indefinite power
op. cit.	opere citato (in the work cited)
o.s.p.	obiit sine prole (died without issue)
ors.	others
P/E	Price/Earnings Ratio
p.p.a.	per power of attorney
pro tem.	pro tempore (temporarily; for the time being)
q.	quaere (a query; inquire)
q.c.f.	quare clausum fregit (because he broke the close)

Q.E.D.	quod erat demonstradum (which was to be demonstrated)
q.t.	qui tam (who as well)
q.v.	quod vide (which see)
® OR T.M., Reg.	Registered; trade-mark
Reg. T.M.	registered trade-mark
sci. fa.	scire facias (revival of judgment)
s.e.o.o.	sauf erreur ou omission (errors or omissions excepted)
seq. (Sing.)	sequens, sequente, sequitur (the following; and in what follows)
seqq. (Pl.)	sequentes, sequentia, sequentibus (the following; in the following places)
s.l.p.	sine legitima prole (without lawful issue)
s.p.	sine prole (without issue)
ss.	scilicet (to wit)
sub.nom.	sub nomine (in the name of; under the title of)
Sub. Pro.	supplementary proceedings
t/a	trading as
T.M.	Reg. T.M.; trade-mark; registered
t/n	true name
u/w OR u/w/o	under the will of
u/w/a	under written agreement
ux.	uxor (wife)
v. OR vs.	versus (against)
f. OR vid.	vide (see)
viz.	videlicet (namely)
X	by; symbol used by one who is unable to write his name for signature purposes; a symbol indicating place for a signature.

B. Abbreviations Used *Within* Citations [*Denotes Words Also Appearing Under "Frequently Used Abbreviations of English Words and Foreign Terms"]

admr.	administrator
admrx.	administratrix
affd. OR aff'd	affirmed
affg.	affirming

a.k.a. OR a/k/a*	also known as
amdg.	amending
amendt.	amendment
Art.	Article
Arts.	Articles
Assn. OR Ass'n	Association
C. OR c.	Chapter
cert. den.	certiorari denied
cf.*	confer (compare)
c.t.a.*	cum testamento annexo (with the will annexed)
d/b/a OR d.b.a.*	doing business as
d.b.n.*	de bonis non (of goods not yet administered)
den.	denied
dept. or dep't	department
ed., Ed.	edition
eds.	editions
eff.	effective
et al.*	et aliae, et alii, et alibi, et alius (and others)
Exh.	Exhibit
Exhs.	Exhibits
ex rel.*	ex relatione (on the relation of)
FICA	Federal Insurance Contributions Act
fn. OR n.	footnote
fol.	folio
fols.	folios
f/u/b*	for use and benefit
ibid., ib.*	ibidem (in the same place)
id.*	idem (the same)
L.	Laws
loc. cit.*	loco citato (in the place cited; in passage already quoted)
mod.	modified
modfg.	modifying
m.o.g.	modified on other grounds
MS. OR ms.*	manuscript
MSS. OR mss.*	manuscripts
n. OR fn.	footnote
nem. con.*	nemine contradicente (no one contradicting)
nem. diss.*	nemine dissentiente (no one dissenting)
n.o.r.	not officially reported
n. othw. rep.	not otherwise reported
op. cit.*	opere citato (in the work cited)
p.	page
pp.	pages

par. OR ¶	paragraph
pars. OR ¶ ¶	paragraphs
q.v.*	quod vide (which see)
reh.	rehearing
renum.	renumbered
rev.	revised
revd.	reversed
revd. o.g.	reversed on other grounds
revg.	reversing
s.c.	same case
Sec. OR §	Section
Secs. OR § §	Sections
sl. op.	slip opinion
subd.	subdivision
subds.	subdivisions
sub. nom.*	sub nomine (in the name of; under the title of)
subsec.	subsection
subsecs.	subsections
t/a*	trading as
Tit.	Title
Vol.	Volume
Vols.	Volumes
w.o.	without opinion

C. Abbreviations Frequently Used in Citation Reports

Abbreviations of legal reports, reporters, and authorities are not standardized. In view of the variants of abbreviations, the following random sampling is far from complete, but the list may serve as a convenient guide.

A	Atlantic
A 2d	Atlantic Reporter, Second Series
ABAJ	American Bar Association Journal
A&E	Admiralty and Ecclesiastical Cases, Eng.
A&E (NS)	Adolphus and Ellis, Queens Bench Reports, Eng., New Series
Abb Adm	Abbott's Admiralty Reports (Austin Abbott)
Abb Ct App	Abbott's New York Court of Appeals Decisions
Abb N Cas	Abbott's New Cases
Abb Pr (NY)	Abbotts' New York Practice Reports (Austin and Benjamin Abbott)
Abb Pr. NS (NY)	Abbotts' New York Practice Reports, New Series
AC	Advance California Reports
AC	Appeal Cases
AD 2d	Appellate Divisions Reports, Second Series
AFTR	American Federal Tax Reports
Ala	Alabama Reports
Ala App	Alabama Appeals Reports
Ala Sel Cas	Alabama Select Cases
Alaska	Alaska Reports
ALR	American Law Reports
AM&E Ann Cas	American and English Annotated Cases
Am&E Corp Cas	American and English Corporation Cases
Am&E Encyc	American and English Encyclopedia of Law
Am&E Ry Cas	American and English Railway Cases
Am Ann Cas	American Annotated Cases
Am Bankr NS	American Bankruptcy, New Series
ABAR	American Bar Association, Annual Reports
AMC	American Maritime Cases
Am Civ LJ	American Civil Law Journal (New York)
Am Corp Cas	American Corporation Cases, Chicago
Am Cr Rep	American Criminal Reports
Am Dec	American Decisions
Am Dig	American Digest
Am J Int L	American Journal of International Law, New York
Am Jur	American Jurisprudence; American Jurist
Am L Cas	American Leading Cases
Am LJ	American Law Journal (Phila.)
Am L Rec	American Law Record
Am Prac Rep	American Practice Reports
Am Rep	American Reports, Albany
Am Ry Cas	American Railway Cases, Boston
Am Ry Rep	American Railway Reports, New York
Am St Rep	American State Reports
App Cas	House of Lords and Privy Council, Appeal Cases, Eng., to 1890
App Div	Appellate Division Reports
Atl	Atlantic Reporter
Austr CLR	Australia Commonwealth Law Reports
Bail L (SC)	Bailey Law

Bald	Baldwin, U.S. Circuit Court Reports, Third Circuit	CCA	U.S. Circuit Court of Appeals Reports
Bann & Ard	Banning and Arden, Patent Cases, U.S. Courts	CCH	Commerce Clearing House
Barb	Barbour's Supreme Court reports, New York	CCPA (Customs)	U.S. Court of Customs and Patent Appeals
Barb Ch	Barbour's Chancery Reports, New York	CCPA (Patents)	U.S. Court of Customs and Patent Appeals
Barr (Pa)	Barr	CCR	Crown Cases Reversed, Eng.
Beasl	Beasley, New Jersey Equity	Cent Rep	Central Reporter, Rochester, New York
Bell CC	Crown Cases, Reserved, Eng.		
Ben	Benedict, U.S. District Court Reports, S.D., New York	CFR	Code of Federal Regulations
Benn FI Cas	Bennett, Fire Insurance Cases, New York	CFR Cum Supp	Code of Federal Regulations Cumulative Supplement
Bibb (Ky)	Bibb	Ch	Chancery Appeal, Eng.
Bi-Mo L Rev	Bi-Monthly Law Review	Ch D	Chancery Division, Eng., from 1891
Bl Com	Blackstone, Commentaries on Laws of England	CJ	Corpus Juris
Black (US)	Black, U.S. Supreme Court	CJS	Corpus Juris Secundum
Blatchf (F)	Blatchford, U.S. Circuit Court Reports	Clarke Ch	Clarke's Chancery Reports, New York
Bosw	Bosworth's Superior Court Reports, New York	CLR (Austr)	Commonwealth Law Reports
		CLS	Consolidated Laws Service
Bouv L Dict	Bouvier's Law Dictionary	Cong Rec	Congressional Record
Bradb	Bradbury's Pleading and Practice Reports, New York	Conn	Connecticut Reports
		Conn S	Connecticut Supplement
Bradf	Bradford's Surrogate's Reports, New York	Connoly	Connoly's New York Surrogate Reports
Branch	Branch's Reports, Florida	Const	Constitutional Reports
Brit Col (Can)	British Columbia	Cornell LQ	Cornell Law Quarterly
B Reg	National Bankruptcy Register, U.S. Courts	Cow	Cowen's New York Reports
		Cow Cr Rep	Cowen's Criminal Reports, New York
BTA	U.S. Board of Tax Appeals Decisions	CP	Common Pleas, Eng.
Burnett (Ore)	Burnett	CPA	Civil Practice Act, New York
Cadwalader	Cadwalader Cases, U.S. District Court, Eastern District of Pennsylvania	CPLR	Civil Practice Law and Rules [became effective September 1, 1963]
CA	U.S. Court of Appeals Reports	Cr App R	Criminal Appeal Reports, Eng.
CAA	Civil Aeronautics Authority Reports	Cranch, CC	Cranch, U.S. Circuit Court Reports, District of Columbia.
CAB	Civil Aeronautics Board Reports	Cranch Pat Dec (NS)	Cranch's Patent Decisions, New Series
Cal	California Reports	Ct Cl	U.S. Court of Claims Reports, New York
Cal 2d	California Reports, Second Series	Ct Cl (NY)	Court of Claims Reports, New York
Cal App	California Appellate Reports	Cummins (Idaho)	Cummins
Cal App 2d	California Appellate Reports, Second Series	Cum Supp	Cumulative Supplement
Canal Zone	Canal Zone	Cust Ct	Customs Court
Can LT	Canadian Law Times	C-Wait Encycl NY Prac	Carmody-Wait Encyclopedia of New York Practice
Cardoza, Judicial Process	Cardoza's Growth of the Law	Cyc	Cyclopaedia of Law and Procedure
Case & Com	Case & Comment		

Dak L Rev	Dakota Law Review
Dall	Dallas, U.S. Reports
Daly	Daly's Common Pleas Reports
Day (Conn)	Day
DC App	District of Columbia Appeals Reports
Del	Delaware Reports
Dem	Demarest's Surrogates' Reports, New York
Detroit L Rev	Detroit Law Review
Duer	Duer's Superior Court Reports, New York
E Rep	Eastern Reporter
Edinb LJ	Edinburgh Law Journal
El B&S	Ellis, Best, and Smith's Reports, Queen's Bench, Eng.
Eng Ch	English Chancery Reports
Eng Rep	English Reports
Eng Rep R	English Reports, Full Reprint
Eng Rul Cas	English Ruling Cases
EO	Executive Orders [Presidential]
Eq	Equity Division, Law Reports and Law Journal, Eng.
Estee (Hawaii)	Estee's District Court of Hawaii
Ex D	Exchequer Division, High Court of Justice, Eng.
Ex Proc	Presidential Proclamations
F	Federal Reporter
F 2d	Federal Reporter, Second Series
FCA	Federal Code Annotated
FCC	Federal Communications Commission Decisions, Reports, and Orders
Fed	Federal Reporter
Fed Cas	Federal Cases
Fed LQ	Federal Law Quarterly (Indianapolis)
Fed Supp	Federal Supplement
Fla	Florida Reports
Flipp (F)	Flippin, U.S. Circuit Court
FPC	Federal Power Commission Opinions and Decisions
FR	Federal Register
FRCP	Federal Rules of Civil Procedure
FRCrP	Federal Rules of Criminal Procedure
FRD	Federal Rules Decisions
FTC	Federal Trade Commission Decisions
Ga	Georgia Reports
Ga App	Georgia Appeals Reports
Gibbons (NY)	Gibbons (Surrogate)

Gunby (La)	Gunby's Appeal Decisions
Hall	Hall's Superior Court Reports, New York
Harv L Rev	Harvard Law Review
Hawaii Dist	U.S. District Court of Hawaii
Hill	Hill's Reports, New York
Hilt	Hilton's Common Pleas Reports, New York
Hitch, Pr & Proc	Hitch's Practice & Procedure in the Probate Court of Massachusetts
HL	House of Lords Cases, Eng.
HLSc	House of Lords, Scotch, and Divorce Appeals, Eng.
How	Howard, U.S. Reports
How App Cas	Howard's New York Court of Appeals Cases
How Prac	Howard's Practice Reports, New York
How Prac (NS)	Howard's Practice Reports, New Series, New York
Hun (NY)	Hun (Supreme)
ICC	Interstate Commerce Commission
Idaho	Idaho Reports
Ill	Illinois Reports
Ill App	Illinois Appellate Court Reports
Ill Cir Ct	Illinois Circuit Court
Ind	Indiana Reports
Ind App	Indiana Appellate Court Reports
Iowa	Iowa Reports
Int Rev Bull	Internal Revenue Bulletin
IRC	Internal Revenue Code
J Air Law	Journal of Air Law
Jeff (Va)	Jefferson
J Jur	Journal of Jurisprudence
Johns Cas	Johnson's New York Cases
Johns Ch	Johnson's New York Chancery Reports
Jud C	Judicial Code
Jud Rep	Judicial Repository, New York
Justice's LR (Pa)	Justice's Law Reporter
Kan	Kansas Reports
KB	King's Bench, Eng., from 1901
Kent's Commen	Kent's Commentaries
Key	Keyes' Reports, New York
Ky	Kentucky Reports
La	Louisiana Reports
La Ann	Louisiana Annual Reports

La App	Louisiana Court of Appeals Reports
LD	Dept. of Interior, Public Lands Decisions
L Ed	U.S. Supreme Court Reports, Lawyers' Edition
Lan Dec (US)	Lands Decisions (US)
LAR	Labor Arbitration Reports
LJ (NS) Adm	Law Journal Reports, New Series, Admiralty, Eng.
LJ (NS) Bank	Law Journal Reports, New Series, Bankruptcy, Eng.
LJ (NS) CP	Law Journal Reports, New Series, Common Pleas, Eng.
LJ (NS) KB	Law Journal Reports, New Series, King's Bench, Eng.
LJ (NS) Mat Cas	Law Journal Reports, New Series, Divorce and Matrimonial Cases, Eng.
LJ (NS) MC	Law Journal Reports, New Series, Magistrate's Cases, Eng.
LJ (NS) P	Law Journal Reports, New Series, Probate, Eng.
LJ (NS) PC	Law Journal Reports, New Series, Privy Council, Eng.
LL LR	Lloyd's List Law Reports, Eng.
LR	Law Reports, Eng.
LRA	Lawyers Reports Annotated
LRA (NS)	Lawyers Reports Annotated, New Series
LT (Eng)	Law Times Journal
Luders' Elec Cas (Eng)	Luders' Election Cases
Mass	Massachusetts Reports
MCC	Motor Carrier Cases, Interstate Commerce Commission Reports
McQuillan, Municipal Corporations	McQuillan on Municipal Corporations
Md	Maryland Reports
Me	Maine Reports
Med Leg J	Medical Legal Journal
Mich	Michigan Reports
Michie, Banks	Michie's Banks & Banking
Minn	Minnesota Reports
Misc	Miscellaneous Reports, New York
Misc 2d	Miscellaneous Reports, New York, Second Series
Miss	Mississippi Reports
Mo	Missouri Reports
Mo App	Missouri Appeals Reports
Mont	Montana Reports

Month L Bull (NY)	Monthly Law Bulletin
MPR (Can)	Maritime Provinces Reports
Nat L Rep (US)	National Law Reporter
NC	North Carolina Reports
ND	North Dakota Reports
NE	Northeastern Reporter
NE 2d	Northeastern Reporter, Second Series
Neb	Nebraska Reports
Nev	Nevada Reports
NH	New Hampshire Reports
N Ir	Northern Ireland Law
NJ	New Jersey Reports
NJ Eq	New Jersey Equity Reports
NJL	New Jersey Law Reports
NJLJ	New Jersey Law Journal
NJ Misc	New Jersey Miscellaneous Reports
NJ Super	New Jersey Superior Court
NLB	National Labor Board Decisions
NLRB	National Labor Relations Board Decisions and Orders
NM	New Mexico Reports
NY	New York Court of Appeals Reports
NY 2d	New York Court of Appeals Reports, Second Series
NY Ann Cas	New York Annotated Cases
NYLC Ann	New York Leading Cases, Annotated
NYLJ	New York Law Journal
NYLRB	New York State Labor Relations Board
NYS	New York Supplement
NYS 2d	New York Supplement, Second Series
NY St Rep	New York State Reporter
NW	Northwestern Reporter
NW 2d	Northwestern Reporter, Second Series
NY Civ Proc	New York Civil Procedure Reports
Ohio	Ohio Reports
Ohio St.	Ohio State Reports
Okla	Oklahoma Reports
Okla Cr	Oklahoma Criminal Reports
Ont L	Ontario Law Reports
Op Att Gen	Dept. of Justice, Opinions of U.S. Attorneys General
Ops Sol POD	Official Opinions of Solicitor of Post Office Dept.
Ore	Oregon Reports
Overt (Tenn)	Overton

Pa	Pennsylvania State Reports
Pac	Pacific Reporter
P 2d	Pacific Reporter, Second Series
Page, Wills	Page on Wills
Paige Ch.	Paige's Chancery Reports
Patton & H (Va)	Patton & Heath
PC	Privy Council, Eng.
Pet	Peters, U.S. Reports
Philippine	Philippine Reports
PL	Public Laws
Prob D	Probate Division, Law Reports, Eng.
PSC	Reports of New York Public Service Commission
Puerto Rico F	Puerto Rico Federal Reports
PUR	Public Utilities Reports
PUR (NS)	Public Utilities Reports, New Series
QB	Queen's Bench, Eng.
QB Div	Queen's Bench Division, Law Reports, Eng.
Quebec Pr (Can)	Quebec Practice
Queens LJ (Austr)	Queensland Law Journal
RCL	Ruling Case Law
RCP	Rules of Civil Practice, New York
Redf.	Redfield's Surrogates' Reports, New York
Remington, Bankruptcy	Remington on Bankruptcy
Rev Stat	Revised Statutes
RI	Rhode Island Reports
RLB	Railroad Labor Board Decisions
Ry & C Cas (Eng)	Railway and Canal Cases
Sawy (F)	Sawyer, U.S. Circuit Court
SC	South Carolina Reports
S Ct	U.S. Supreme Court Reporter
SD	South Dakota Reports
SE	Southeastern Reporter
SE 2d	Southeastern Reporter, Second Series
SEC	Securities and Exchange Commission Decisions
Sen Doc	Senate Document
Shep (Ala)	Shepherd, Reports
So	Southern Reporter
So 2d	Southern Reporter, Second Series
Stat	Statutes at Large
Summers, Oil & Gas	Summers on Oil & Gas
SW	Southwestern Reporter
SW 2d	Southwestern Reporter, Second Series
Sweeney (NY)	Sweeney (Superior)
TC	Tax Court of the U.S. Reports
Tax L Rev	Tax Law Review
Tenn	Tennessee Reports
Tex	Texas Reports
Tex Cr Rep	Texas Criminal Reports
Thacher Crim Cas (Mass)	Thacher Criminal Cases
Tiffany, Real Property	Tiffany on Real Property
UCC	Uniform Commercial Code
UCMJ	Uniform Code of Military Justice
ULA	Uniform Laws Annotated
US	United States Supreme Court Reports
US Av	United States Aviation Reports
USC	United States Code
USCA	U.S. Code Annotated
USCMA	Official Reports, United States Court of Military Appeals
USC Supp	U.S. Code Supplement
USL Week	The United States Law Weekly
USPQ	U.S. Patent Quarterly
Utah	Utah Reports
Va	Virginia Reports
Vent (Eng)	Ventris (Common Pleas)
Vt	Vermont Reports
Virgin Islands	Virgin Islands
Wait's NY Prac	Wait's New York Practice
Walk Ch (Mich)	Walker's Chancery Reports
Wall	Wallace, U.S. Reports
Ware (F)	Ware, U.S. District Court
Wash	Washington State Reports
Wash 2d	Washington State Reports, Second Series
Wash Jur	Washington Jurist
Wend	Wendell's Reports
Wharton, Crim Proc	Wharton's Criminal Law & Procedure
Wheat	Wheaton, U.S. Reports
Wheel Cr Cas	Wheeler's Criminal Cases
Wigmore, Evidence	Wigmore on Evidence
Wis	Wisconsin Reports
WL Gaz (Ohio)	Western Law Gazette

WN	Weekly Notes, Eng.		C.M.	colored male
W Va	West Virginia Reports		C.M.F.	colored married female
Wyo	Wyoming Reports		C.M.M.	colored married male
Yale LJ	Yale Law Journal		C.N.S.	central nervous system
Yukon Terr	Yukon Territory		CO_2	carbon dioxide
Zab (NJ)	Zabriskie's Report		C.P.C.	Clinical Pathological Conference
			C.S.F.	cerebrospinal fluid

D. Commonly Used Medical Abbreviations

			C.S.F.	colored single female
			C.S.M.	colored single male
			C.S.R.	corrected sedimentation rate
abd.	abdomen		C.V.	cardiovascular
A.C.D.	absolute cardiac dullness		C.V.A.	cerebrovascular accident
A.C.S.	American College of Surgeons		c.v.a.	costovertebral angle, cerebrovascular accident
ACTH	adreno-corticotropic hormone			
a.d.	(auris dextra) right ear		C.V.R.	cardiovascular-respiratory
ad lib.	(ad libitum) as much as needed		D & C	dilatation and curettage
			decub.	(decubitus) lying down
adv.	(adversum) against		D_1 & D_2	first and second dorsal vertebrae
A/B Ratio	albumin-globulin ratio			
$AgNO_3$	silver nitrate		de d. in d.	(de die in diem) from day to day
A.J.	ankle jerks			
A.M.A.	American Medical Association		def.	defecation
amp.	ampoule		dieb. alt.	(diebus alternis) on alternate days
amt.	amount			
Anes.	anesthesia		D.O.A.	dead on arrival
a.s.	(auris sinistra) left ear		Dx	diagnosis
AV	auriculoventricular		E.A.H.F.	eczema, allergy, hay fever
A.Z.	Ascheim-Zondek test for pregnancy		ECG	electrocardiogram
			E.D.C.	expected date of confinement
Ba	barium		E.E.G.	electroencephalogram
B.C.	bone condition		E.E.N.T.	eye, ear, nose, and throat
B.C.G.	Bacillus Calmette Guerin		EKG	electrocardiogram
B.E.	barium enema		E.N.T.	ear, nose, and throat
B.M.	bowel movement		E.O.M.	extraocular movements
B.M.R.	basal metabolic rate		E.S.R.	erythrocyte sedimentation rate
BNA	Basle Nomina Anatomica (Anatomical Nomenclature)		exam.	examination
B.P.	blood pressure		F.H.	family history
B.P.H.	benign prostatic hypertrophy		F.H.S.	fetal heart sounds
B.R.P.	bathroom privileges		Fl.	fluid
B.S.	breath sounds		F.U.O.	fever of unknown origin
B. & S.	Bartholin's and Skene's glands		G.A.	gastric analysis
BUN	blood-urea-nitrogen test		G.B.	gallbladder
$\bar{c}$	(cum) with		GC	gonorrhea
C_1 & C_2	first and second cervical vertebrae		G.E.	gastroenterology
			G.G.E.	generalized glandular enlargement
CA	chronological age			
Ca	cancer		G.I.	gastrointestinal
c.b.c.	complete blood count		G.O.E.	Gas, oxygen, and ether anesthesia
C.C.	chief complaint OR current complaint			
			G.S.W.	gunshot wound
C.F.	colored female		gt.	(gutta) drop
C_3H_6	cyclopropane		gtt.	(guttae) drops
C.I.	color index		G.U.	genito-urinary (uro-genital)
c.m.	costal margin		Gyn.	gynecology

Hb	hemoglobin	OC	onset and cause
HCl	hydrochloric acid	OD	(oculus dexter) right
Hct.	hematocrit		eye
H.C.V.D.	hypertensive cardiovascular	O.O.B.	out of bed
	disease	O.P.C.	out-patient clinic
Hg.	hemoglobin	O.P.D.	outpatient department
ht.	height	Ophthal.	ophthalmology
I.M.	intramuscular	O.R.	operating room
inf.	infusion	Orth.	orthopedics
I.Q.	intelligence quotient	O.S.	(oculus sinister) left eye
I.S.	intercostal space	O.U.	each eye
I.U.	international unit		
IV	intravenous	P.	pulse
IVP	intravenous pyelogram	P. & A.	percussion and auscultation
KG.	kilogram	Path.	pathology
KI	potassium iodide	P.E.	physical examination OR
K.J.	knee jerk		physical evaluation
K.U.B.	kidneys, ureters, bladder	P.H.	past (previous) history
L & A	light and accommodation	P.I.	present illness
lb.	pound	P.I.D.	pelvic inflammatory disease
L.B.D.	left border of dullness (of	P.M.	(post mortem) after death
	heart to percussion)	P.M.I.	point of maximal impulse
L.D.A.	left dorso-anterior	P.M.P.	previous menstrual period
L.D.P.	left dorso-posterior	P. Op.	postoperative
L_1 & I_2	first and second lumbar verte-	prep	preparation
	brae	p.r.n.	(pro re nata) whenever neces-
L.F.A.	least fatal disease		sary
L.F.P.	left fronto-posterior	Prog.	prognosis
L.L.Q.	left lower quadrant	PSP	phenosulfonphthalein test
L.M.A.	left mentum anterior		(kidney)
L.M.D.	local medical doctor	P.T.	physical therapy
L.M.P.	last menstrual period	pt.	patient
L.M.T.	left mentum transverse	pulv.	(pulvis) powder
L.O.A.	left occiput anterior	P.x.	physical examination
L.O.P.	left occiput posterior	px.	pneumothorax
L.O.T.	left occiput transverse	P.Z.I.	protamine zinc insulin
L.S.A.	left sacrum anterior	R.	respiration
L.S.K.	liver, spleen, and kidneys	r.	right
L.S.P.	left sacrum posterior	Ra	radium
L.S.T.	left sacrum transverse	R.B.C.	red blood count
L.U.Q.	left upper quadrant	R.B.D.	right border of dullness (heart
M.A.	mental age		percussion)
McB pt.	McBurney's point	R.D.A.	right dorso-anterior
M.C.L.	mid-clavicular line	R.D.P.	right dorso-posterior
M.L.D.	minimum lethal dose	resp.	respiration
M.M.	mucous membranes	R.F.A.	right fronto-anterior
M.S.L.	mid-sternal line	R.F.P.	right fronto-posterior
neg.	negative	Rh.	Rhesus factor
N.F.	National Formulary	R.L.Q.	right lower quadrant
N.N.R.	New and Nonofficial Reme-	R.M.A.	right mentum anterior
	dies	R.M.P.	right mentum posterior
N_2O	nitrous oxide	R.M.T.	right mentum transverse
NPN	nonprotein nitrogen	R.O.A.	right occiput anterior
N.P.O.	nothing by mouth	R.O.P.	right occiput posterior
O	(octarius) a pint	R.O.S.	review of systems
Ob. OR O.B.,	obstetrics	R.O.T.	right occiput transverse
obs.			

R.R. & E.	round, regular, and equal (of pupils)	T & A	tonsillectomy and adenoidectomy
R.S.A.	right sacrum anterior	T.A.	toxin-antitoxin
R.S.P.	right sacrum posterior	T.A.T.	tetanus antitoxin
R.S.T.	right sacrum transverse	T.B. OR (tbc)	tuberculosis, or tubercle bacilli
R.U.Q.	right upper quadrant	temp.	temperature
Rx.	treatment, therapy	T.P.	total protein
s̄	(sine) without	T.P.R.	temperature, pulse, respiration
SA	sino-auricular	U.C.H.D.	usual childhood diseases
s.c.	subcutaneous	ung.	ointment
S.H.	social history	Ur.	urine
S.O.B.	short of breath	U.R.I.	upper respiratory infection
solve	dissolve	U.S.P.	United States Pharmacopoeia
S.O.S.	(si opus sit) if necessary	V.D.	venereal disease
sp. gr.	specific gravity	V.D.S.	venereal disease (syphilis)
S.R.	sedimentation rate	v.f.	field of vision
s.s.	soapsuds	W.B.C.	white blood cells OR white blood count
Staph.	staphylococcus OR staphylococcal	w/d	well developed
		W.F.	white female
stat.	(statim) at once	W.M.	white male
STD	skin test done	w/n	well-nourished
STS	serology test for syphilis	W.r.	Wassermann reaction
Subcu.	subcutaneous	w/v	weight by volume
T.	temperature	X	unit of x-ray dosage

Part III

PART III, "Spelling," consists of legal words which present spelling difficulties; a list of words ending in "able" and "ible"; plurals of certain words; and the spelling of compound terms.

The list was partially derived from a study of word frequency in legal documents. The author went through a number of briefs, litigation papers, leases, wills, patent formats, corporate documents, and letters written in law offices, at the same time making a list of words which appeared again and again. In addition, a number of legal handbooks were examined for vocabulary content. Omission of certain words was intentional. For example, an attempt was made to omit the 500 words which account for almost three-fourths of all words used in business, since these words are included in general dictionaries.

A secretary who works for an attorney who has an extensive vocabulary—such as a trial lawyer, or a lawyer in a highly specialized area—may have to resort to an unabridged lawyer's dictionary if a particular word is not found in this book. This section will, however, be a means of helping most legal secretaries become familiar with the spelling and word division of legal words most frequently used.

Spelling

A. Legal Words Presenting Spelling Difficulties

abandonment
abeyance
abridgment
abrogate
abscond
absence
acceptor supra protest
accidentally
accretion
acknowledged
acknowledgment
adapter
addenda
adduced
adjudication
adjuster
admiralty
admittance
adverse possession
adviser
affidavit
aging
aleatory
align or aline
allegation
allege
allonge
allowance
ambiguous
amendment
anesthetic
annulment
antedated
appall
apparently
appellant
appellate
appellee
applicable
appurtenance
arbitration
arbitrators
arraign
ascendance
assignee
assignor
attorney in fact
attorneys
aye
bankruptcy
barreled, barreling
belatedly
beneficiary

beveled, beveling
biased
blond
bona fide
boulder
boycott
brier
caliber
canceled
canceling
cancellation
catalog
caveat emptor
cessation
cestui que trust
chancellor
chancery
channeled
channeling
chose in action
cigarette
coconut
codicil
collateral
combated, combating
commencement
commitment
committed
comparable
compelling
complainant
concealment
confer
confiscation
connector
consanguinity
consequential
consignor
contention
continuity
contributory negligence
controversy
convenience
conversion
converter
conveyance
conveyor
corporeal
corpus delicti
corpus juris
corruption
councilor
counseled

counselor
counseling
courtesy (good manners)
credulity
curing
curtesy (life estate)
decedent
de facto
defendant
defense
de jure
del credere
delinquent
demurrer
deponent
deposition
descendant
development
diagramed
diagraming
dialed
dialing
dike
disk
dissenting
distinguish
diversity
domiciliary
dower
draft
drought
duress
easement
egress
embezzlement
emblements
eminent domain
employee
enclose
enclosure
encumbrance
enforcible
entrust
equaled
equaling
equity of redemption
eradicate
erroneous
escheat
escrow
esthetic
estoppel
excavate

excavations
executor
exhibitor
existence
extradition
facsimile
favor
felony
femme sole
fiduciary
finalized
flier
focused
focusing
forbade
foreclosure
forgery
fulfill
fuse
garnishment
gasoline
goodby
graveled
graveling
gray
grudging
guarantee (n. or v.)
guaranty (n.)
habeas corpus
harassment
horizontal
impanel
inaction
inartfully
inartistically
incidentally
inconsistent
incorporeal
indemnity
indenture
inexplicable
ingress
injunction
in personam
insolvency
intern
intestate
in transitu
ipso facto
irrevocable
jacketing
jackknife
jeweled

jeweler
jewelry
judgment
judicial
jurisdictional
kerosene
kidnaped
kidnaper
kidnaping
labeled
labeling
legacy
leveled
leveler
leveling
libelant OR libellant
libeled
libeler
libeling
libelous
license
lien
likable
limitations
liquidate
lis pendens
litigants
litigate
litigation
locus sigilli
malfeasance
mandamus
maneuver
maneuverability
marshal
marshaled
marshaling
marvelous
meager OR meagre
medieval
meter
misapplication
misdemeanor
misfeasance

misinterpretation
mistrial
modeled
modeling
modular
mold
money
moneys OR monies
monolog
movable
municipal
negatively
niece
nolo contendere
non compos mentis
nonfeasance
nonplused
notary public
novation
nullity
occur
occurred
offense
originally
oscillation
ostensible
penciled
penciling
percent
performance
perfunctory
perjury
personal (relating to an
    individual)
personality (personal
    existence)
personalty (personal
    property as distin-
    guished from real
    property)
personnel (employees)
petitioner
plaintiff
pleadings

plow
post mortem
practice
pre-bid inspection
prefer
preferred
prejudicial
preliminary
preparatory
presence
prima facie evidence
principal (chief)
principle (rule)
probate
procedure
programed
programer
programing
propriety
provocation
pursuant
quasi contract
quo warranto
reasonable
recital
recognizance
reconnaissance
referable
referring
remand
remedied
removal
replevin
requisite
residency
respondent
ridiculous
salable
salability
signaled
signaling
skillful
specialty
statutory

stenciled
stenciling
stretching
subpena OR subpoena
subrogation
subsequent
subsidiary
substance
succinctly
sulfur OR sulphur
superintendent
surrogate
talisman
technical
technically
testator
theater OR theatre
totaled
totaling
traveled
traveler
traveling
trover
unassailability
uniformity
usury
vacating
venire
venue
verbiage
verification
vicissitude
visa
visaed
vitamin
willful
woolen
woolly
worshiped
worshiper
worshiping

B. Words Ending in "able" and "ible"

acceptable
accessible
accountable
adjustable
admirable
admissible
agreeable
appreciable

apprehensible
audible
avoidable
breakable
certifiable
changeable
charitable
collapsible

combustible
comparable
compatible
comprehensible
compressible
conceivable
conducible
conductible

congestible
considerable
consumable
contemptible
controvertible
convertible
convincible
corrigible

corruptible	identifiable	lamentable	reprehensible
credible	illegible	legible	repressible
creditable	imaginable	manageable	reproducible
crucible	impassable OR im-	marketable	resistible
culpable	passible	negligible	responsible
deducible	impeachable	negotiable	reversible
deductible	impeccable	noticeable	revertible
defeasible	imperceptible	omissible	risible
defectible	imponderable	ostensible	salable OR saleable
defensible	impossible	payable	seducible
delectable	inaccessible	perceptible	sensible
deniable	inadmissible	perfectible	sociable
deplorable	inaudible	perishable	submergible
desirable	incombustible	permissible	submersible
destructible	incompatible	persuasible	subvertible
diffusible	imcomprehensible	pervertible	suggestible
digestible	incorrigible	plausible	supersensible
disagreeable	incredible	pleasurable	suppressible
discernible	indelible	portable	susceptible
discreditable	indispensable	possible	suspensible
dissectible	indivertible	predictable	tenable
divisible	ineligible	preferable	terrible
edible	inexcusable	perishable	tolerable
educable	infallible	probable	traducible
eligible	inflammable	producible	transferable
employable	inflexible	productible	transmissible
enforceable	infractible	questionable	transvertible
enjoyable	infrangible	reasonable	tripartible
enviable	instructible	receptible	uncorruptible
equitable	intangible	redeemable	unexhaustible
exchangeable	intelligible	redemptible	unexpressible
expansible	interruptible	reducible	uninhabitable
expendable	intractable	reflectible	unintelligible
explosible	invariable	reflexible	unresponsible
expressible	invincible	refragable	unsinkable
extensible	irascible	refrangible	unsusceptible
fallible	irreconcilable	refutable	valuable
favorable	irreducible	regrettable	variable
feasible	irrepressible	reliable	vendible
flexible	irresistible	remissible	veritable
forcible	irresponsible	renascible	vincible
foreseeable	irreversible	renderable	visible
fusible	irrevocable	rendible	vulnerable
horrible	justifiable	renewable	workable
		replaceable	

C. Singular and Plural Forms

1. Selected words which cause difficulty

Singular	Plural	Singular	Plural
addendum	addenda	ally	allies
adieu	adieus	alumna (fem.)	alumnae
agency	agencies	alumnus (masc.)	alumni
agendum	agenda	antenna	antennas (antennae, scientific)
alias	aliases		

Singular	Plural	Singular	Plural
appendix	appendixes OR appendices	larynx	larynxes
army	armies	lens	lenses
attorney	attorneys	life	lives
automaton	automatons	locus	loci
axis	axes	loss	losses
banjo	banjos	madam	mesdames
basis	bases	mass	masses
beau	beaus	matrix	matrices OR matrixes
biography	biographies	maximum	maximums
buffalo	buffaloes	medium	media OR mediums
bus	buses OR busses	memorandum	memoranda OR memorandums
cameo	cameos		
canoe	canoes	minimum	minimums
cargo	cargoes OR cargos	minutia	minutiae
chassis	chassis (same as singular)	money	moneys OR monies
		monkey	monkeys
		monsieur	messieurs
city	cities	motto	mottoes OR mottos
copy	copies	nucleus	nuclei
crisis	crises	oasis	oases
criterion	criteria	octopus	octopuses
curriculum	curricula OR curriculums	opus	opera OR opuses
		ox	oxen
datum	data	parenthesis	parentheses
dilettante	dilettanti	penny	pennies
do	do's OR dos	phenomenon	phenomena
don't	don'ts	plaintiff	plaintiffs
echo	echoes	plateau	plateaus
ellipsis	ellipses	podium	podiums
equilibrium	equilibriums (equilibria, scientific)	pony	ponies
		proof	proofs
erratum	errata	radio	radios
executrix	executrices OR executrixes	radius	radii
		radix	radixes
focus	focuses	ratio	ratios
folio	folios	rebuff	rebuffs
folium	folia	referendum	referendums
formula	formulas	rodeo	rodeos
fungus	fungi	safe	safes
genius	geniuses	sanatorium	sanatoriums
genus	genera	sanitarium	sanitariums
giraffe	giraffes	secretary	secretaries
gladiolus	gladiolus (same as singular)	shelf	shelves
		sheriff	sheriffs
handkerchief	handkerchiefs OR handkerchieves	ski	skis
		solo	solos
hypothesis	hypotheses	soprano	sopranos
index	indexes (indices, scientific)	species	species
		stadium	stadiums
insigne	insignia	staff	staffs OR staves
key	keys	stimulus	stimuli
kimono	kimonos	stratum	strata
lady	ladies	studio	studios
larva	larvae	stylus	styluses

Singular	Plural	Singular	Plural
syllabus	syllabuses OR syllabi	tornado	tornadoes
symposium	symposia	torpedo	torpedoes
synopsis	synopses	turkey	turkeys
tableau	tableaus	valley	valleys
tariff	tariffs	vertebra	vertebras (verte-
tax	taxes		brae, scientific)
taxi	taxis	veto	vetoes
terminus	termini	virtuoso	virtuosos
testatrix	testatrices	volcano	volcanoes
thesaurus	thesauri OR thes-	vortex	vortexes
	auruses	wife	wives
thesis	theses	wolf	wolves
thief	thieves	woman	women
thorax	thoraxes	workman	workmen
tobacco	tobaccos	yourself	yourselves
tooth	teeth	zero	zeros
		zoo	zoos

2. Compound terms

Singular	Plural	Singular	Plural
adjutant general	adjutants general	crepe suzette	crepes suzette
aide-de-camp	aides-de-camp	daughter-in-law	daughters-in-law
ambassador at large	ambassadors at large	deputy chief of staff	deputy chiefs of staff
assistant attorney	assistant attorneys	deputy judge	deputy judges
assistant attorney general	assistant attorneys general	deputy sheriff	deputy sheriffs
assistant chief of staff	assistant chiefs of staff	eye-opener	eye-openers
assistant commissioner	assistant commissioners	follow-up	follow-ups
assistant comptroller general	assistant comptrollers general	forget-me-not	forget-me-nots
		general counsel	general counsels
assistant corporation counsel	assistant corporation counsels	get-together	get-togethers
		governor-elect	governors-elect
assistant director	assistant directors	governor general	governors general
assistant general counsel	assistant general counsels	grandmother	grandmothers
		grant-in-aid	grants-in-aid
assistant secretary	assistant secretaries	hand-me-down	hand-me-downs
assistant surgeon general	assistant surgeons general	heir at law	heirs at law
		higher-up	higher-ups
attorney at law	attorneys at law	in-law	in-laws
attorney general	attorneys general	inspector general	inspectors general
billet-doux	billets-doux	jack-in-the-pulpit	jack-in-the-pulpits
bill of fare	bills of fare	judge advocate	judge advocates
brigadier general	brigadier generals	judge advocate general	judge advocate generals
brother-in-law	brothers-in-law	lieutenant colonel	lieutenant colonels
businessman	businessmen	major general	major generals
chargé d'affaires	chargés d'affaires	man-of-the-earth	men-of-the-earth
coat of arms	coats of arms	manservant	menservants
commander in chief	commanders in chief	master at arms	masters at arms
comptroller general	comptrollers general	man buyer	men buyers
consul general	consuls general	man cook	men cooks
court-martial	courts-martial	man employee	men employees
		man-of-war	men-of-war

Singular	Plural	Singular	Plural
minister-designate	ministers-designate	sergeant at arms	sergeants at arms
mother-in-law	mothers-in-law	sergeant major	sergeants major
notary public	notaries public	shareholder	shareholders
passerby	passersby	son-in-law	sons-in-law
pick-me-up	pick-me-ups	stepchild	stepchildren
play-off	play-offs	stockholder	stockholders
postmaster general	postmasters general	storekeeper	storekeepers
president-elect	presidents-elect	surgeon general	surgeons general
prisoner of war	prisoners of war	trademark	trademarks
provost marshal	provost marshals	trade union	trade unions
provost marshal general	provost marshal generals	under secretary	under secretaries
quartermaster general	quartermasters general	vice chairman	vice chairmen
right-of-way	rights-of-way	vice president	vice presidents
runner-up	runners-up	will-o'-the-wisp	will-o'-the-wisps
salesgirl	salesgirls	woman aviator	women aviators
secretary general	secretaries general	woman student	women students
secretary-treasurer	secretary-treasurers OR	woman writer	women writers
	secretaries-treasurers	write-up	write-ups

Part IV

PART IV, "Courts," presents a brief outline of the Supreme Court, the Courts of Appeal, the District Courts of the United States, and the court system in the various states. Also included are forms of address for justices, judges, and state and municipal dignitaries.

The purpose is to acquaint the secretary with the American legal system and the hierarchy of the various courts in the United States. The American legal organization is a dual court system consisting of one Federal court system and 50 State court systems. There is some diversity among the various State systems since the jurisdiction of the courts in any state is limited by the constitution and statutes of that state.

A distinctive characteristic of the American legal system is the adversary system, which is a competitive system under which the attorneys for each side prepare and present a case for their respective clients, and the judge's role is to maintain an objective point of view.

Whether the legal secretary is in the office of an attorney, an Associate Justice, a Justice, or a Chief Judge, her duties will be concerned with legal practice, and she should have some idea of her place in the realm of law and the far-reaching significance and importance of care and accuracy in the production of every legal document. To this end, this brief section on "Courts" has been included in the book.

Courts

Characteristic of the American legal system is the dual system of law consisting of Federal laws and the laws of the 50 states. Attorneys practice law under both legal systems and represent clients in Federal and State courts. While the legal secretary will receive instructions from the attorney, she will be able to work more efficiently and intelligbly in a variety of cases if she has some understanding of the hierarchy of the American legal system. The purpose of this chapter, therefore, is to present a concise outline of the legal system of the United States.

A.   Federal Courts

The principal Federal courts of the United States are the

1. Supreme Court
2. Courts of Appeal
3. District Courts

In addition, there are courts of special or limited jurisdiction, such as the

District of Columbia Court of Appeals
District of Columbia Tax Court
Court of Claims
Court of Customs and Patent Appeals
    (Customs Court, Patent Office, and
    Tariff Commission)
Tax Court of the United States
Courts of the Territories and Insular
    Possessions

1. The *Supreme Court,* the highest court in the United States, consists of a Chief Justice and eight associate justices, all appointed by the President, with the consent of the Senate. The Supreme Court has original jurisdiction in cases concerning ambassadors, consuls, and other public ministers, and in cases where a state is a party. Primarily, it is an appellate court, with jurisdiction both as to law and to fact, subject to regulation by Congress.

The Supreme Court meets in Washington, D.C. Each year the term begins on the first Monday in October and continues in session until the requirements of its business are met. Six members constitute a quorum. Usually the Court adjourns some time during the month of June.

Subject to review by the Supreme Court are the State Courts, Court of Customs and Patent Appeals, Court of Claims, District Courts of the United States, Courts of Appeal of the United States,

Customs Courts, and Courts of the Territories and Insular Possessions.

2. The *Courts of Appeal* are intermediate appellate courts which handle appeals from the United States District Courts and some administrative bodies. Unless a case has permission to appeal to the Supreme Court, it is directed to the proper circuit. The United States is divided into 11 judicial circuits, with a United States Court of Appeals for each circuit. With the exception of the District of Columbia, each circuit includes three or more states. The number of divisions for each court of appeals varies according to the population of the circuit. Each circuit has a Circuit Judge, with additional judges assisting. Rules vary from one court to another, since each court of appeals publishes its own rules.

Ordinarily each court of appeals is divided into divisions with three judges in each division. The court may sit *en banc* with all judges present; the agreement of any two judges, however, is binding. The courts of appeal have authority to review decisions of the district courts, except in unusual circumstances where a case has been granted permission to appeal directly to the Supreme Court of the United States. Appellate procedure involves an appeal to the Court of Appeals from the decision of a United States District Court, and further appeal to the Supreme Court from the Court of Appeals.

3. The *District Courts* are frequently referred to as Federal courts. These courts have jurisdiction over civil actions arising under the Constitution, laws, or treaties of the United States, in cases where diversity of citizenship exists between the parties and where the amount in controversy exceeds $10,000.

UNITED STATES COURTS OF APPEALS JUDICIAL CIRCUITS

Judicial Circuit	*U.S. District Courts Included, District of:*
District of Columbia	Columbia
First	Maine New Hampshire Massachusetts Rhode Island Puerto Rico
Second	Vermont Connecticut northern New York southern New York

	eastern New York
	western New York
Third	New Jersey
	eastern Pennsylvania
	middle Pennsylvania
	western Pennsylvania
	Delaware
	Virgin Islands
Fourth	Maryland
	northern West Virginia
	southern West Virginia
	eastern Virginia
	western Virginia
	eastern North Carolina
	middle North Carolina
	western North Carolina
	eastern South Carolina
	western South Carolina
Fifth	northern Georgia
	middle Georgia
	southern Georgia
	northern Florida
	southern Florida
	northern Alabama
	middle Alabama
	southern Alabama
	northern Mississippi
	southern Mississippi
	eastern Louisiana
	western Louisiana
	northern Texas
	southern Texas
	western Texas
	Canal Zone
Sixth	northern Ohio
	southern Ohio
	eastern Michigan
	western Michigan
	eastern Kentucky
	western Kentucky
	eastern Tennessee
	middle Tennessee
	western Tennessee
Seventh	northern Indiana
	southern Indiana

	northern Illinois
	eastern Illinois
	southern Illinois
	eastern Wisconsin
	western Wisconsin
Eighth	Minnesota
	northern Iowa
	southern Iowa
	eastern Missouri
	western Missouri
	eastern Arkansas
	western Arkansas
	Nebraska
	North Dakota
	South Dakota
Ninth	northern California
	southern California
	Oregon
	Nevada
	Montana
	eastern Washington
	western Washington
	Idaho
	Arizona
	Alaska
	Hawaii
	Territory of Guam
Tenth	Colorado
	Wyoming
	Utah
	Kansas
	eastern Oklahoma
	western Oklahoma
	northern Oklahoma
	New Mexico

Each state has at least one district court and some larger states have several district courts. There is at least one department in each district court and as many as 24 departments in some district courts. For each department, there is one judge and a separate courtroom, with some districts having several judges wherein the senior judge acts as chief judge.

Concerning the Federal District Courts, House Document No. 180 ("The United States Courts"), published by the United States Government Printing Office, states: "There are 92 of these courts, 87 in the 50 States, including Alaska and Hawaii and one each in the District of Columbia, the Canal Zone, Guam, Puerto Rico, and the Virgin Islands."

In regard to court procedure, the Federal courts and most State courts have similar rules of practice and procedure. A number of states have modeled their rules on the Federal court rules. Following is a brief outline of the procedure generally followed by most courts:

Contested cases:

1. Filing the complaint and issuance of summons
2. Service of summons and complaint
3. Appearance
4. Depositions
5. Setting for trial
6. Pretrial
7. Notice of trial
8. Subpenas
9. Preparation of jury instructions
10. Trial
11. Judgment
12. Cost bill
13. Notice of entry of judgment
14. Motion for new trial and notice of ruling
15. Recording abstract of judgment
16. Execution
17. Supplementary proceedings
18. New trial
19. Appeal

Uncontested cases:

1. Filing the complaint and issuance of summons
2. Service of summons and complaint
3. Appearance
4. Default entry
5. Hearing
6. Judgment
7. Recording abstract of judgment
8. Execution
9. Supplementary proceedings

The United States District Courts are the principal trial courts in the United States court system. The types of cases handled in these courts are generally civil, criminal, and bankruptcy.

In civil actions, the district courts have original jurisdiction in the following areas:

1. Federal questions in general
2. Citizenship of parties

3. Admiralty, maritime, and prize cases
4. Agriculture
5. Arbitration
6. Air pollution control
7. Attachment or sequestration; garnishment
8. Atomic energy; idemnification for nuclear incidents
9. Bankruptcy
10. Banks and other corporations
11. Bonds executed under Federal statutes
12. Civil rights
13. Commerce and anti-trust
14. Conservation
15. Customs
16. Electronic product radiation
17. Eminent domain
18. Federal property procurement and disposition
19. Fines, penalties, forfeitures, seizures
20. Flood insurance
21. Food, drugs, and cosmetics
22. Habeas corpus
23. Indians
24. Internal revenue
25. International claims; action for return of property
26. Interpleader actions involving money or property of value of $500 or more claimed by citizens of different states
27. Interstate land sales
28. Intoxicating liquors
29. Labor
30. Livestock and poultry; protection against introduction and dissemination of diseases
31. Mandamus; action to compel officer or employee of United States to perform duty
32. Meat inspection
33. Motor vehicle standards
34. Narcotic addicts; civil commitment
35. Natural gas pipelines
36. Patents, copyrights, trademarks, unfair competition
37. Postal matters
38. Poultry and poultry products inspection
39. Railroads
40. Real property; minerals
41. Small business controversies
42. Small business investment companies; forfeitures of rights, privileges, and franchises; restraining orders
43. State taxes
44. Telegraphs, telephones, and radio
45. Transportation

46. United States as plaintiff generally
47. United States as defendant generally
48. Water pollution, interstate compacts

The district courts are concerned with review and enforcement of administrative orders in the following areas:

1. Judicial review of actions of administrative agencies
2. Administrator of Federal Aviation Agency
3. Civil Aeronautics Board
4. Civil Service Commission
5. Commissioner of Education
6. Federal Communications Commission
7. Federal Deposit Insurance Corporation
8. Federal Home Loan Bank Board
9. Federal Maritime Commission
10. Federal Petroleum Board
11. Federal Power Commission
12. Federal Savings and Loan Insurance Corporation
13. Federal Trade Commission
14. Interstate Commerce Commission
15. Patents and Trademarks (orders concerning)
16. Railroad and air transport adjustment and arbitration boards; Railroad Retirement Board
17. Secretary of Agriculture
18. Secretary of the Army; Chief of Engineers
19. Secretary of Health, Education, and Welfare
20. Secretary of the Interior
21. Secretary of Labor
22. Deputy Commissioner
23. Secretary of Transportation
24. Secretary of the Treasury
25. Securities and Exchange Commission
26. Small Business Administration
27. Tariff Commission
28. War contract termination claims
29. Enforcement of subpenas

The district courts have original jurisdiction in criminal cases, as follows:

1. All offenses against the laws of the United States; criminal proceedings against Federal officers in State court removed to Federal court
2. United States Magistrates

The judicial circuit of the District of Columbia has original jurisdiction:

1. Same as other U.S. District Courts
2. Certain actions involving (a) alien property; (b) Commissioner of Patents; (c) Hoover Dam; (d) Library of Congress Trust Fund; (e) narcotic addicts; (f) nonresident patentees; (g) Secretary of the Interior; (h) voting rights
3. General jurisdiction
4. Outer Continental Shelf, leases, determinations of Secretary of Interior
5. Naturalization
6. Attachment and garnishment
7. Business corporations
8. Change of name
9. Education; removal of members of Board of Education
10. Elections; recount of votes
11. Eminent domain
12. Habeas corpus
13. Partition and assignment of dower
14. Probate proceedings
15. Quieting title
16. Quo warranto

B.   State Courts

In the United States there are actually 51 court systems: one Federal court and 50 State court systems. The jurisdiction of the courts in a state is in accordance with the constitution and statutes of that state; consequently, the organization of the various State courts is not uniform. Each state has trial courts or courts of original jurisdiction, an intermediate court of appeals, specialized courts, and a court of last resort. In the majority of the states, the Supreme Court is the highest court; in other states, the highest court may be the Court of Appeals, Justice Court, the Supreme Judicial Court, or the Supreme Court of Appeals.

The legal secretary is concerned with typing legal documents. In the preparation of documents, there are more similarities than differences in rules in the various states, counties, or municipalities. An efficient legal secretary should have no difficulty in adapting her legal experience in one situation to the preparation of legal documents in another area. The greatest difference from state to state is in the form of the caption. The principal point is to maintain consistency within a particular geographical area.

The hierarchy of the court system in the various states of the United States is as follows:

State	Names of Courts
State	*Names of Courts*
Alabama	Supreme Court
	Court of Appeals
	Circuit Courts
	Courts of Probate
	County Courts
	Justice Courts
	Recorders' Courts
Alaska	Supreme Court
	Superior Courts
	District Magistrate Courts
	Deputy Magistrate Courts
Arizona	Supreme Court
	Superior Courts
	Justice Courts
	Police Courts
Arkansas	Supreme Court
	Chancery & Probate Courts
	Circuit Courts
	County Courts
	Courts of Common Pleas
	Justice Courts
	Municipal Courts
	Police Courts
California	Supreme Court
	District Courts of Appeal
	Superior Courts
	Municipal Courts
	Justice Courts
Colorado	Supreme Court
	District Courts
	County Courts
	Superior Court
	Juvenile Court
	Municipal Courts
	Justice Courts
	Small Claims Courts
	Police Magistrate Courts
Connecticut	Supreme Court of Errors
	Superior Court
	Court of Common Pleas
	Circuit Court
	Juvenile Court
	Probate Courts
Delaware	Supreme Court
	Court of Chancery
	Superior Court
	Courts of Common Pleas
	Family Court
	Municipal Courts
	Justice Courts
Florida	Supreme Court
	District Courts of Appeal
	Circuit Courts
	Civil Courts of Record
	Criminal Courts of Record
	Civil and Criminal Courts of Record
	County Judges' Courts
	Court of Crimes
	Juvenile & Domestic Relations Courts
	Small Claims Courts
	Justice Courts
	Municipal Courts
	Metropolitan Courts
Georgia	Supreme Court
	Court of Appeals
	Superior Courts
	Courts of Ordinary and Probate
	County Courts
	Municipal Courts
	City Courts
	Justice Courts
	Juvenile Courts
Hawaii	Supreme Court
	Circuit Court
	District Courts
Idaho	Supreme Court
	District Courts
	Probate Courts
	Justice Courts
	Municipal Courts
Illinois	Supreme Court
	Appellate Courts
	Circuit Courts
	Superior Court
	City Courts
	County Courts
	Court of Claims
	Probate Courts
	Municipal Courts
	Town Courts
	Village Courts
	Police Courts
	Justice Courts
Indiana	Supreme Court
	Appellate Court
	Circuit Courts
	Superior Courts
	Criminal Courts
	Probate Courts
	Municipal Courts
	Justice Courts
	Magistrates' Courts
	Juvenile Courts

Iowa	Supreme Court		Court of Claims
	District Courts		Superior Court
	Superior Courts		Recorder's Court
	Municipal Courts		Probate Courts
	Justice Courts		Common Pleas Court
	Mayors' Courts		Municipal Courts
	Police Courts		Justice Courts
Kansas	Supreme Court	Minnesota	Supreme Court
	District Courts		District Courts
	Probate Courts		Probate Courts
	Court of Common Pleas		Municipal Courts
	City Courts		Justice Courts
	County Courts	Mississippi	Supreme Court
	Justice Courts		Chancery Courts
	Police Courts		Circuit Courts
	Juvenile Courts		County Courts
Kentucky	Court of Appeals		City Courts
	Circuit Courts		Justice Courts
	Quarterly Courts	Missouri	Supreme Court
	County Courts		Courts of Appeals
	Justice Courts		Circuit Courts
	Police Courts		Courts of Common Pleas
Louisiana	Supreme Court		Probate Courts
	Courts of Appeal		Court of Criminal Corrections
	District Courts		Magistrates' Courts
	City Courts		Municipal Courts
	Juvenile Courts	Montana	Supreme Court
	Mayors' Courts		District Courts
	Justice Courts		Municipal Courts
	Traffic Court		Justice Courts
	Family Court		Police Courts
	Municipal Court	Nebraska	Supreme Court
Maine	Supreme Judicial Court		District Courts
	Superior Court		County Courts
	Probate Courts		Municipal Courts
	District Courts		Juvenile Courts
	Trial Justices		Justice Courts
Maryland	Court of Appeals		Workmen's Compensation Court
	Circuit Courts		Court of Industrial Relations
	Courts of Baltimore City		
	Orphans' Courts		
	People's Courts	Nevada	Supreme Court
	Municipal Court		District Courts
	Trial Magistrates		Municipal Courts
Massachusetts	Supreme Judicial Court		Justice Courts
	Superior Court	New Hampshire	Supreme Court
	Land Court		Superior Courts
	Probate Courts		Probate Courts
	Municipal Courts		Municipal Courts
	District Courts	New Jersey	Supreme Court
	Juvenile Court		Appellate Division of Superior Court
Michigan	Supreme Court		Superior Court
	Circuit Courts		

County Courts
County District Courts
Juvenile & Domestic Relations
   Court
Municipal Court

New Mexico
Supreme Court
District Courts
Probate Courts
Justice Courts

New York
Court of Appeals
Supreme Courts
County Courts (except in the
   City of New York)
Surrogates' Courts
Court of Claims
City Courts (some cities)
Civil Court of the City of New
   York
Criminal Court of the City of
   New York
Justice Courts
Courts of Special Sessions
Other Courts
   Municipal Courts
   Police Courts
   Recorders' Courts

North Carolina
Supreme Court
Superior Courts
County Courts
Juvenile Courts
City Courts
Domestic Relations Courts
Recorders' Courts
Justice Courts
Mayors' and Police Courts

North Dakota
Supreme Court
District Courts
County Courts
Justice Courts
Police Magistrates

Ohio
Supreme Court
Courts of Appeals
Courts of Common Pleas
Probate Courts
Juvenile Courts
Municipal Courts
County Courts
Police Court

Oklahoma
Supreme Court
Court of Criminal Appeals
District Courts
Superior Courts
County Courts

Courts of Common Pleas
Juvenile Courts
Justice Courts

Oregon
Supreme Court
Circuit Courts
Tax Courts
District Courts
County Courts
Justice Courts
Municipal Courts

Pennsylvania
Supreme Court
Superior Court
Common Pleas Courts
County Courts
Orphans' Courts
Magistrates' Courts

Puerto Rico
Supreme Court
Superior Court
District Court
Justice Courts

Rhode Island
Supreme Court
Superior Court
District Courts
Probate Courts
Juvenile Court
Police Court

South Carolina
Supreme Court
Circuit Courts
County Courts
Probate Courts
Magistrates' Courts
Civil & Criminal Courts
City Recorders' Courts
Juvenile & Domestic Relations
   Courts

South Dakota
Supreme Court
Circuit Courts
County Courts
Municipal Courts
Justice Courts

Tennessee
Supreme Courts
Court of Appeals
Chancery Courts
Circuit Courts
Criminal Courts
County Courts
Courts of General Sessions
Municipal Courts
Juvenile Courts

Texas
Supreme Court
Court of Criminal Appeals
Court of Civil Appeals
District Courts

		Washington	Supreme Court
	County Courts		Superior Courts
	Courts of Domestic Relations		Justice Courts
	Justice Courts		Municipal Courts
Utah	Supreme Court	West Virginia	Supreme Court of Appeals
	District Courts		Circuit Courts
	Juvenile Courts		Court of Claims
	City Courts		Common Pleas Court
	Justice Courts		Criminal Courts
Vermont	Supreme Court		Intermediate Courts
	County Courts		Domestic Relations Court
	Probate Courts		County Courts
	Municipal Courts		Justice Courts
	Justice Courts	Wisconsin	Supreme Court
Virginia	Supreme Court of Appeals		Circuit Courts
	Circuit Courts		County Courts
	Corporation and Hustings		Justice Courts
	Courts		Police Justices
	Juvenile and Domestic Rela-	Wyoming	Supreme Court
	tions Courts		District Courts
	County and Municipal Courts		Justice Courts

C.   Forms of Address for Justices and Judges

Person and Address	Salutation

UNITED STATES:

Chief Justice

The Honorable (name)	Sir
Chief Justice of the United States	Dear Sir
Washington, D.C. 20544	Dear Mr. Chief Justice
	Dear Mr. Chief Justice (name)
The Chief Justice of the	My dear Mr. Chief Justice
United States	My dear Mr. Chief Justice (name)
Washington, D.C. 20544	

Associate Justice

The Honorable (name)	Sir
Associate Justice of the	Dear Sir
Supreme Court	Dear Mr. Justice
Washington, D.C. 20544	Dear Mr. Justice (name)
	My dear Mr. Justice
The Honorable (name)	My dear Mr. Justice (name)
Justice	
Supreme Court of the	
United States	
Washington, D.C. 20544	

DISTRICT COURT:

Chief Judge

The Honorable (name)	Sir
Chief Judge of the United States	Dear Sir
District Court for the	Dear Chief Justice
Southern District of New York	Dear Chief Justice (name)
New York, N.Y. 10014	My dear Chief Justice
	My dear Chief Justice (name)

Judge

The Honorable (name)	Sir
Judge, United States District Court	Dear Sir
for the Southern District of	Dear Judge
New York	Dear Judge (name)
New York, N.Y. 10014	My dear Judge
	My dear Judge (name)

STATE SUPREME COURT:

Chief Justice

The Honorable (name)	Sir
Chief Justice	Dear Sir
California Supreme Court	Dear Chief Justice
Sacramento, California 95614	Dear Chief Justice (name)
	My dear Chief Justice
The Chief Justice	My dear Chief Justice (name)
California Supreme Court	
Sacramento, California 95614	

Justice

The Honorable (name)	Sir
Associate Justice of the	Dear Sir
Iowa Supreme Court	Dear Mr. Justice
Des Moines, Iowa 50309	Dear Mr. Justice (name)
	My dear Mr. Justice
The Honorable (name)	My dear Mr. Justice (name)
Justice	
Iowa Supreme Court	
Des Moines, Iowa 50309	

COURT OF APPEALS:

Chief Judge

The Honorable (name)	Sir
Chief Judge of the Court of	Dear Sir
Appeals of the State of	Dear Chief Judge (name)
New York	My dear Chief Judge
Albany, New York 12207	My dear Chief Judge (name)

Associate Judge

The Honorable (name)	Sir
Associate Judge, Court of	Dear Sir
Appeals of the State of	Dear Judge
New York	Dear Judge (name)
Albany, New York 12207	My dear Judge
	My dear Judge (name)

Presiding Justice

The Honorable (name)	Sir
Presiding Justice, Appellate	Dear Sir
Division, First Judicial	Dear Mr. Presiding Justice
Department	Dear Mr. Presiding Justice (name)
New York Supreme Court	My dear Mr. Presiding Justice
New York, N.Y. 10014	My dear Mr. Presiding Justice (name)

Associate Justice

The Honorable (name)	Sir
Associate Justice	Dear Sir
Appellate Division	Dear Mr. Justice
First Judicial Department	Dear Mr. Justice (name)
New York Supreme Court	My dear Mr. Justice
New York, N.Y. 10007	My dear Mr. Justice (name)
The Honorable (name)	Sir
Justice of the District	Dear Sir
Court of Appeals	Dear Mr. Justice
Court of Appeals Building	Dear Mr. Justice (name)
San Diego, California 92101	My dear Mr. Justice
	My dear Mr. Justice (name)

SUPERIOR COURT

The Honorable (name)	Sir
Judge of the Superior Court	Dear Sir
Superior Court Building	Dear Judge (name)
Tacoma, Washington 98660	My dear Judge (name)

OTHER COURTS

Surrogate

The Honorable (name)	Sir
Surrogate's Court	Dear Sir
Nassau County	Dear Mr. Surrogate
Mineola, New York 11501	Dear Mr. Surrogate (name)
	My dear Mr. Surrogate
	My dear Mr. Surrogate (name)

Court Clerk

Thomas J. Burke, Esq.	Sir
United States District Court	Dear Sir

Office of the Clerk   Dear Mr. Burke
Eastern District of New York   My dear Mr. Burke
Cadman Plaza East
Brooklyn, New York 11201

John F. Fenton, Esq.   Sir
Clerk of the Court of Appeals   Dear Sir
    of the State of New York   Dear Mr. Fenton
Albany, New York 12207   My dear Mr. Fenton

District Attorney
Honorable (name)   Sir
District Attorney, New York   Dear Sir
    County   Dear Mr. (name)
New York, N.Y. 10013   My dear Mr. (name)

GOVERNOR

The Honorable (name)   Dear Governor
Governor of the State of Pennsylvania   Dear Governor (name)
The Capitol   My dear Governor
Harrisburg, Pennsylvania 17101   My dear Governor (name)

MAYOR

The Honorable (name)   Dear Mayor
Mayor of the City of Chicago   Dear Mayor (name)
City Hall   My dear Mayor
Chicago, Illinois 60602   My dear Mayor (name)

COUNCILMAN

Honorable (name)   Dear Councilman
The Council of The City of   Dear Councilman (name)
    New York   My dear Councilman
City Hall   My dear Councilman (name)
New York, N.Y. 10007

COMMISSIONER

Honorable (name)   Dear Commissioner
The Council of the City of   Dear Commissioner (name)
    New York   My dear Commissioner
City Hall   My dear Commissioner (name)
New York, N.Y. 10007

ATTORNEY

Thomas J. Burke, Esq.   Dear Sir
Patent Counsel   Dear Mr. Burke
(name) Corporation   My dear Mr. Burke
10889 Wilshire Blvd.

Los Angeles, California 90024

Note: In all of the preceding situations, an acceptable complimentary close would be:

Very truly yours
(or)
Sincerely yours

Part V

PART V presents miscellaneous legal forms which are germane to any law office, whether a one-man office, a giant legal partnership, or the legal department of a large corporation.

The forms included are the ones frequently used by the secretary as an addendum to legal documents, forms utilized in various office routines, and certain forms which the secretary may have the responsibility for organizing and executing.

Legal documents are tailor-made to suit the client and the particular case at hand, for which instruments the attorney is responsible, and examples of which forms are provided in lawyers' desk books. Some of these forms, of course, are deliberately omitted here since this book is designed especially for the legal secretary.

Reference to forms included in Part V should eliminate needless waste of time and energy on the part of the secretary. Every legal secretary will have occasion to refer to these forms again and again, and instead of having to shuffle through shelves of papers when looking for a form of acknowledgment, verification, affidavit of service, or other commonly used form, she will simply have to refer to this book.

32 Model Forms for the Legal Secretary

In selecting the legal forms for inclusion in this chapter, the principal consideration was frequency of use. Whether the work of the legal secretary is concerned with general practice, corporation law, litigation, or tax law, she will have to make use of many of these forms in connection with legal papers. Having such frequently used forms readily accessible will shorten the time of the secretary in completing a legal instrument. While an attorney may spend hours and even days in the preparation of a legal document, he expects the secretary to complete the document by typing in the appropriate clauses, and usually time is of the essence.

A. Acknowledgment

It is the duty of a notary public to acknowledge the execution of documents and to attest the execution of some documents under oath, such as affidavits and verified pleadings. In witnessing a document, it is not necessary that the notary know the contents thereof. The notary may ask if the signer knows the contents, if he is signing of his own free will, and he may also ask for proof that the person signing is the person described in the legal instrument.

Sample forms of the various types of acknowledgments are outlined below:

1. Individual acknowledgment

STATE OF   )
                                   :SS.:
COUNTY OF   )

On the   day of   , 19   , before me personally came   (name of person)   to me known to be the individual described in and who executed the foregoing instrument, and (he, she) acknowledged to me that (he, she) executed the same.

_____
Notary Public

2. Corporate acknowledgment

STATE OF   )
                                   :SS.:
COUNTY OF   )

On the   day of   , 19   , before me personally came   (name of person)   to me known who, being by me duly sworn, did depose and say that (he,

she) resides at   , that (he, she) is the
      (office)   of   (name of corporation)   , the
corporation described in and which executed the foregoing instrument; that (he, she) knows the seal of said corporation; that the seal affixed to said instrument is such corporate seal; that it was so affixed by order of the board of directors of said corporation, and that (he, she) signed (his, her) name thereto by like order.

_____
Notary Public

3. Acknowledgment for two officers of a corporation

STATE OF   )
                    :SS.:
COUNTY OF   )

I, the undersigned, a Notary Public in and for the jurisdiction aforesaid, do HEREBY CERTIFY that before me personally appeared   (name of person)   and   (name of person)   Vice President and   Secretary, respectively, of   (name of corporation)   , a corporation organized under the laws of the State of (name of State),   duly qualified to do business in the State of (name of other State), to me known to be the persons described in and who executed the foregoing instrument bearing date as of the   day of   , 19   , and who severally acknowledged the execution thereof to be their free act and deed as such officers, for the uses and purposes therein mentioned, that they had full authority to execute said instrument on behalf of said corporation, and that they affixed thereto the official seal of said corporation.

WITNESS my hand and official seal in the County and State aforesaid, this   day of   , 19

_____
Notary Public

4. Alternate form of corporate acknowledgment

STATE OF   )
                    :SS.:
COUNTY OF   )

BEFORE ME, the undersigned authority in and for the said County, on this day personally appeared   (name of person), (office held)   of   (name of corporation), (a, an) (state in which incorporated)   corporation, known to me to be the person whose name is subscribed to the foregoing instrument, and (he, she) acknowledged to me that the same was the act of said   (name of corporation),   and that (he, she) executed the same as the act of such corporation for the purposes and considerations therein expressed in the capacity therein stated.

GIVEN UNDER MY HAND AND SEAL OF OFFICE THIS DAY OF   , 19

—————————————

Notary Public

5. Acknowledgment for witness to an instrument

STATE OF   )
                            :SS.:
COUNTY OF   )

On the   day of   , 19   , before me personally came   (name of witness)   , the subscribing witness to the foregoing instrument, with whom I am personally acquainted, who, being by me duly sworn, did depose and say that (he, she) resides at   , that (he, she) knows   (name of person)   to be the individual described in and who executed the foregoing instrument; that (he, she), said subscribing witness, was present and saw   (name of person)   execute the same; and that (he, she), said witness, at the same time subscribed (his, her) name as witness thereto.

—————————————

Notary Public

B.   Affidavit of Service

Affidavits of service are usually found on litigation backs and on the back of a summons or other notice. The original affidavit of service is affixed to any original paper where proof of service is required. All affidavits must have a *venue* (STATE OF   , COUNTY OF   ) and a *jurat* (sworn to before me this   day of   , 19   ).

1. Service by mail upon one attorney

STATE OF   )
                            :SS.:
COUNTY OF   )

(name of deponent)   being duly sworn, deposes and says, that deponent is not a party to the action, is over 18 years of age and resides at   ; that on the   day

of   19   , deponent served the within   (name of document)   upon   attorney
for   in this action, at   , the address designated by said attorney for that purpose, by depositing a true copy of
same enclosed in a postpaid properly addressed wrapper in (a post
office, an official depository) under the exclusive care and custody
of the United States Post Office Department within the State of

_____

Sworn to before me
this   day of
              , 19

_____

Notary Public

2. Affidavit of service upon two or more attorneys

AFFIDA VIT OF SER VICE BY MAIL

STATE OF   )
                       :SS.:
COUNTY OF   )

              (name of deponent)   being duly sworn, deposes
and says that deponent is not a party to the action, is over 18 years
of age, and resides at   ; that on the   day
of   , 19   , deponent served the
within   (name of document)   upon
                       (name of attorney
                          address)
                          and
                       (name of attorney
                          address)
attorneys for   in this action, at the addresses designated by said attorneys for that purpose, by depositing a true copy
of same enclosed in a postpaid, properly addressed wrapper in (a
post office, an official depository) under the exclusive care and
custody of the United States Post Office Department within the
State of

_____

Sworn to before me
this   day of
19

_____

Notary Public

3. Personal service

STATE OF   )
                            :SS.:
COUNTY OF   )

(name of deponent)   being duly sworn, deposes and says, that deponent is not a party to the action, is over 18 years of age and resides at   ; that on the   day of   , 19   , at   (place of service)   , deponent served the within   (name of document) upon   (name of party served)   the   herein, by delivering a true copy thereof to (her, him) personally. Deponent knew the person so served to be the person mentioned and described in said papers as the   therein.

_____

Sworn to before
me this   day
of   , 19

_____

Notary Public

4. Substituted service

STATE OF   )
                            :SS.:
COUNTY OF   )

(name of deponent)   , being duly sworn, deposes and says:
I am over the age of 18 years, not a party to this action, and reside at   . On   , 19   , I served the annexed   (name of document)   in the above-entitled action upon the defendant   (name)   at   (address)   , that being the residence (or business) address of the defendant, by depositing the same in the mail chute maintained by the United States Post Office at   , properly enclosed and sealed in a post-paid wrapper addressed to the said defendant at the aforementioned address, and by leaving a copy of said (name of document) at the residence (or business) address of said defendant at
with   [name (wife, husband, sister, brother, mother, etc.)] [or any other description showing the person to be of suitable age]
                            OR
by affixing to the outer door of defendant's residence   (business address)   a copy of said   (name of document).

Sworn to before me
this   day of
                , 19

_____

Notary Public

5. Matrimonial

STATE OF   )
                           :SS.:
COUNTY OF   )

     (name of deponent)   , being duly sworn, deposes
and says that he resides at   ; that he is over 18 years of
age and is not a party to the   within action.

     That on the   day of   , 19 , at
                , deponent served the   in the above action
upon   , the defendant therein named, by delivering to
and leaving with him personally a true copy thereof.

     Deponent further says that at the time of such service, he
knew the person served as aforesaid to be the same person named
and described in said   as the defendant in this action,
and that the sources of deponent's knowledge and the grounds of his
belief as to the identity of said person so served are   (papers,
photo, etc. annexed).

     Deponent further says that said Summons served as aforesaid
had the words "Action for Separation" legibly written upon the face
thereof.

_____

Sworn to before me
this   day of
                , 19

_____

Notary Public

C. Affidavit of Title

STATE OF   )
                           :SS.:
COUNTY OF   )

     being duly sworn, deposes and says that (he,
she) is one of the sellers of premises   in the town
of   , County of   , City and State

of   , said premises being known and designated as

The deponent has not been known by any other name or names for more than   years from the date hereof; that this affidavit is made with knowledge that   (title co.)   relies on the statements herein made for the purpose of insuring title.

_____

Sworn to before
me this   day of
             19

_____

Notary Public

D. Attorney's Affirmation

[an attorney may use an "affirmation"
in lieu of an "affidavit"]

STATE OF   )
                          :SS.:
COUNTY OF   )

The undersigned, being an attorney duly admitted to practice in the courts of the State of   shows: that (he, she)

the attorney(s) of record, or an attorney acting as of counsel with the attorney of record, for the   in the within action; that (he, she) has read the foregoing

and knows the contents thereof; that the same is true to (his, her) own knowledge, except as to those matters therein stated to be alleged upon information and belief, and that as to those matters (he, she) believes them to be true. (He, She) further states that the reason this affirmation is made by (him, her) and not by the

The grounds of (his, her) belief and sources of information as to all matters not stated upon (his, her) knowledge are as follows:

The undersigned affirms that the foregoing statements are true, under the penalties of perjury, pursuant to 2106 CPLR.

_____

Signature

_____

Typed

Dated: _____

[alternate form of attorney's affirmation]

STATE OF   )
                             :SS.:
COUNTY OF   )

         (attorney's name)   , an attorney at law, duly admitted to practice in the State of   , hereby affirms that the foregoing statement is true under penalty of perjury.

                                 _____

                                   Attorney's name
                                 Office & P.O Address

DATED: _____

            _____ day of _____ 19 ____

E.   Attorney's Certification

STATE OF   )
                             :SS.:
COUNTY OF   )

    The undersigned attorney certifies, pursuant to Section 2105 CPLR, that the within has been compared by the undersigned with the original on file in the office of   and found to be a true and complete copy.

                                 _____

                                   Signature

                                 _____

                                   Typed

DATED: _____

F.   Bill for Services Rendered

                                               (date of bill)

(name of client
  address of client)

                        –In Account With–

                                   (name of attorney
                                    address of attorney)

For Professional Services Rendered

$

(list of services)
(dates of services)

Disbursements:

(list of disbursements) $

TOTAL $_____

G.   Closing Statement on Sale of House

[sample form]

Premises: _____

Seller: _____

Buyer: _____

Held at: Address: _____

_____

Date: _____

Present: [list all persons at closing]

Due to Seller:
   Purchase price, etc.
   Seller's credits:

Buyer's Credits:

Balance, Paid as Follows:

Expenses:

H. Consent to Change of Attorneys

STATE OF   )
                             :SS.:
COUNTY OF   )

---X

TITLE OF ACTION   CONSENT

---X

IT IS HEREBY CONSENTED that the attorneys of record for   (plaintiff or defendant)   be changed, and that   (new attorneys)   of   (address)   be substituted as attorneys for said   (plaintiff or defendant)   in the above entitled action in place and stead of   (attorneys of record)   of   (address) Asheville

DATED: _____
                                    Client

                          _____
                                Attorneys of Record

                          _____
                                New Attorneys

Acknowledgment of Client

I. Notice of Consent to Change of Attorneys

STATE OF   )
                             :SS.:
COUNTY OF   )

---X

TITLE OF ACTION   CONSENT

---X

PLEASE TAKE NOTICE that, pursuant to Section 321 of the

Civil Practice Law and Rules, the attorney of record for the (plaintiffs, defendants) is changed, and that we have been substituted as attorneys for   , the (plaintiffs, defendants) above named by Consent, filed with the Clerk of this Court on the   day of   19 , and that we appear for the said (plaintiffs, defendants) and demand that all papers in this action be served upon us at our office at   County of   , City and State of

DATED:

_____

(new attorney)
Office & P.O. Address

TO:

Name of Other Attorney
Address

J.   Memorandum Enclosing Newspaper Clipping or Report

DATE:

NAME OF FIRM
ADDRESS

Tel. No.

_____

Enclosure Memo

To:
Re:

Herewith the following:

(e.g., Copy of article in *The Wall Street Journal,* of (date)

(alternate paragraph)

As per our telephone conversation, I am enclosing herewith information concerning the above. If you wish to pursue it, I will bring the details up to date.

(NAME OF FIRM)

By_____

K. Payment of Physician's Fee by Attorney

Address of Patient

Date of Authorization

Name of Doctor
Address of Doctor

    I,   (name of patient)   , in consideration of medical services rendered by   (name of doctor)   for injuries sustained in an accident which occurred on   (date)   and for treatment of same, DO HEREBY AUTHORIZE   (name of attorney)   to deduct and pay over to my doctor aforementioned the sum of $, out of any monies that may become payable by reason of the claim, suit, or settlement brought to recover damages.

_____

(patient)

Witnessed by

_____

Address of Attorney:

_____

_____

L. Power of Attorney

POWER OF ATTORNEY

    KNOW ALL MEN BY THESE PRESENTS, that
_____ o f
_____, County of
_____ in the State of
_____ has made, constituted, and appointed, and BY THESE PRESENTS does make, constitute, and appoint _____, of the City of
_____, County of
_____, State of
_____, my true and lawful attorney, for me and in my name, place and stead to   (state powers given)   , giving and granting unto   (name of person appointed)   , said attorney, full power and authority to do

and perform all and every act and thing whatsoever requisite and necessary to be done in and about the premises, as fully, to all intents and purposes, as I might or could do if personally present at the doing thereof, with full power of substitution and revocation, hereby ratifying and confirming all that (name of person appointed) , said attorney, or (her, his) substitute shall lawfully do or cause to be done by virtue thereof.

IN TESTIMONY WHEREOF, I have hereunto set my hand and seal this day of , 19

          _____(L.S.)

                    Signature

(Witness, if desired
or required)

M.   Retainer   [sample]

TO: [name of attorney(s)]
     address

RETAINER

The undersigned (name of client) residing at (street, City, and State), hereby retains the firm of (attorneys) to prosecute or adjust a claim for damages arising out of the death of (name of husband) ,the husband of the undersigned, which death occurred as a result of an airplane accident in or about the City of (City and State), on (date of accident).

The undersigned hereby grants to the firm of (attorneys) exclusive right to take all legal steps necessary and appropriate to enforce any claim she may have as widow, or as a legal representative of the estate of her deceased husband, and agrees not to settle in either capacity any claims she may have arising out of the aforementioned accident without the written consent of (attorneys).

In consideration of the services rendered or to be rendered by you, the undersigned agrees to pay you an amount as directed by a Court of competent jurisdiction on any infant's claim, and you are authorized to retain out of any monies that may come into your hand by reason of the above referred to claim:

One-third of any recovery, whether by
settlement or otherwise.

Such percentage shall be computed on the net sum recovered after deducting taxable costs and disbursements, including expenses for expert testimony, investigative or other services properly chargeable to the enforcement of the claim or the prosecution of this action.

Provided, that in the event extraordinary services are required, you may apply to the Court for greater compensation pursuant to the Special Rules of the Appellate Division regulating the conduct of Attorneys.

It is understood that your obligations under this retainer are subject to the results of your initial investigation of the facts surrounding the accident, and it is agreed by me that, if, following your initial investigation of the facts, you in your own judgment conclude that you do not wish to represent me, then you may notify me in writing of such decision, and this retainer will thereafter be of no further force and effect. It is understood that you will make every attempt to make an early determination as to whether you intend to proceed with the representation in accordance with this retainer.

DATED:

_____
                                    Name of Client

Witness: _____

_____
     (print name of witness)

Address: _____

_____

N.   Retainer Statement Filed Nunc Pro Tunc

(This type of affidavit is used when Retainer Statement to Judicial Conference has been overlooked.) [Sample as follows:]

(name of attorney)   Esq., being duly sworn, deposes and says that he is an attorney-at-law and a member of the firm of   attorneys for   ,the plaintiff herein.

That he makes this affidavit to explain the unintentional late filing of a Retainer Statement to the Judicial Conference of the State of

That after deponent was consulted about the claim, and the retainer signed, there was a   (reason for late filing)   and therefore the Retainer Statement to the Judicial Conference was overlooked.

WHEREFORE, deponent respectfully requests that the statement be accepted for filing nunc pro tunc.

_____
                                    Attorney

Sworn to before
me this   day of
          , 19

O. Verification

A verification is a sworn statement that the information contained in a pleading paper is true. Some states have a statutory requirement that certain papers be verified. The papers commonly verified are complaints, answers, petitions, and bills of particulars. The verification is usually made by a party to the action, but a party's agent or attorney may verify a pleading. The lawyer indicates who is to make the verification.

1. Individual verification

STATE OF   )
                      :SS.:
COUNTY OF   )

             (name of person)   , being duly sworn, deposes and says that deponent is   , the   in the within action; that deponent   has read the foregoing   and knows the contents thereof; that the same is true to deponent's own knowledge, except as to the matters therein stated to be alleged upon information and belief, and as to those matters deponent believes it to be true.

_____

Sworn to before
me this   day of
          , 19

_____

2. Corporate verification

STATE OF   )
                      :SS.:
COUNTY OF   )

             (name of person)   being duly sworn, deposes and

says that deponent is the   (office held)   of   (name
of corporation)   ,the Corporation named in the within action;
that deponent has read the foregoing   (name of document)
and knows the contents thereof; and that the same is true to
deponent's own knowledge, except as to the matters therein stated
to be alleged upon information and belief, and as to those matters
deponent believes it to be true.

This verification is made by deponent because   is
a   corporation. Deponent is an officer thereof, to wit,
its   . The grounds of deponent's belief as to all matters
not stated upon deponent's knowledge are as follows:

_____

Sworn to before me
this   day of
          , 19

_____

3. Attorney's verification

STATE OF   )
                            :SS.:
COUNTY OF   )

          (name)   being duly sworn, deposes and says:
that he is the attorney for the   (plaintiff)   (defendant)
in the within action; that he resides at   ;that he has
read and knows the contents of the foregoing   ; and
that the same is true of his own knowledge, except as to the matters
therein stated to be alleged on information and belief; and as to
those matters, he believes it to be true.

That the reason this verification is made by deponent and not
by   (plaintiff) (defendant)   is that the   (plaintiff)   (defendant)   is not   within the County of
          where deponent has his office. The grounds of
deponent's belief as to all matters not stated upon deponent's
knowledge are as follows:

The undersigned affirms that the foregoing statements are true
under the penalties of perjury.

_____

DATED:

P.   Wills

A Will is an instrument in which a person sets forth the manner in which he wishes his property disposed of after his death. A man who makes a Will is called the testator; a woman is called the testatrix.

1. Types of wills

  a. *Conditional,* which by its terms is made conditional upon the occurrence of a specified event, such as death from an accident, operation, or disease.

  b. *Formal,* which meets the strict formalities as stated by law.

  c. *Holographic,* which is in the handwriting of the testator or testatrix.

  d. *Joint,* which is executed by two or more parties.

  e. *Nuncupative,* which is an oral Will made in the presence of witnesses. This is effective only in unusual circumstances; for example, in contemplation of death by a person involved in military action on the field of battle, or on a vessel at sea.

  f. *Reciprocal,* which contains reciprocal or mutual provisions, and is executed by different testators.

2. Principal elements of a will

Title
Introductory paragraph
  Revocation clause
Text or body
  Payment of debts, including funeral expenses
  Dispositive clauses
    Devises
    Bequests
    Trust provisions
    Residuary clause
  Appointment of executor
  Appointment of guardian
  Precatory provisions
Testimonium clause
Signature and seal
Attestation clause; signatures of witnesses
Witnesses' affidavit

Notes:

1. A new page cannot begin with the signature clause; at least one line of the Will should be on the page with the signature clause. The same holds true for the attestation clause; at least one line should be on the same page as the signature.

2. Although most states require only two witnesses, it is desirable to have three whenever possible. Having a choice among three witnesses makes it easier to obtain two witnesses at probate.

3. Attestation clause; signatures of witnesses

The foregoing instrument, consisting of this and (number of pages) preceding typewritten pages, each identified by the signature of the Testator (Testatrix), was signed, sealed, published, and declared by the above-named Testator (Testatrix) (N A M E) as and for (his, her) Last Will and Testament, in the presence of us who were all present at the same time and who, in the presence of the Testator (Testatrix), at (his, her) request, and in the presence of each other, have hereunto subscribed our names as witnesses thereto and hereto this

day of   nineteen hundred and

_____ residing at _____

                         _____

_____ residing at _____

                         _____

_____ residing at _____

                         _____

(Alternate form of attestation clause)

Signed, sealed, published, and declared by the above-named Testator (Testatrix)   (N A M E)   as and for (his, her) Last Will and Testament, in the presence of us who, at (his, her) request, in (his, her) presence and in the presence of each other, have hereunto subscribed our names as attesting witnesses the day and year above written.

_____ address _____

_____

_____ address _____

_____

_____ address _____

_____

4. Witnesses' affidavit

STATE OF   )
                           :SS.:
COUNTY OF   )

Then and there personally appeared the within-named
(1)   ,(2)   ,and (3)   , who, being severally duly
sworn, depose and say:

That they are acquainted with   (N A M E)   the
within-named (Testator, Testatrix); that they witnessed the execution of the within Will of the above-named (Testator, Testatrix);
that said (Testator, Testatrix) subscribed said Will in their presence
and in the presence of each other; that the said (Testator,
Testatrix) in their presence and hearing and in the presence
and hearing of each of them declared the same to be (his, her) Last
Will and Testament; that each subscribed the same as a witness of
the execution and publication thereof at the request of the said
(Testator, Testatrix) in (his, her) presence and in the presence of
each other; that the said (Testator, Testatrix) at the time of the
execution of said Will was more than 21 years of age and was of
sound and disposing mind, memory, and understanding and not
under any restraint or in any way incompetent to make a Will; and
that they make this affidavit at the request of the said (Testator,
Testatrix).

_____

_____

_____

Sworn to before me
this   day of
        19

Notary Public

(Alternate form of witnesses' affidavit)

STATE OF   )
                            :SS.:
COUNTY OF   )

(1)   ,(2)   , and (3)   , being duly and severally sworn, each deposes and says that:

1. Affiant resides at the address set forth opposite (his, her) signature on the last page of the foregoing instrument.

2. Affiant is acquainted with   , hereafter referred to as the (Testator, Testatrix).

3. On   , 19 , at   (address where signed)   the (Testator, Testatrix) in the presence and sight of all of the undersigned affiants, signed (his, her) name to the end of the foregoing instrument, and thereupon in the presence and hearing of all the undersigned affiants, first declared the foregoing instrument to be (his, her) Last Will and Testament, and then requested that all of the undersigned affiants sign their names as subscribing witnesses, which each of the undersigned affiants in the presence and sight of the (Testator, Testatrix) and in the presence and sight of each other, thereupon did.

4. Affiant has examined the signatures at the end of the foregoing instrument and such signatures are the signatures affixed by the (Testator, Testatrix) and by each of the undersigned affiants.

5. The (Testator, Testatrix) at the time of the execution of the foregoing instrument, was over the age of 21 years, was of sound mind, memory, and understanding, was in all respects competent to make a Will, and was not under any restraint.

6. The foregoing instrument was executed by the (Testator, Testatrix) and witnessed by each of the undersigned affiants under the supervision of   , an attorney-at-law.

7. The (Testator, Testatrix) immediately after the execution of the foregoing instrument, requested each of the undersigned affiants to make this affidavit as to the foregoing.

_____

_____

_____

Sworn to before me by each of
the three foregoing subscribers

this   day of
19 .

_____

Notary Public

Q.   Board of Directors' Meeting

Corporations are usually under the jurisdiction of the Department of State in each state. The requirements and forms may vary to some extent from state to state. If a law firm is engaged in extensive corporation work, a copy of the Business Corporation Act of the respective state, along with pertinent printed forms, should be kept on file in the attorney's office.

Included in this section are four of the most commonly used forms relating to directors' meetings: waiver of notice, notice, proxy, and minutes.

1. Waiver of notice

WAIVER OF NOTICE OF
SPECIAL MEETING OF
SHAREHOLDERS OF
(name of corporation)

We, the undersigned, being all of the shareholders of (name of corporation), a (state of incorporation) corporation, hereby call a special meeting of said shareholders, waive all notice thereof, whether provided by statute or otherwise, and consent and agree that such special meeting of shareholders shall be held on (month, day, year), at (time of day) at (address).

DATED: (city)   (date)

_____

(name of shareholder)

(type line for *each* shareholder,
with name typed under line)

2. Notice of meeting

TO THE STOCKHOLDERS OF (NAME OF CORPORATION)

PLEASE TAKE NOTICE that a Deferred Annual Meeting of Stockholders of (name of corporation) will be held on the 30th day of September, 19 , at 10:30 a.m., in Suite 8976, (address: street, city, state), for the purpose of electing Directors of the Corporation, and for the transaction of such other business as may lawfully come before the meeting.

In the event that you do not expect to be present at the meeting, would you kindly sign and return immediately the proxy form appearing at the bottom of this notice (or enclosed with this notice).

By order of the Board of Directors.

DATED: (city) (date)

_____
                                            Secretary

3. Proxy

PROXY

The undersigned hereby appoints   (name)   his proxy, with full power of substitution and revocation for and in the name, place, and stead of the undersigned, to vote upon and act with respect to all of the shares of stock of (name of corporation) standing in the name of the undersigned, or with respect to which the undersigned is entitled to vote and act at a meeting to be held on September 30, 19 , at 10:30 a.m., in Suite 8976, (address: street, city, state), and at any adjournment thereof.

The undersigned hereby ratifies and confirms all that the said attorney, agent, and proxy, or his substitute may lawfully do by virtue hereof.

DATED: _____

4. Minutes

(NAME OF CORPORATION)
MINUTES OF ANNUAL MEETING
OF
BOARD OF DIRECTORS

The Annual Meeting of the Board of Directors of the (name of corporation) was held at the office of the Corporation,   (address)   on   (date)   at 10:30 a.m.

Present were:

(list of persons present)

constituting all of the Directors.

(name)   acted as Chairman, and   (name)   acted as Secretary of the meeting.

On motion duly made, seconded, and carried, the following officers were elected:

(name)   President
(name)   Executive Vice President
(name)   Vice President
(name)   Treasurer
(name)   Secretary

(name)   announced that he had received the resignation of (name) as Vice President, to be effective on (date). The Board appreciated (person's name) personal reasons in the matter, and the resignation was accepted with regret.

On motion duly made and seconded, the President was authorized to continue the appointments of all of the foregoing officers at the compensation prevailing at this time, except as hereinafter specified.

On motion duly made and seconded, the salaries of certain officers were stipulated at the respective amounts set forth after their names:

(name) $150,000
(name)   125,000
(name)   100,000
(name)   90,000
(name)   75,000

The Board discussed the financial operations of the Corporation. After some discussion, and upon motion duly made, seconded, and carried, it was

RESOLVED, that the semi-annual dividend on shares of preferred stock of the Corporation, in the amount of $300,000, be paid to preferred stockholders of record as of April 1, 19 , and be charged against paid-in surplus; and it was further

RESOLVED, etc.

There being no further business to come before the meeting, it adjourned at 3:30 p.m.

_____
                                        Secretary